I D E A

Erwin Panofsky

IDEA

A Concept in Art Theory

TRANSLATED BY

JOSEPH J. S. PEAKE

University of South Carolina Press

COLUMBIA / 1968

FOREWORD
to the Second German Edition

THE SUGGESTION TO REPUBLISH a little book that appeared more than thirty-five years ago and has been long out of print is uncommonly flattering to the book's author. But at the same time it presents him with a problem of conscience. It is only too clear that in such a long time not only has scholarship as such gone forward, but also the opinions of the author himself, even if fundamentally unchanged, have been altered in many details.

To take this development into account would be possible only if the author could bring himself to write a completely new book probably three or four times as big; but for this he lacks the time, the strength, and—*ut aperte loquar*—the inclination. The alternative is an unchanged reprint with corrections limited to a number of typographical and factual errors. In particular the final paragraph of the chapter on "Mannerism" and note 239a that belonged with it have been deleted, for Giulio Clovio's report about a meeting with El Greco (published by Hugo Kehrer) referred to there has turned out to be a "patriotic" forgery. It must be left to the reader to supplement and correct the old text—*questo saggio antico*, to quote an Italian colleague—in the light of new publications; may this be made easier for him by a few indications.

For the chapter on classical antiquity there are several among the numerous new works on Plato's attitude toward art that should be cited, for information on which I thank Prof. Harold F. Cherniss: P. M. Schul, *Platon et l'art de son Temps*, 1st edn. (Paris, 1933), 2d edn. (Paris, 1952); H. J. M. Broos, *Plato's Beschouwing van Kunst en schoonheid* (Leiden, 1948); E. Huber-Abrahamowicz, *Das Problem der Kunst bei Platon* (Winterthur, 1954); B. Schweitzer, *Plato und die bildende Kunst der Griechen* (Tübingen, 1954); E. Wind, "Theios Phobos: Untersuchungen über die platonische Kunstphilosophie," *Zeitschrift für Aesthetik und Allgemeine Kunstwissenschaft*, XXVI (1932), 349 ff.; A. W. Bijvanck, "Platon et l'art grec," *Bulletin van de Vereeniging tot Bevordering der Kennis van de Antieke Beschaving*, XXX (1955), 35 ff.; idem, "De beeldende kunst in den tijd van Plato," *Mededelingen der Königliche Nederlandse Akademie van Wetenschappen*, Afd. Letterkunde, n.s. XVIII (1955), 429 ff. (with a summary in French); H. F. Bouchery, "Plato en de beeldende kunst," *Gentse: Bijdragen tot de Kunstgeschiedenis*, XI (1954), 125 ff.; H. J. M. Broos, "Platon en de kunst," *Bulletin van de Vereeniging tot Bevordering der Kennis van de Antieke Beschaving*, XXIII (1948), 1 ff.; R. Bianchi-Bandinelli, "Osservazioni storico-artistiche a un passo del Sofista Platonico," *Studi in onore di Ugo Enrico Paoli* (Florence, 1956), pp. 81 ff.; T. B. L. Webster, "Plato and Aristotle as Critics of Greek Art," *Symbolae Osloenses*, XXIX (1952), 8 ff.; and further, B. Schweitzer, *Xenokrates von Athen* (Schriften der Königsberger Gelehrten Gesellschaft, Geisteswissenschaftliche Klasse, IX, 1; Halle a. d. Saale, 1932); H. Jucker, *Vom Verhältnis der Römer zur bildenden Kunst der Griechen* (Frankfurt, 1950), especially pp. 126–40.

The chapter on the Middle Ages should be supplemented above all by E. de Bruyn's monumental *Etudes d'esthétique médiévale* (Bruges, 1946), and by an essay as short as it is enlightening: M. Schapiro, "On the Aesthetic Attitude of the Romanesque Age," *Art and Thought* (London, 1948), pp. 130 ff.

To the chapters on the Renaissance, "Mannerism," and Classicism should be added: A. Blunt, *Artistic Theory in Italy* (Oxford, 1940); idem, "Poussin's Notes on Painting," *Journal of the Warburg Institute*, I (1938), 344 ff.; and R. W. Lee, "Ut Pictura Poesis: The Humanistic Theory of Painting," *Art Bulletin*, XXII (1940), 197 ff. But most important is the fact that Giovanni Pietro Bellori's *Idea del pittore, dello schultore, e dell' architetto*, the "Magna Charta" of the classicistic interpretation of art that was first published in 1672, which considered the "idealistic" style of the Carracci and of Domenichino to be the final solution of the conflict between "unnatural" Mannerism and "raw" Naturalism, has turned out to be the summary and codification of trains of thought that were already current in the circle of those very painters and that had already been formulated previously in the manuscript papers of their countryman, friend, and patron, the learned Monsignor Giovanni Battista Agucchi (or Agucchia), between 1607 and 1615: D. Mahon, *Studies in Seicento Art and Theory* (Studies of the Warburg Institute, Nr. XVI; London, 1947). On a treatise by Agucchi that goes beyond the realm of art theory and on the aesthetic convictions of his friend Galilei, see E. Panofsky, *Galileo as a Critic of the Arts* (Utrecht, 1954).

Also for the chapter on Michelangelo and Dürer the author might refer to two of his own publications: *Studies in Iconology: Humanistic Themes in the Art of the Renaissance* (New York, 1949; Harper Torchbooks, 1962), pp. 242 ff.; and *Albrecht Dürer*, 3rd edn. (Princeton, 1948), pp. 279 ff.

Put briefly, the reader of the work reprinted here should always keep in mind that it was written more than a generation ago and has in no way been "modernized." If books were subject to the same laws and regulations as pharmaceutical products, the dust jacket of every copy would have to bear the label "Use with Care"[1]—or as it used to say on old medicine containers: CAVTIVS.

ERWIN PANOFSKY

Princeton, October 1959

---

1. The same warning must be given in regard to an Italian translation that appeared in Florence in 1952: *Idea: Contributo alla storia dell' estetica*, introduced and translated by E. Cione.

F O R E W O R D

to the First German Edition

T HE PRESENT STUDY is closely connected with a lecture
given by Prof. Ernst Cassirer at the Warburg Library
whose subject was "The Idea of the Beautiful in Plato's
Dialogues" and which will appear in the second volume of
Vorträge der Bibliothek Warburg. My investigation traces
the historical destiny of the same concept whose systematic
meaning was explained in Cassirer's lecture. It was the intent
of both authors that this connection should be manifest in the
way of public presentation; but the present study—primarily
by the addition of notes that in some places have swollen into
small excursuses and of excerpts from sources which in this
case can hardly be dispensed with—has become too extensive to be included in the Warburg Library's lecture series.
Thus the undersigned must content himself with specially
referring the reader of this little book to the above-mentioned
lecture on Plato and with expressing his sincerest gratitude
to Prof. Cassirer himself for various suggestions and an
oft-tried readiness with gracious help.

Cordial thanks are also due to Dr. Gertrud Bing, who
undertook the laborious task of preparing the index.

E. PANOFSKY

Hamburg, March 1924

CONTENTS

ILLUSTRATIONS

⌈1⌉

INTRODUCTION

IDEA

⌈1⌉

Plato, who established once and for all the metaphysical meaning and value of the beautiful, and whose
doctrine of Ideas has become ever more important for the
aesthetics of the representational arts, was nevertheless
unable to do full justice to these representational arts themselves. To be sure, it would be going too far to say that
Plato's philosophy is simply opposed to art as such or that
it summarily denies the painter or sculptor the ability to
envision Ideas.[1] As Plato distinguished between genuine
and false, legitimate and illegitimate practices in every
area of life—especially in the field of philosophy itself—he
occasionally contrasted, when speaking of the representational arts, the much-maligned practitioners of μιμητιχὴ
τέχνη (imitative representation), who know how to render
only the sensory appearances of the material world, with
those artists who, insofar as possible in activities limited
to empirical reality, try to do justice to Idea in their works
and whose labors may even serve as a paradigm for those
of the lawgiver. Of these "poietic" or "heuretic" painters,
to use Platonic terms, he says:

> When they finally commence the execution of their work
> [that is, after having carefully prepared the panel and
> sketched the principal lines], they let the eye, frequently
> alternating, dwell now on this, now on that side, once on
> that which is truly beautiful, just, rational, and otherwise
> pertinent in this context, and then again on that which
> merely passes for all this among men; and by blending
> and mixing they produce from their materials that human
> image in the conception of which they let themselves be

3

guided by what Homer described as divine and godlike when met with among mankind.[2]

But despite these and similar statements [3] one is still justified in characterizing Plato's philosophy as, if not exactly hostile, at least indifferent to or unfamiliar with art, and it is understandable that practically all later philosophers, especially Plotinus, understood Plato's countless attacks on the "mimetic" arts to be a wholesale condemnation of representational art as such. For since Plato applied to the products of sculpture and painting the concept—utterly foreign to their nature—of cognitive truth (i.e., correspondence to the Ideas) as a measure of value, his philosophic system could have no room for an aesthetics of representational art as an intellectual realm *sui generis*. (In fact, a systematic separation of aesthetics from the theoretical and ethical spheres was not attained before the eighteenth century.)

Thus he was forced to determine the circle of those artistic phenomena that he could approve from his standpoint very narrowly; and even within this restricted circle art could have, in his view, only a qualified value: if it be the duty of art to be, in the sense of the Ideas, "true"—that is, in a sense, to compete with rational cognition—then its goal must be to reduce the visible world to unalterable, universally and eternally valid forms, thus renouncing that individuality and originality in which we are accustomed to see the principal criterion of artistic accomplishment. Quite logically Plato contrasts "undisciplined" Greek art with the "law-bound" art of the Egyptians, whose works, always conceived in the same style, were no more beautiful and no uglier in Plato's own time than they had been ten thousand years before.[4] But even if the goal of art has been achieved to the best of human ability, the work of art can never claim a higher rank than that of εἴδωλον (image), which, though apparently accurate, falls short of its Idea

4

in many respects and can approach the latter no more closely than does the ὄνομα (name) which the philosopher necessarily uses to express his insights.[5]

Thus Plato determined the value of a work of art in the same way as he did that of a scientific investigation—by measuring the amount of theoretical and especially mathematical insight invested in it[6]—and by far the largest part of that which has been and is still esteemed as art, even great art, he did classify as μιμητικὴ τέχνη, against which he hurled his famous condemnations in Book Ten of the *Republic* and in the *Sophist:* either the artist produces copies, conscientious at best, of given objects, in which case his μίμησις εἰκαστική (copying exactly) reproduces the components of sense-perceptible reality—but absolutely nothing more than the components of senseperceptible reality—and this would amount to a pointless duplication of the world of appearances, which in turn only imitates the world of Ideas;[7] or he begets unreliable and deceptive illusions, which by way of μίμησις φανταστική (copying imaginatively) make the large small and the small large in order to mislead our imperfect eyes,[8] and then his product increases the confusion in our soul; its truth value is less than even that of the world of appearances, a τρίτον τι ἀπὸ τῆς ἀληθείας (third remove from truth).[9]

In a well-known poem by John Tzetzes, Phidias, taking account as an ὀπτικός and γεωμέτρης of the apparent reduction in size of things placed at great heights, is said to have given objectively incorrect proportions to a statue of Athena and by precisely this to have carried off the victory over Alcamenes.[10] For Plato this work would have been a standard example of that sham art which he blamed, almost as if expressly referring to this statue by Phidias, for setting forth, in deference to perspective distortion, not τὰς οὔσας συμμετρίας (the actual proportions) but τὰς δοξούσας εἶναι καλάς (those which seem beautiful).[11] Taking all this into consideration, it is understandable that Plato's ideal was met by the works of those Egyptian painters and sculptors who not only seemed to adhere eternally to firmly established formulas but also abhorred any concession to visual perception. And ultimately it was not the artist but the dialectician whom Plato entrusted with the task of revealing the world of Ideas. For while art stops with the production of images, it is the exalted privilege of philosophy to use "words" merely as the lowest step of a stairway to knowledge which for the artist ends with the completion of his εἴδωλον.[12]

Melanchthon

When we now consult, by contrast, a thinker of the sixteenth century—an age that customarily understood representational art as μίμησις, though not merely as imitation in the sense of "realism"—about his notion of the nature of the Platonic Idea, we read in Melanchthon, for instance: *Certum est, Platonem ubique vocare Ideas perfectam et illustrem notitiam, ut Apelles habet in animo inclusam pulcherrimam imaginem humani corporis* [13] (It is certain that Plato everywhere calls Ideas a perfect and lucid notion, as Apelles carries in his mind the most beautiful image of the human body). This interpretation, admittedly an attempt to reconcile Plato with Aristotle,[14] is distinguished from a genuine Platonic definition by two things: first, the Ideas are no longer metaphysical substances existing outside the world of sensory appearances as well as outside the human intellect in a ὑπερουράνιος τόπος (supercelestial place), but they are notions or conceptions residing in the mind of man; second, it appears to be self-evident to a thinker of this time that the Ideas preferably reveal themselves in artistic activity. The painter, and no longer the dialectician, is now adduced as an example when the concept "idea" is discussed.[15]

Melanchthon's pronouncement (he was actually not an art theorist, nor did he even show an especially lively interest in the visual arts) seems important for two reasons: for one thing, it foreshadows the fact that from now on art theory as such will take possession of the doctrine of ideas with ever greater zeal, or better, that art-theoretical thought will be increasingly influenced by this doctrine; for another thing, Melanchthon makes us wonder how it was possible that precisely the concept of "idea," from which Plato himself had so often deduced the inferiority of artistic activity, is now used almost as a specifically art-theoretical concept. A solution to this problem is suggested by Melanchthon himself. For his interpretation of the idea concept he refers us to Cicero,[16] thus indicating that classical antiquity itself had transformed the Platonic concept of "idea" into a weapon against the Platonic view of art, thereby preparing the ground, as it were, for that of the Renaissance.

ANTIQUITY

C ICERO, IN HIS *Orator*, a self-apology disguised as a theoretical and didactic treatise,[1] compares the perfect
speaker with an "idea," which we cannot encounter in experience but only imagine, and which in this respect resembles the object of artistic representation; it, too, cannot be
seen with the eyes in its full perfection but lives in the artist's
consciousness as a mere image:

Atque ego in summo oratore fingendo talem informabo,
qualis fortasse nemo fuit. non enim quaero quis fuerit,
sed quid sit illud, quo nihil esse possit praestantius, quod
in perpetuitate dicendi non saepe atque haud scio an numquam, in aliqua autem parte eluceat aliquando, idem
apud alios densius, apud alios fortasse rarius. sed ego
sic statuo, nihil esse in ullo genere tam pulchrum, quo
non pulchrius id sit, unde illud, ut ex ore aliquo quasi
imago, exprimatur; quod neque oculis neque auribus
neque ullo sensu percipi potest, cogitatione tantum et
mente complectimur, itaque et Phidiae simulacris, quibus
nihil in illo genere perfectius videmus, et iis picturis
quas nominavi[2] cogitare tamen possumus pulchriora,
nec vero ille artifex, cum faceret Jovis formam aut Miner-
vae, contemplabatur aliquem, e quo similitudinem
duceret, sed ipsius in mente insidebat species pulchritudinis eximia quaedam, quam intuens in eaque defixus
ad illius similitudinem artem, et manum dirigebat. ut
igitur in formis et figuris est aliquid perfectum et excellens, cuius ad cogitatam speciem imitando referuntur
ea, quae sub oculos ipsa non cadunt,[3] sic perfectae eloquentiae speciem animo videmus, effigiem auribus quaerimus.
has rerum formas appellat ἰδέας ille non intelle-
gendi solum sed etiam dicendi gravissimus auctor et

magister Plato, easque gigni negat et ait semper esse ac
ratione et intellegentia contineri: cetera nasci occidere,
fluere, labi nec diutius esse uno et eodem statu. quidquid
est igitur de quo ratione et via disputetur, id est ad ultimam
sui generis formam speciemque redigendum.[4]

(And in imagining the perfect orator I shall depict him as
such a man as has perhaps never existed. For I do not ask
who he was, but what is that quality which is superior to
everything else, which does not always and perhaps never
shines out unremittingly in his speeches but sometimes in
some part, more frequently with some, more seldom perhaps with others. But I do believe that there is nothing in
any genre so beautiful that that from which it was copied,
like a portrait of a face, may not be more beautiful; this
we cannot perceive either with eyes or ears or any other
sense, but we comprehend it with out mind and with our
thoughts; thus we can imagine things more beautiful than
Phidias's sculptures, which are the most beautiful we have
seen in their genre, and those pictures which I have spoken about; [2] and indeed that artist, when he produced his
Zeus or his Athena, did not look at a [scil. real] human
being whom he could imitate, but in his own mind there
lived a sublime notion of beauty; this he beheld, on this he
fixed his attention, and according to its likeness he directed his art and hand. As there is in the world of shapes
and figures something perfect and sublime, to which imagined form those objects not accessible to sensory perception [scil. the divine beings to be represented] can be
related by way of imitation,[3] so do we see the image of
perfect eloquence in the mind and only seek to comprehend its copy with the ears. Plato, that mighty master and
teacher not only of thought but also of speech, calls these
forms of things "ideas"; he denies that they come into
being and asserts that they exist eternally, being contained in our reason and our intellect: all else is born and
dies, remains in a state of flux, glides down and does not
long remain in one and the same state. Thus whatever is

to be discussed with regard to principles and method must be reduced to the final form and species of its class.)

Beauty and Truth to Nature

In this enraptured, rhetorical description of artistic creation the Platonic concept of "idea" serves to give the lie to the Platonic conception of art. Here the artist is neither an imitator of common and deceptive appearances, nor is he a pathfinder for a metaphysical οὐσία (substance) who is bound to rigid norms and whose exertions are yet doomed to ultimate failure. Instead, in his own mind there dwells a glorious prototype of beauty upon which he, as a creator, may cast his inner eye. Although the absolute perfection of this inner model cannot enter into the work he creates, the finished work will reveal a beauty that is more than a mere copy of an attractive "reality" (which is presented only to the easily deceived senses), yet something else than the mere reflection of a "truth" essentially accessible only to the intellect.

It is clear that such a turn in Platonic thought—hardly occurring for the first time with Cicero—was possible only under two conditions: the conception of the nature of art must have shifted to an un-Platonic, even anti-Platonic position; and the conception of the nature of the Idea must have shifted likewise. Concerning the first of these conditions, it appears that the prestige of art and the artist had powerfully increased in the Hellenistic-Roman milieu. First the painter,[5] then the sculptor (whose dirty and tiresome labors must have been especially distasteful to the minds of the Greek golden age) [6] was recognized more and more as a privileged and blessed individual.[7] Painting, if we can believe Pliny, was expressly received into the ranks of the liberal arts [8] (i.e., arts worthy of a freeborn person), art connoisseurship and art criticism began to flourish, the collector's instinct was aroused, and the favor of princes and the rich did more to raise the prestige of the arts. If for the sake of truth the "mimetic arts" were to be banished from Plato's republic,[9] Philostratus says in the introduction to his Εἰκόνες (remarkably anticipating a well-known pronouncement by Leonardo da Vinci):[10] Ὅστις μὴ ἀσπάζεται τὴν ζωγραφίαν, ἀδικεῖ τὴν ἀλήθειαν, ἀδικεῖ δὲ καὶ σοφίαν (He who does not love painting, does an injustice to truth and does an injustice to wisdom).[11] This statement shows that the higher valuation of the arts in all outward appearances was connected with a greater esteem for the internal values of art—that ever more general recognition was accorded to what Plato was inclined either to deny completely or to consider attainable only by a sacrifice of artistic freedom and originality: the autonomy of art in relation to deceptive and imperfect reality.

Insofar as art was an object of thought in classical antiquity, two opposing motives were from the very beginning set naïvely side by side (exactly as happened later during the Renaissance). There was the notion that the work of art is inferior to nature, insofar as it merely imitates nature, at best to the point of deception; and then there was the notion that the work of art is superior to nature because, improving upon the deficiencies of nature's individual products, art independently confronts nature with a newly created image of beauty. Side by side with the endlessly varied anecdotes about painted grapes that attract sparrows, painted horses that real ones neigh at, a painted curtain that fools even the artist's eye, and the countless epigrams about the deceptive lifelikeness of Myron's sculpted cow,[12] there is the admission that the works of Polycletus had lent the human figure "a grace surpassing truth,"[13] there is the disapproval of that Demetrius who went too far in being faithful to nature, preferring versimilitude to beauty,[14] and there are the numerous poetic passages in which the almost supernatural beauty of a human being is extolled by a comparison with statues or paintings. Socrates, for instance, found nothing wrong with the supposition that, "since you do not easily come upon a human being who is faultless in all his parts," the painter should be obliged and enabled to combine the most beautiful parts from a number of human bodies in order to make the figure to be represented appear beautiful, even though painting in itself is an εἰκασία τῶν ὁρωμένων.[15] Then there was a story, repeated *ad nauseam* (especially later, during the Renaissance): Zeuxis—the same artist who was said to have painted the sparrow-deceiving grapes—was also said to have requested the five most beautiful maidens from the city of Croton, in order to copy the most beautiful parts of each in his picture of Helen (or Venus).[16] Even the "antiartistic" Plato compared in a most remarkable instance his paragon for the perfect state, an adequate example of which can never actually exist, to the procedure of a painter who in his work presents a paradigm of the most beautiful human being; and such a painter, Plato asserts, must be considered an excellent artist, not although, but precisely because he could not prove the empirical existence of so perfect a creature.[17] Aristotle formulated this basic view in his characteristically lapidary manner: "Great men are distinguished from ordinary men in the same way as beautiful people from plain ones, or as an artfully painted object from a real one, namely, in that that which is dispersed has been gathered into one (τῷ συνῆχϑαι τὰ διεσπαρμένα εἰϛἕν)."[18]

Thus despite its adherence to the concept of μίμησις, ancient Greek thought was thoroughly familiar with the notion that the artist's relation to nature is not only that of an obedient copyist but also that of an independent rival, who by his creative ability freely improves on her necessary imperfections. And with the increasing emphasis on an intellectual as opposed to a sensory approach, characteristic of the devel-

opment of late Greek philosophy (one has only to consider
the allegorization of myths in the Stoic diatribes), the conviction grew that a supreme art can even dispense entirely
with the model perceived by the senses, that it can completely emancipate itself from the impression of that which
is actually observed. The result of this second line of Hel-
lenic thought—for the other continues unchanged alongside
it—is marked by statements like the following ones, both of
them significantly referring to Phidias's *Zeus*.[19] Dion
Chrysostom says in his *Olympic:* "Not even a madman
would suppose that in his size and beauty the Olympian
Zeus of Phidias resembles any mortal being." [20] And to an
Egyptian who sneeringly asked whether Phidias or the
other Greek artists had been in Heaven and seen the gods in
their true forms, the elder Philostratus has his Apollonius of
Tyana give this memorable answer: "That was done by imagination, which is a better artist than imitation, for imitation can only depict what it saw, but imagination what it has
not seen." [21]

Aristotle

We have now come to the point where Cicero's equation of
the Platonic Idea with an "artistic notion" inherent in the
mind of the painter or sculptor begins to be understandable.
As art criticism—passionately taking sides against the icon-
oclastic tendency already felt in pagan antiquity, and to
some extent attacking it with its own spiritualistic arguments—had come to raise the object of representation from
the level of external, perceivable reality to the level of an internal, spiritual image, so did philosophy more and more
strongly incline to pull down the principle of knowledge,
that is, the Idea, from the level of a metaphysical οὐσία (essence) to that of a mere ἐννόημα (thought): in the same de-

gree that the artistic object had risen from the sphere of empirical reality, the philosophic Idea had sunk from the ὑπερουράνιος τόπος. This means that both reality and Idea had come to be located in the human consciousness (though not as yet in a psychological sense), within which they could blend into a unity.

On the one hand, the Stoa had reinterpreted the Platonic Ideas to mean those innate ἐννοήματα, or *notiones anticipatae*, which precede experience (we can hardly call them "subjective" in the modern sense, but they are nevertheless opposed to transcendental essences in that they are thought of as immanent contents of consciousness).[22] On the other hand, however—and in our context this seems still more important—Aristotle had replaced, in the domain of epistemology, the antithetic dualism between the world of Ideas and the world of appearances by the synthetic interaction between the general concept and the single, particular notion; and, in the domain of natural philosophy and aesthetics, by the synthetic interaction between form and matter: Γίγνεται πᾶν ἔκ τε τοῦ ὑποκειμένου καὶ τῆς μορφῆς. That is to say, whatsoever is formed by nature or the hand of man, is no longer formed as the imitation of a definite Idea by a definite appearance, but by the entrance of a definite form into a definite substance. An individual man is "this particular form in this particular flesh and blood";[23] and as far as works of art are concerned, they are distinguished from the creations of nature only in that their form, before it enters into matter, is in the mind of man: Ἀπὸ τέχνης δὲ γίγνεται, ὅσων τὸ εἶδος ἐν τῇ ψυχῇ.[24]

Cicero's Compromise Between Aristotle and Plato

This Aristotelian definition of art included all *artes*, even those of medicine and agriculture; it was to take on infinitely greater meaning for the thought of the Middle Ages than those other ideas in Aristotle's *Poetics*, which concern art in the narrower sense and which came to life again only in the Renaissance. Under the influence of this definition the ancient world was able with particular ease to equate "artistic conception" with Idea, especially since Aristotle had retained the Platonic designation εἶδος for form in general as well as, in particular, for that "inner form," which is present in the soul of the artist and is transferred by his activity to matter. Thus Cicero's formulation, we might say, amounts to a compromise between Aristotle and Plato—a compromise, however, which in itself presupposes the existence of an anti-Platonic conception of art: that *forma* or *species*, present in the mind of Phidias and which he looked at when he created his *Zeus*, is, as it were, a hybrid of the Aristotelian ἔνδον εἶδος, with which it shares the attribute of being a notion immanent in consciousness, and of the Platonic Idea, with which it shares the attribute of absolute perfection, *perfectum et excellens*.

This Ciceronian compromise, however, precisely because it is a compromise, contains a peculiar problem that demanded solution, even if the intellect was not necessarily aware of its existence. If that inner image which is the actual object of the work of art were really nothing but a notion contained in the mind of the artist, a *cogitata species*, what guarantees that it has that perfection by which it shall surpass all appearances of reality? And conversely, if it does in fact have such perfection, must it not then be something else altogether than a mere *cogitata species?* Ultimately there were only two possible choices between these alternatives: either to deny to the Idea, now always synonymous with "artistic notion," its quality of higher perfection, or to legitimize this perfection on metaphysical grounds. Seneca chose the former, the Neoplatonists the latter.

Seneca

Seneca does not hesitate to admit that the artist may be able to imitate a notion conceived in his mind instead of a visible natural object; but not only does he see no particular difference in value, he also sees no difference in the natures of the one and the other. To him, the question whether the artist work according to a real or an ideal model, whether his object be an outward appearance in front of his eyes or an inner notion existing in his mind, is no longer a question of value or ethical conviction but a mere question of fact. In his Letter Nr. 65 he begins by enumerating four "original causes" of the work of art (in agreement with Aristotle):

Dicunt, ut scis, Stoici nostri duo esse in rerum natura, ex quibus omnia fiant, causam et materiam. Materia iacet iners, res ad omnia parata, cessatura, si nemo moveat. Causa autem, id est ratio, materiam format et quocumque vult versat, ex illa varia opera producit. Esse ergo debet, unde fiat aliquid, deinde a quo fiat. Hoc causa est, illud materia.

Omnis ars naturae imitatio est. Itaque quod de universo dicebam, ad haec transfer, quae ab homine facienda sunt. Statua et materiam habuit, quae pateretur artificem, et artificem, qui materiae daret faciem. Ergo in statua materia aes fuit, causa opifex. Eadem condicio rerum omnium est; ex eo constant, quod fit, et ex eo, quod facit. Stoicis placet unam causam esse, id, quod, facit. Aristoteles putat causam tribus modis dici: "Prima," inquit, "causa est ipsa materia, sine qua nihil potest effici; secunda opifex. Tertia est forma, quae unicuique operi inponitur tamquam statuae"; nam hanc Aristoteles idos vocat. "Quarta quoque," inquit, "his accedit, propositum totius operis." Quid sit hoc, aperiam. Aes prima statuae causa est. Numquam enim facta esset, nisi fuisset id, ex quo funderetur ducereturve. Secunda causa artifex est. Non potuisset enim aes illud in habitum statuae figurari, nisi accessissent peritae manus. Tertia causa est forma. Neque enim statua ista doryphoros aut diadumenos vocaretur, nisi haec illi esset inpressa facies. Quarta causa est faciendi propositum. Nam nisi hoc fuisset, facta non esset. Quid est propositum? Quod invitavit artificem, quod ille secutus fecit; vel pecunia est haec, si venditurus fabricavit, vel gloria, si laboravit in nomen, vel religio, si donum templo paravit. Ergo et haec causa est, propter quam fit; an non putas inter causas facti operis esse numerandum, quo remoto factum non esset?

His quintam Plato adicit exemplar, quam ipse idean vocat: hoc est enim, ad quod respiciens artifex id, quod destinabat, effecit. Nihil autem ad rem pertinet, utrum foris habeat exemplar, ad quod referat oculos, an intus, quod ibi ipse concepit et posuit. Haec exemplaria rerum omnium deus intra se habet numerosque universorum, quae agenda sunt, et modos mente conplexus est; plenus his figuris est, quas Plato ideas appellat, immortales, inmutabiles, infatigabiles. Itaque homines quidem pereunt, ipsa autem humanitas, ad quam homo effingitur, permanet, et hominibus laborantibus, intereuntibus illa nihil patitur. Quinque ergo causae sunt, ut Plato dicit: id ex quo, id a quo, id in quo, id ad quod, id propter quod. Novissime id quod ex his est. Tamquam in statua, quia de hac loqui coapimus, id ex quo aes est, id a quo artifex est, id in quo forma est, quae aptatur illi, id ad quod exemplar est, quod imitatur is, qui facit, id propter quod facientis propositum est, id quod ex istis est, ipsa statua est. Haec omnia mundus quoque, ut ait Plato, habet. Facientem: hic deus est. Ex quo fit: haec materia est. Formam: haec est habitus et ordo mundi, quem videmus. Exemplar, scilicet, ad quod deus hanc magnitudinem operis pulcherrimi fecit. Propositum, propter quod fecit. Quaeris, quod sit propositum deo? Bonitas. Ita certe Plato ait: "Quae deo faciendi mundum fuit causa? Bonus est; bono nulla cuiusquam boni

invidia est. Fecit itaque quam optimum potuit." Fer ergo,
iudex, sententiam et pronuntia, quis tibi videatur verissimum dicere, non quis verissimum dicat. Id enim tam
supra nos est quam ipsa veritas.[25]

(As you know, our Stoics say that there are two principles in nature from which all things are made—cause and
matter. Matter lies inert, a thing ready for all purposes,
and it will lie fallow if no one works upon it. But cause,
i.e. reason, shapes matter and turns it wherever it wishes,
and produces various objects from it. Thus there must be
that from which something is made and, next, that by
which it is made. The first is matter, the second is cause.

All art is imitation of nature. Therefore transfer what
I have said of things in general to those things which must
be made by man. A statue has had both matter, which had
to submit to the artist, and the artist, who had to give
shape to the matter. Therefore in the statue the matter
was bronze, the cause the artisan. The same applies to all
things: they consist of that which is made, and of that
which makes. The Stoics believe that there is one
cause—that which makes. Aristotle thinks cause can be
taken to mean three things. "The first cause," he says, "is
matter itself, without which nothing can be made; the
second is the artisan. The third is the form, which is
imposed on every work, such as a statue"; for this is what
Aristotle calls *idos*. "A fourth also," he says, "is added to
these—the purpose of the whole work." What this may
be, I will reveal. Bronze is the first cause of the statue. For
it could never have been made, had there not been that
from which it could be cast or chased. The second cause is
the artist. For that bronze could not have been formed into
the appearance of the statue, had not expert hands
come near it. The third cause is the form. For this
[individual] statue could not be called either *Doryphoros*
or *Diadumenos*, had not this shape been impressed upon
it. The fourth cause is the purpose of what is to be made.
For had this not existed, it would not have been made.

What is the purpose? That which lured the artist, that which he pursued as he worked; either this is money, if he made it to sell, or glory, if he worked for fame, or religion, if he prepared a gift for a temple. Thus this also is a cause—the reason for which it was made; or do you not think that that reason without which it would not have been made, should be included among the causes of the work produced?

To these [causes] Plato added a fifth—the model [exemplar], which he himself calls "idea"; this is that at which the artist looked when he made the thing he intended. But it does not matter whether this model was an external one, to which he directed his eyes, or one within himself, which he himself conceived and installed there. God has within himself these models of all things, and he comprises in his mind the numbers and measures of all things which are to be made; he is full of these forms, which Plato calls "ideas"—immortal, immutable, inexhaustible. Thus men perish, but humanity itself, according to which a man is created, persists; and while men suffer and die, it undergoes nothing. Therefore there are five causes, as Plato says: the *e quo* [matter], the *a quo* [the maker], the *in quo* [the shape], the *ad quod* [the model], and the *propter quod* [the purpose]. Lastly there is the thing which results from these. As in the statue—because we began to talk about this—the matter is bronze, the maker is the artist, the shape is the form which is made to fit it, the model is the exemplar which the maker copies, the purpose is the reason for which it was made, the thing which results from all these is the statue itself. The world too, as Plato says, has all these things. The maker is God. The material is matter. The shape is the appearance and order of the world which we see. The model is of course that according to which God made this great quantity of most beautiful things. The purpose is the reason for which he made it. You ask what is God's purpose? Goodness. Thus, at least, Plato says: "What cause was there for God to make the world? He is good; a good man does not begrudge anything good. And so he created the best he could." Therefore pronounce an opinion, judge, and say who seems to you to speak most truly, not who does speak most truly. For that is as far beyond us as truth itself.)

Understood in terms of the italicized passage, Seneca's concept of artistic Idea basically coincides with the concept of object of representation as opposed to form of representation, and this object he designates, with total disregard for Platonic usage, as *idos* = εῖδος. In fact, the concept of artistic Idea may actually be applied to the natural model. In another letter Seneca says:

Nunc ad id, quod tibi promisi, revertor, quomodo quaecumque sunt, in sex modos Plato partiatur. Primum illud "quod est" nec visu nec tactu nec ullo sensu conprenditur; cogitabile est. Quod generaliter est, tamquam homo generalis, sub oculos non venit; sed specialis venit, ut Cicero et Cato. Animal non videtur; cogitatur. Videtur autem species eius, equus et canis.

Secundum ex his, quae sunt, ponit Plato quod eminet et exsuperat omnia. Hoc ait per excellentiam esse. Poeta communiter dicitur, omnibus enim versus facientibus hoc nomen est, sed iam apud Graecos in unius notam cessit; Homerum intellegas, cum audieris poetam. Quid ergo hoc est? Deus scilicet, maior ac potentior cunctis.

Tertium genus est eorum, quae proprie sunt; innumerabilia haec sunt, sed extra nostrum posita conspectum. Quae sint, interrogas. Propria Platonis supellex est; ideas vocat, ex quibus omnia, quaecumque videmus, fiunt et ad quas cuncta formantur. Hae inmortales, inmutabiles, inviolabiles sunt. Quid sit idea, id est, quid Platoni esse videatur, audi: *"Idea est eorum, quae natura fiunt, exemplar aeternum."* Adiciam definitioni interpretationem, quo tibi res apertior fiat: volo imaginem tuam facere. Exemplar picturae te habeo, ex quo capit aliquem habitum mens nostra, quem operi suo inponat. Ita illa, quae me docet et* *instruit facies, a qua petitur imitatio, idea est.* Talia ergo exemplaria infinita habet rerum natura, hominum, piscium, arborum, ad quae quodcumque fieri ab illa debet, exprimitur.

Quartum locum habebit idos. Quid sit hoc idos, attendas oportet et Platoni inputes, non mihi, hanc rerum difficultatem. Nulla est autem sine difficultate subtilitas. Paulo ante *pictoris* imagine utebar. *Ille cum reddere Vergilium coloribus vellet, ipsum intuebatur. Idea erat Vergilii facies, futuri operis exemplar. Ex hac quod artifex trahit et operi suo inposuit, idos est.* Quid intersit, quaeris? Alterum exemplar est, alterum forma ab exemplari sumpta et operi inposita. Alteram artifex imitatur, alteram facit. *Habet aliquam faciem statua; haec est idos. Habet aliquam faciem exemplar ipsum, quod intuens opifex statuam figuravit; haec idea est.* Etiamnunc si aliam desideras distinctionem, idos in opere est, idea extra opus nec tantum extra opus est, sed ante opus.[26]

(Now I return to that which I promised you, how Plato divides all things in six ways. The first thing "which is," can be comprehended neither by vision nor touch nor any other sense; it can only be thought. That which is generic, like "man" in general, does not come before the eyes; but the particular does, such as Cicero and Cato. "Animal" is not seen; it is thought. However a species of it, like horse or dog, is seen.

As the second of "things which are" Plato regards that which stands out and surpasses everything else. This he calls "being" par excellence. "Poet" is used generally, for this name is given to all who make verses; but among the Greeks it has become the mark of one person; you understand "Homer" when you hear "poet." But what is this? God, of course, greater and more powerful than all others.

The third genus is things which "are" in the proper sense of the word; these are innumerable, but are situated outside our sight. What may they be, you ask? It is Plato's own equipment; he calls "ideas" that from which all things visible are made and according to which all things are shaped. They are immortal, immutable, inviolable. Hear what an idea is, that is, what it seems to Plato to be: *"Idea is the eternal model of the things which are made by nature." I will add an interpretation to the definition, in order to make the matter clearer to you: suppose I wished to paint your portrait. As a model for the painting I have you, and from you my mind takes a certain appearance which it expresses in its work. Thus that countenance which instructs and guides me, according to which a likeness is sought, is the idea.* Thus nature has an infinite number of such models of things—men, fish, trees—according to which everything that must be made by her is modeled.

The fourth place is held by form [*idos*]. It is necessary that you be attentive to what this form may be, and blame this difficulty of things on Plato, not me. But there is no sophistication without difficulty. A moment ago I referred to the *painter. When this painter wanted to make a picture of Virgil, he looked at him. His idea was the countenance of Virgil, the model of the work of art. That which the artist takes from the model and puts into his work is the* idos [=εἶδος; here, as above, meaning "form"]. *What may the difference be, you ask? The former is the model, the latter the form, taken from the model and put into the work. The one is imitated by the artist, the other he makes. The statue has a countenance; this is the* idos. *The natural model has a countenance, looking at which the artist fashioned the statue; this is the* idea. And now if you desire another distinction, the form is in the work; but the idea is outside the work, and not so much is it outside the work as it is prior to the work.)

Plotinus

To Seneca then, the inner notion of an object did not assume the slightest precedence over the outward inspection of an object—indeed, he could apply the term "idea" to the one as well as to the other.[27] Plotinus, by contrast, ventured in his philosophy to secure for the ἔνδον εἶδος of the artist a metaphysical claim to the rank of "perfect and sublime archetype." Plotinus consciously opposed Platonic attacks on μιμητικὴ τέχνη :

> When someone looks down upon the arts because they are concerned with imitating nature, it must first be replied that also the things of nature, too, imitate other things; then you must know that artists do not simply reproduce the visible, but they go back to the principles [λόγοι] in which nature itself had found its origin; and further, that they on their own part achieve and add much, whenever something is missing [*scil.* for perfection], for they are in possession of beauty. Phidias produced his *Zeus* according to nothing visible, but he made him such as Zeus himself would appear should he wish to reveal himself to our eyes.[28]

Thus the artistic idea has been assigned a completely new position. Divested of the rigid immobility that seems to have characterized it in Plato's philosophy, the Idea beheld by the artist's mind became the living "vision" of the artist.[29] Yet over and above its existence as a part of human consciousness it can claim the rank of metaphysical validity and objectivity, quite in contrast to Cicero's *cogitata species*. The inner notions of the artist have the right to confront reality as fully autonomous εἴδη that surpass reality itself in beauty: first, because these inner notions are identical (or at least can be identical) with the very principles in which nature itself originated and which are revealed to the artist in an act of intellectual contemplation; second, because these notions, although from the viewpoint of the psychology of art nothing more than just "notions" in the sense of the Ciceronian *species* or *formae*, possess a supernatural and superindividual existence when looked at from the viewpoint of

art metaphysics. It was far more than a mere figure of
speech when Plotinus said that Phidias represented his
Zeus in such a way as he would have appeared should he
have chosen to reveal himself to the eyes of men: according
to Plotinian metaphysics the "picture" that Phidias carried
in his inner self was not only the notion but the very essence
of Zeus.

Plotinus, then, considered the artist's mind to share the
nature and, if we may say so, the fate of the creative Νοῦς,
that likewise constitutes an actualized form of the Unfath-
omable One, the Absolute. For according to Plotinus the
Νοῦς also engenders ideas by and within itself (while the
Platonic δημιουργός only looks at them as something outside himself); and the Νοῦς, too, "overflows" and must pour
its pure and incorporeal thoughts into a spatial world where
form and matter come asunder, a world in which the purity
and unity of the original image are lost. Just as Plotinus
considers the beauty of nature to be a radiance of the Idea
shining through matter formed after its image but never
completely formable,[30] so does he consider the beauty of a
work of art to depend upon the "injection" of an ideal form
into matter, overcoming the latter's natural inertia and in-
spiriting, spiritualizing, enlivening it—or at least attempt-
ing to do so.[31]

Thus art is fighting the same battle as the Νοῦς, the battle for victory of form over the formless,[32] and under this
aspect the Aristotelian disjunction, ὕλη and εἶδος (for it
really is Aristotelian), takes on a completely new meaning.
Aristotle had also stated that the form of a work of art is
present in the soul of the artist long before being translated
into matter,[33] and in order to support this claim he had used
the same examples later cited by Plotinus—the house conceived in the architect's mind and the statue imagined by
the sculptor.[34] He too had contrasted the indivisibility of
the pure form with the divisibility of its material incarna-

tion.[35] And for him, too, form was superior to matter in every respect: form is more being, more substance, more nature, more of an original thing than is matter; it is something better and more godlike. Nevertheless Aristotle is far from attributing to matter an inherent resistance, or even a basic indifference, to the process of becoming formed. On the contrary, according to his view, ὕλη (which he expressly did not wish to be considered a κακόν = evil thing) possesses the potential for becoming completely formed to the same extent as the εἶδος possesses the actual power for the act of forming; moreover, matter "longs for form as its fulfillment, as the female longs for the male." [36]

By contrast, Plotinus conceived of ὕλη as something essentially evil, nay, nonexistent. Never capable of being perfectly formed,[37] it is not truly enlivened by the εἶδος but retains its negative, sterile, and hostile character even in the situation of (apparently) being formed. It is a substance that cannot be affected by form (ἀπαθές)[38] and, because it remains alien to the εἶδος, must resist (seen from the point of view of εἶδος itself) the latter's operation. Accordingly, Plotinus, to whom εἶδος meant not only "form" in Aristotle's sense but also "Idea" in Plato's sense, saw the confrontation of form and matter as a struggle between strength and weakness (which operates as resistance to strength), between beauty and ugliness, good and evil. Aristotle would have considered it pointless to compare the value of the imagined house and the house actually built or of the imagined and the actual statue, since before form is translated into matter a house simply cannot be "house" or a statue "statue." [39] Plotinus, on the other hand, for whom the structures belonging to the world of appearances were imitations of Ideas rather than incarnated forms, considered the material, sense-perceptible αἰσθητόν (object of sensation) to be so inferior to the ideal νοητόν (object of thought) in aesthetic and ethical value that it could be called "beautiful" only insofar as it allowed the νοητόν to be recognized or perceived in it. "How can the architect adjust the externally apparent house to the internal εἶδος of the house and insist that it is beautiful? Only for this reason, that the external house, if the stones are imagined away, *is* the internal εἶδος, divided of course with regard to the mass of matter, but indivisible in essence, even though appearing in multiple form." [40] Since for Plotinus the progression from unity to plurality always meant a decline from the perfect to the imperfect, it is logical that he combatted with real passion the definition of beauty—obligatory for classical antiquity as well as for the classical Renaissance—as συμμετρία and εὔχροια, that is, "proportional correspondence of the parts to each other and to the whole, coupled with pleasing color." [41] Such a "harmony of parts" necessarily presupposes parts, and acknowledging such a definition would imply that only compounds, not single entities, could be beautiful. In other words, an external aspect of beauty, dependent only upon the divisibility of the material structure, would be elevated to the very principle of beauty. But in truth, according to Plotinus's view, the beauty of nature as well as of art is founded exclusively upon that μετοχὴ τοῦ εἴδους (participation in the Idea) [42] that only out of necessity is expressed in the purely phenomenal characteristics of συμμετρία and εὔχροια.

All this goes to show that Plotinus's essentially "poietic" or "heuretic" view of the pictorial arts, in the way he wished it understood, was just as much of a threat to the position of art as the essentially "mimetic" view stressed by Plato—only that the lines of attack came from opposite directions: according to the mimetic view, art is merely imitation of sensory objects, and its right to existence is denied because its goals are not worth striving for; according to the heuretic view, art has the sublime task of "injecting" an εἶδος into resistant matter, and the possibility of its success is disputed because the goal is unattainable. True, something beautiful does arise when the sculptor "removes and scrapes off, smoothes and polishes until he has provided a beautiful countenance for his work," [43] but a higher kind of beauty exists where the Idea is spared the descent into the material world altogether. True, it is a good thing to see form triumph over matter, but it is better yet if this triumph (which can never be complete) is unnecessary in the first place:

> Suppose two blocks of stone were lying next to each other, one unformed and untouched by art, the other artfully worked into a statue of a god or a man—if of a god, perhaps into the likeness of a Muse or a Grace; if of a man, into the image not of just anyone, but of such a one as only art has composed from all beautiful people. [44] Then the block of stone formed by art into an image of the beautiful will appear beautiful, not because it is a block of stone (for then the other one would be just as beautiful) but because of the shape art has lent to it. The material did not possess this shape, but it was in the mind of him who envisaged it (ὁ ἐννοήσας) [45] before it came into the stone. And it resided in the artist's mind, not insofar as he had eyes and hands, but only insofar as he partook of art. This beauty, then, was much greater in art. For the beauty inherent in art does not itself enter into the stone, but it remains unto itself, and that which enters into the stone is only a lesser beauty derived from it; and even this does not remain pure unto itself and such as the artist desired it, but is revealed only insofar as the stone was obedient to art. [46]

Consequently the thoughts of a "Raphael without hands" are actually more valuable than the paintings of the real Raphael ("for the more beauty, entering into matter, is dispersed therein, the weaker it will be, compared to that beauty that remains unto itself"). [47] And while according to the "mimesis" theory that the works of art produced by man are mere copies of sensory deceptions, under the aspect of "heuresis" they are mere hints of an unrealized and actually unrealizable νοητὸν κάλλος (intelligible beauty) which in the final analysis is identical with the "greatest good." The path to contemplation of this "intelligible beauty, that resides, as it were, in a hidden temple" [48] leads ever onward— even beyond the work of art as such: "What, then, does this inner eye perceive? For just awakened, it will not immediately be able to bear the highest brilliance. The soul must become accustomed first to the sight of beautiful deeds, then to the sight of beautiful works, not so much those brought forth by art as those achieved by good men, and finally it must look at the souls of those who make the beautiful works." [49] In one of the most impressive passages in his book on the beautiful, Plotinus says:

For he who contemplates physical beauty must not lose himself therein, but he must recognize that it is an image and a vestige and a shadow, and he must flee to that of which it is a likeness. For if one were to rush forth and to grasp for truth that which is only a beautiful reflection in the water, then the same thing will happen to him that happened to the one about whom a meaningful myth tells how he, wanting to grasp a mirrored reflection, vanished in the depths of the waters; in the same way, he who holds on to physical beauty and will not let go of it, will sink, not with his body but with his soul, into the dark abysses, horrible for the mind to behold, where he will languish blindly in Orcus, consorting with shadows there as he did here. [50]

Thus the Platonic attack accuses the arts of continually arresting man's inner vision within the realm of sensory images, that is, of actually obstructing his contemplation of the world of Ideas; and the Plotinian defense condemns the arts to the tragic fate of eternally driving man's inner eye beyond these sensory images, that is, of opening to him the prospect of the world of Ideas but at the same time veiling the view. Understood as copies of the sensory world, works of art are divested of a more elevated spiritual or, if you will, symbolic meaning; understood as revelations of Ideas, they are divested of the timeless validity and self-sufficiency which properly belongs to them. It seems that unless the theory of Ideas gives up its own metaphysical standpoint, it must perforce deny to the work of art either the one or the other.

THE MIDDLE
AGES

[3]

THE VIEW EXPRESSED by Mörike in the words *Was aber schön ist, selig scheint es in ihm selbst* (That which is beautiful shines blessedly in itself) stands in sharp contrast to that of Neoplatonic aesthetics. According to this latter, each manifestation of the beautiful is merely an insufficient symbol for another, higher form of beauty; thus visible beauty is in a way a reflection of an invisible beauty, which is in turn only a reflection of Beauty in the absolute. This aesthetic attitude, so curiously in harmony with the symbolical and spiritual character that distinguishes the art of late antiquity from that of the classic period, could be taken over almost without alteration by early Christian philosophers. St. Augustine, too, acknowledged that through art a kind of beauty is revealed that, far from being merely derived from the creations of nature and transferred to the work of art by a simple act of copying, lives in the mind of the artist himself and is directly translated by him into matter. But St. Augustine, too, saw visible beauty as only a feeble likeness of the invisible, and his admiration for single beautiful figures, borne in the soul of the master artist who, as a kind of mediator between God and the material world, then made them visible in his work, leads him to adore the one supreme Beauty that is "above the souls." The *pulchra* (beautiful things) that the artist can conceive in his mind and reveal with his hand are all derived from that one *pulchritudo* that must be worshiped not in individual works of art but in something beyond them:

Quam innumerabilia variis artibus et opificiis in vestibus, calciamentis, vasis et cuiuscemodi fabricationibus, pic-

turis etiam diversisque figmentis atque his usum necessarium atque moderatum et piam significationem longe
transgredientibus addiderunt homines ad inlecebras ocu-
lorum, foras sequentes quod faciunt, intus relinquentes a
quo facti sunt et exterminantes quod facti sunt. at ego,
deus meus et decus meum, etiam hinc tibi dico hymnum et
sacrifico laudem sacrificatori meo, quoniam pulchra
traiecta per animas in manus artificiosas ab illa pulchritudine veniunt, quae supra animas est, cui suspirat anima
mea die ac nocte. sed pulchritudinum exteriorum opera-
tores et sectatores inde trahunt adprobandi modum, non
autem inde trahunt utendi modum.[1]

(How endlessly have men perfected the various arts and
accomplishments in the making of clothes, shoes, vessels
and all kinds of utensils, also paintings and various images—and indeed far beyond necessary and temperate use
or pious meaning, but rather as a charm for the eye—
seeking outwardly that which they make, but in their
souls forsaking Him by Whom they were made and for-
getting that they were made. But I, my God and my glory,
sing to Thee here also and consecrate praise to Thee who
hast consecrated me; for all those beautiful things that
here are conveyed through the souls into the artful hands
come from that Beauty that is above the souls and for
which my soul sighs day and night. Those, however, who
work at and run after external beauty learn from it only
the way it should be appreciated but not the way it should
be used.)

If the artistic attitude of Augustine and his followers [2] was in
absolute agreement with that of Neoplatonism, so his understanding of the nature of "Idea" was at least decisively prepared by pagan philosophy in late antiquity. As far as
terminology was concerned, he was able to lean on Cicero,
whose definition he needed to alter by only a small albeit
important addition, in order to get a formulation of the Idea
concept suitable to his new view of the world.[3] As far as es-

sential content was concerned, the interpretation of the Ideas as independent οὐσίαι—unacceptable from the Christian point of view—had already been sufficiently adjusted by his Jewish and pagan predecessors to permit him a direct assimilation. Plato's metaphysical essences, found already in existence by the δημιουργός at his formation of the world (the concept of a "creation" in the sense of the Bible apparently was foreign to the mythos of Greek antiquity),[4] were (quite apart from their transformation in Stoic and Peripatetic philosophy) already considered by Philo to be immanent in the divine mind as its own creations;[5] and the issue of whether they exist inside or outside the Νοῦς had been decided by Plotinus in favor of the first alternative.[6] Thus Augustine had only to replace the impersonal world soul of Neoplatonism with the personal God of Christianity in order to gain an interpretation acceptable to a Christian and in fact authoritative for the entire Middle Ages:

> Ideas igitur latine possumus vel formas species dicere, ut verbum e verbo transferre videamur. Si autem rationes eas vocemus, ab interpretandi quidem proprietate vocemus . . . sed tamen, quisquis hoc vocabulo uti voluerit, a re ipsa non errabit. Sunt namque principales formae quaedam vel rationes rerum, stabiles atque incommutabiles, quae ipsae formatae non sunt, ac per hoc aeternae ac semper eodem modo se habentes, quae divina intelligentia continentur. Et cum ipsae neque oriantur neque intereant, secundum eas tamen formari dicitur omne, quod oriri et interire potest, et omne, quod oritur et interit.[7]

(In Latin, therefore, we can call Ideas either *formas* or *species*, so that we seem to give a literal translation. If, however, we should call them *rationes* [principles], we should name them after their interpretative significance . . . yet whoever might wish to use this word will not be far wrong. For they are the original forms or principles of things, constant, and unchangeable, that themselves have not been formed. They are therefore eternal, persisting in one and the same condition and are contained in the divine intelligence; and while they themselves do not arise and perish, everything that can and does arise and perish is said to be formed according to them.)

That there must be Ideas follows immediately from the fact that God has created the world according to a principle (*ratio*) which, commensurate with the variety of single things and beings, can only be imagined as individualized. That Ideas may be imagined only as contents of the divine consciousness itself follows from the fact that to postulate extradivine models which would have guided God's creative activity would be equivalent to blasphemy.[8] Thus the Ideas, to which Platonism assigned a being absolute in every respect, were transformed, in the course of a development only brought to a climax by St. Augustine,[9] first into the contents of a creative world soul and finally into the thoughts of a personal God. That is, their original, transcendental-philosophical significance was remodeled first (a development already prepared by Plato himself) into a cosmological and finally into a theological meaning.

More and more it was forgotten that the concept "Idea" had originally been intended to explain—or, rather, to legitimize—the accomplishments of the human mind. It had been meant to demonstrate the possibility of an unconditionally reliable and definite cognition, of an unconditionally good and ethical behavior, and of an unconditionally pure and "philosophical" love of beauty. Such a vindication of human cognition, behavior, and feeling seemed less and less important in comparison to the insight into the meaning and coherence of the entire universe and its unfoldment. Ultimately the theory of Ideas, originally a philosophy of human reason, was transformed almost into a logic of divine thought. In this signification—and only in this signification—it outlasted the entire Middle Ages, even beyond the great Aristo-

telian revival in the thirteenth century, and there were always the same *drie hôher Fragen* (three high questions), as
Meister Eckhart put it, that occupied the minds of those
thinkers, basically the same which St. Augustine had already asked and answered. First, does God have Ideas or,
again in Meister Eckhart's words, *vorgêndiu bilde* (antecedent images) of created things? Second, if so, does He have
many Ideas or only one? Third, can God conceive the
created things only by means of the Ideas? As with St.
Augustine the answers to all three questions were nearly
always affirmative. Only the Pseudo-Dionysius took a divergent position and was therefore attacked by later writers
with ever new, yet essentially identical arguments, all to
a large extent literally dependent on the statements of St.
Augustine.[10] The definition of "Idea" as such was also borrowed by everyone from St. Augustine's discussion,[11] since
the Aristotelian interpretation of Idea as a nontranscendental
"inner form" (also in relation to the human mind) was no
less unsatisfactory from the Christian standpoint than the
Platonic interpretation of Idea as an essence existing per se
(also in relation to the divine mind).[12]

The Artist's "Quasi-idea"

It is clear that under these circumstances there could hardly
be much concern with an artistic "idea" in the proper sense.
Scholasticism in general, just like Plato, showed far less
interest in the problem of art than in the problem of the
beautiful, much more compelling because of its amalgamation with the problem of the good.[13] To bring forth and
to harbor Ideas became almost a privilege of the divine
mind, and whenever these "antecedent images" conceived
and enclosed in God were thought of at all in relation to
man, it was less as objects of logical cognition or picto-

rial imitation than as objects of mystical vision.[14] The relationship of the artistic mind to its inner notions and its external works, however, could well be paralleled with the relationship of the divine intellect to its inner Ideas and to the world it created; so that the artist, even if he does not have an Idea as such, can nevertheless be thought of as having a "quasi-idea" (as Thomas Aquinas once literally put it). This is in fact how medieval philosophy represented the artistic creative process—comparing the artist with the *deus artifex* or *deus pictor*,[15] not in order to honor art[16] but in order to make it easier to understand the nature and the working of the divine mind or, less often, in order to make possible the solution of other theological questions:[17] the passages in which we can recognize—or, rather, from which we can interpret—the aesthetic views of medieval Scholasticism are no more than auxiliary constructions for theological trains of thought. Thus Thomas Aquinas, in a discussion of the Idea concept that was to be a model for all posterity,[18] again revived the Aristotelian example of the "architect" that had been used by Philo and Plotinus:[19]

> . . . nisi inquantum similitudo formae est in ipso. Quod quidem contingit dupliciter: in quibusdam enim agentibus praeexistit forma rei fiendae secundum esse *naturale* . . . sicut homo generat hominem, et ignis ignem. In quibusdam vero secundum esse *intelligibile*, ut in his, quae agunt per intellectum; *sicut domus praeexistit in mente aedificatoris: et haec potest dici idea domus*, quia artifex intendit domum assimilare formae, quam mente concepit. Quia igitur mundus non est a casu factus, sed est factus a Deo per intellectum agentem, necesse est, quod in mente divina sit forma, ad similitudinem cuius mundus est factus. Et in hoc consistit ratio ideae.[20]

> (. . . except in so far as a likeness of the form [*scil.* to be produced] must be in him [*scil.*, the producer]. This happens in a twofold manner: in some effective agents there

pre-exists the form of the thing to be produced by way of *natural* existence, as when . . . man engenders man, or fire engenders fire. But in others it pre-exists by way of *intelligible* existence, as in those beings which operate by the mind; *thus the house pre-existed in the mind of the architect: and this can be designated as the Idea of the house*, because the artist intends to assimilate the [*scil.* real] house to the same form that he has conceived in his mind. Now since the world has not come about by accident but was created by God by an act of His intellect, there must necessarily be present in the divine mind a form according to whose pattern the world was made. And herein consists the conceptual nature of Idea.)

The fact was therefore well established in medieval thought that the artist worked, even if not from an Idea in the real, metaphysical sense, at least from an inner notion of form, or "quasi-idea," that preceded the work.[21] But—and for this reason it is no accident that Scholastic philosophers, when using art for purposes of comparison, preferred to cite the architect—the question of how this inner notion of form could be related to the experience of a natural object could not be raised at all by medieval thinkers.[22] This was prohibited by the parallel of artistic production with divine cognition, to which no object could ever be considered external. It was further prohibited by the predominant Aristotelian view of art that acknowledged a relationship between inner form and matter but did not recognize a relationship between inner form and external objects, compared with which the products of the *artes* were mostly considered inferior in reality value but not as representations striving to reproduce them "realistically."[23] Finally it was prohibited by the very character of medieval art as such, which just as slowly took up working from life and accordingly practiced it just as seldom as medieval natural science took up experimentation: in Scholastic philosophy the "naturalism" of the High

Gothic and the "realism" of the fourteenth and fifteenth centuries had highly meaningful parallels; [24] but they did not find an explicit conceptual characterization, let alone acceptance. And the thesis that art (so far as possible) "imitates" nature—or better, nature's *modus operandi*—was understood, as it had been by Aristotle, only as a parallelism, not as a cause-and-effect relationship. Art—including all the *artes* in addition to our three "arts of design"—does not *imitate* what nature creates, but it *works in the same way as* nature creates, achieving definite ends through definite means, realizing definite forms in definite materials, etc.[25] Thus when a mystic—significantly—added the example of a painter painting a "rose" to the traditional example of an architect building a "house," the rose is painted not from nature but according to an image present in the painter's soul, so that no essential difference existed between the examples from the pictorial arts and architecture:

Diu driu Wort: bilde, forme, gestalt, sint ein dinc. Daz nu eines dinges forme, bilde oder gestalt in einer sêle si, als einer rôsen bilde, das enist niht mê danne ein durch zweier sache willen. Diu ein sache ist, daz ich *nach der gestalt der sêle bilde eine rôsen an eine lîpliche materie*, von der sache ist der rôsen forme ein bilde in einer sêle. Diu ander sache ist, daz ich in dem innern bilde der rôsen die ûzern rôsen einvalteclîche bekenne, ob ich sî joch niemer entwerfen wil, als ich die gestalt des hûses in mir trage, das ich doch niht würken wil. . . .[26]

(The three words "image," "form," and "figure" designate but one thing. Now, that the form, image, or figure of a thing is in a soul, as the image of a rose, is for none other than two reasons. The first is that *after the figure in the soul I paint a rose on a material surface*, and for this reason the form of the rose is an image in a soul. The second is this: that I unequivocally recognize the external rose in its inner image, even if I never want to draw it, just as I carry within me the figure of the house which I do not want to build. . . .)

According to the medieval view, we may say in conclusion, the work of art does not arise by man coming to terms with nature, as the terminology of the nineteenth century puts it, but rather by the projection of an inner image into matter—an inner image that, while it can't be properly designated with the term "Idea" (which had been pre-empted by theology), may well be compared with the content of this term. Dante—he, too, intentionally avoiding the word "idea" in this place—has summarized the medieval view of art in a single lapidary sentence: "Art is found on three levels: in the mind of the artist, in the tool, and in the material that receives its form from art." [27]

THE

RENAISSANCE

[4]

IN CONTRAST TO MEDIEVAL THOUGHT the theoretical and historical literature about the art of the Italian Renaissance emphasized, with an insistence and indefatigability perhaps understandable only from the attitudes discussed in the preceding chapter, that the task of art is the direct imitation of reality. To the modern reader it may seem somewhat strange that Cennino Cennini—whose treatise is otherwise deeply rooted in medieval workshop traditions—advised the artist who wants to depict a mountain landscape to take some rough rocks and copy them in appropriate size and lighting; [1] yet this prescription signifies the beginning of a new cultural epoch. When the painter was advised to use a natural model (even if so strangely chosen as here), art theory lifted from a thousand years of oblivion the notion—self-evident in classical antiquity, purged away by Neoplatonism, and hardly even considered in medieval thought—that the work of art is a faithful reproduction of reality. And not only did art theory lift this notion from oblivion; it consciously elevated it to the status of an artistic program. All this was something extraordinarily new.

From the very beginning the literature of the Renaissance took it for granted that the innovation and the glory of the great artists of the fourteenth and fifteenth centuries was to have called art, "antiquated and childishly deviating from the truth of nature" [2] and founded merely on a usage handed down by tradition,[3] back to "verisimilitude." When Leonardo da Vinci said that "that painting is most praiseworthy that has the most similarity to the thing reproduced, and I say this to refute such painters as want to improve upon the

47

things of nature," [4] he expressed an opinion which for centuries no one would have dared contradict.

Parallel to this idea of "imitation," which included the requirement of formal and objective "correctness," [5] art literature in the Renaissance placed the thought of "rising above nature," just as art literature had done in antiquity. On the one hand, nature could be overcome by the freely creative "phantasy" capable of altering appearances above and beyond the possibilities of natural variation and even of bringing forth completely novel creatures such as centaurs and chimeras. On the other hand, and more importantly, nature could be overcome by the artistic intellect, which—not so much by "inventing" as by selecting and improving—can, and accordingly should, make visible a beauty never completely realized in actuality. The constantly repeated admonitions to be faithful to nature are matched by the almost as forceful exhortations to choose the most beautiful from the multitude of natural objects, [6] to avoid the misshapen, particularly in regard to proportions, [7] and in general—here the notorious painter Demetrius is again a warning example—to strive for beauty above and beyond mere truth to nature. Let us listen to Leone Battista Alberti:

Et di tutte le parti li piacerà non solo renderne similitudine, ma più adgiugniervi bellezza; però che nella pictura la vaghezza non meno è grata che richiesta. Ad Demetrio, antiquo pictore manchò ad acquistare l'ultima lode, che fu curioso di fare cose adsimilliate al naturale molto più che vaghe.

Per questo giovarà pilliare da tutti i belli corpi ciascuna lodata parte, et sempre ad imparare molta vaghezza si contenda con istudio et con industria; qual cosa, bene che sia difficile, perchè nonne in uno corpo solo si truova compiute bellezze, ma sono disperse et rare in più corpi, pure si debba ad investigarla et impararla porvi ogni fatica. Interverrà come a chi s' ausi vogliere e' inprendere

cose maggiori, che facile costui potrà le minori. Ne truo-
vasi cosa alcuna tanto difficile, quale lo studio et assiduità
non vinca.[8]

(And of all the parts [the painter should] not only render a
true likeness but also add beauty to them; for in painting,
loveliness is not so much pleasing as it is required. Demetrius, the ancient painter, failed to gain the highest praise
because he strove to make things similar to nature rather
than lovely.

For this it will help to take from all beautiful bodies
each praiseworthy part, and one must always exert himself with study and skill to learn great loveliness; this may
well be difficult, for perfect beauty is not in one body
alone, but [beautiful parts] are dispersed and rare in
many bodies, yet one must give all his labor to investigate
and learn it. It will happen that one who is accustomed to
aim at and undertake great things will be easily capable of
lesser things. And nothing is so difficult that it cannot be
mastered by study and application.)

With the same enthusiasm with which the anecdotes of the
sparrows and the horses were circulated and occasionally
supplemented by "well-authenticated" examples from recent
times [9] there was repeated—and even more often—that
other anecdote about Zeuxis's selective rendering of the Crotonian maidens. This anecdote even Ariosto did not spare his
readers.[10]

Thus the Renaissance, at first seeing no contradiction
therein, demanded of its works of art truth to nature and
beauty at the same time, just as antiquity had done (the idea
of *imitatio* is, after all, just as much an inheritance from antiquity as is the idea of *electio*). In fact, from the standpoint
of the Renaissance both of these demands, incompatible only
in later times, seemed like the parts of a single postulate: the
demand that the artist confront reality anew in each work of
art, be it as corrector or imitator.[11] Warnings against "imita-

tion" of other masters are characteristic of the Renaissance,[12] but they were not as yet voiced because such imitation would reveal the imitator's poverty of ideas; this could not become important until "idea" had become the central concept of art theory.[13] Rather those warnings were given quite simply because nature is infinitely richer than the works of painters, so that he who imitates other painters' works would lower himself to being the grandchild of nature, when he was capable of being her son.[14]

Birth of an Actual "Art Theory"

Now this double demand, to face reality directly—imitating and nevertheless improving upon it—would have been impossible to fulfill during this epoch if the expressly rejected workshop tradition,[15] which, as it were, spared the artist the necessity of finding his own terms for dealing with nature, had not been replaced by something completely different which made this "coming to terms with nature" possible. The artist was rather like someone driven out of a confined, but protected, residential area into a vast and still uncharted countryside, and there arose, and was bound to arise, that discipline that today is customarily called art theory. In many respects it was built upon antique foundations, but on the whole it is specifically modern. It differs from the earlier literature of art by no longer answering the question "how to do it?" but the quite different and thoroughly unmedieval question "what abilities and, above all, what kind of knowledge enable the artist to confront nature with confidence whenever he is required to do so?"

In its attitude toward art the Renaissance thus differed fundamentally from the Middle Ages in that it removed the object from the inner world of the artist's imagination and placed it firmly in the "outer world." This was accomplished by laying a distance between "subject" and "object" much as in artistic practice perspective placed a distance between the eye and the world of things—a distance which at the same time objectifies the "object" and personalizes the "subject." [16]

One would think that this basically novel attitude would immediately raise the problem that until this day has been the focus of scientific thought about art: the problem of the relationships between "I" and the world, spontaneity and receptivity, given material and active forming power—in short, the problem which for the sake of brevity may be called the "subject-object problem." But the opposite is the case. The purpose of art theory as it was developed in the fifteenth century was primarily practical, only secondarily historical and apologetic, and in no way speculative. That is, it aimed at nothing more than, on the one hand, to legitimize contemporary art as the genuine heir of Greco-Roman antiquity and to wrest a place for it among the *artes liberales* by enumerating its dignity and merits; and, on the other hand, to provide artists with firm and scientifically grounded rules for their creative activity. This second and most important goal, however, could be reached only on the presupposition (quite universally recognized) that above the "subject" as well as above the "object" there exists a system of universal and unconditionally valid laws from which the artistic rules are to be derived, and that the understanding of these laws was the specifically "art-theoretical" task.

As naïvely as this new discipline posed the two demands of correctness and beauty, as naïvely did it believe in its ability to pave and indicate the way to their fulfillment. Formal and objective correctness seemed to be guaranteed if the artist observed, on the one hand, the laws of perspective and, on the other, the laws of anatomy, of the doctrine of psychological and physiological movements, and of physiognomy. He would achieve beauty if he chose a *bella invenzione*,[17] avoided "indecorousness" and "contradictions," and lent to the appearance that harmony that was considered to be a rationally ascertainable *concinnitas* of colors,[18] qualities, and especially proportions. The doctrine of proportion [19] raised the questions of how to ascertain what is harmonious and therefore pleasing, and what constitutes the basis of this pleasingness. The answers, however they might be expressed in an individual case, all agreed that in any event the subjective and individual judgment of the artist does not suffice to legitimize good proportions as "good": if the authors didn't refer to the basic laws of either mathematics or music (which for that time meant almost the same thing), they appealed to the utterances of venerable authorities or to the testimony of antique statues.[20] And even scholars critical or sceptical in this respect, such as Alberti or Leonardo, tried at least to abstract a kind of norm from material sifted by the judgment of public opinion [21] or by the opinion of "experts" [22] and to contrast this norm with judgments based merely on individual taste.

Un-Platonic Orientation of Real Art Theory in the Early Renaissance

Medieval thought saw no problem in artistic creativity, because basically it denied the "subject" as well as the "object": art was nothing more than the materialization of a form that neither depended upon the appearance of a real "object" nor was called into being by the activity of a living "subject"; rather this form pre-existed as a *vorgêndes bilde* (antecedent image) in the mind of the artist.[23] Neither could this problem become apparent to Renaissance thinkers, since they considered the nature and behavior of the "subject" as well as the "object" to be determined by definite rules either valid *a priori* or demonstrable empirically. This explains the peculiar fact that the discipline of art theory, newly arisen in the fifteenth century, was at first almost completely independent of the revival of Neoplatonic philosophy taking place at the same time and within the same Florentine cultural circle. For this metaphysical, even mystical, philosophy that conceived of Plato not as a critical philosopher but as a cosmologist and theologian, that never even sought to distinguish between Platonism and Neoplatonism,[24] that attempted a magnificent combination of the Platonic and the Plotinian, of late Greek cosmology and Christian mysticism, of Homeric myth and Jewish cabala, of Arabic natural science and medieval Scholasticism—such a philosophy could give the most manifold stimulation to a speculative theory *about* art (and, as we will see, later did just that); but it could not be of any essential value for a practical and rationalistically oriented theory *for* art such as the Early Renaissance required and devised.

This kind of art theory was not as yet ready for thoughts such as those that Marsilio Ficino read out of Plotinus and the Pseudo-Dionysius and into Plato. Because of its naturalistic orientation it would have been forced to reject a theory according to which the human soul contains a notion of the perfect man, lion, or horse impressed upon it by the divine mind and according to which it is by this notion that the soul judges the products of nature.[25] The prosaically logical enumeration of the "seven possibilities of motion" [26] in such an art theory had little in common with the mystical doctrine of Neoplatonism, for which straight motion signified the divine initiative, oblique motion the continuity of divine creation, and circular motion the divine identity with itself.[27]

Beauty as Symmetry

At one time Ficino defined beauty, in close accord with Plotinus, as a "clearer similarity of the bodies with the Ideas" or as a "victory of divine reason over matter." [28] At another time he designated it, more nearly approaching Christian Neoplatonism, as a "radiance from the face of God" that first enlightens the angels, then illumines the human soul, and finally the world of corporeal matter.[29] Alberti, fully agreeing with his fellow theorists and predetermining the position of art theory for more than a century, opposed to this metaphysical interpretation of beauty the purely phenomenal definition of the Greek classic age:

. . . statuisse sic possumus pulchritudinem esse quendam consensum et conspirationem partium in eo, cuius sunt, ad certum numerum, finitionem collocationemque habitam, ita uti concinnitas, hoc est absoluta primariaque ratio naturae postularit.[30]

(. . . thus we may say that beauty is a certain agreement and harmony of parts within that to which they belong, with regard to a definite number, proportionality, and order, such as concinnity (i.e., the absolute and primary law of nature) demands.)

An even clearer formulation: "First one must observe that the single members fit together well, and they will fit together well if in relation to size and measure, character, color, and other similar things they harmonize and form one unified beauty." [31] Harmony of proportions and harmony of colors and qualities—this is what Alberti and other art theorists in the Early Renaissance understood to be the nature of beauty. Precisely that definition of beauty to which Plotinus had vigorously objected, because it seized only the external characteristics of appearance but not the inner essence and meaning of beauty, was helped by Alberti to a long-lasting victory: συμμετρία τῶν μερῶν πρὸς ἄλληλα καὶ πρὸς τὸ ὅλον, τό τε τῆς εὐχροίας προστεθέν (proportion of the parts to one another and to the whole, with the addition of a pleasant hue). This definition is important just because it renounces any metaphysical explanation of the beautiful, so that its acceptance loosened for the first time the ancient bond between the *pulchrum* and the *bonum*, even though this was done, at the beginning, less by expressly denying such a bond as by silently suppressing it. The autonomy of the aesthetic experience, which would not be theoretically proved for more than three centuries but which in the interim, as we will see, was quite often in question again, was recognized *de facto* even if not as yet *de jure*.

Thus one may maintain that Early Renaissance art theory in Italy was hardly affected by the revival of Neoplatonism.[32] Art theorists were able to gain access to Euclid, Vitruvius, and Alhazen, on the one side, and to Quintilian and Cicero, on the other; but they could not gain access to Plotinus or Plato, whom Alberti still referred to only as a painter.[33] In fact, Plato's influence became effective on a larger scale for the first time in the *Divina proporzione* (1509) by Luca Pacioli, who was not so much an art theorist in the strict sense of the term as a mathematician and cosmologist.[34]

In only one respect does the Platonic revival seem to have influenced art theory from the beginning: at first only in isolated cases and in relatively unimportant places, but gradually more often and with greater emphasis, one encounters the concept of the artistic "Idea." But perhaps nothing so clearly illuminates the depth of the essential difference between the original premise of art theory and the original premise of Platonism as the fact that it was possible to connect the theory of Ideas with art theory only by sacrificing certain aspects of either the one or the other, and in most cases of both. The more influence the Idea concept had and the closer it approached its inherent (i.e., metaphysical) meaning (which first happened in the so-called "mannerist" period), the further art theory retreated from its originally practical goals and its originally unproblematical premises.

And vice versa, the stronger art theory adhered to these practical goals and unproblematical premises (as was true during the actual Renaissance and then again during the period of "classicism"), the more the Idea concept forfeited its original metaphysical, or at least *a priori*, validity.

Ficino

According to the view of the *Academia Platonica*, as conclusively formulated by Marsilio Ficino, the Ideas are metaphysical realities. They exist as "true substances," while earthly things are only *imagines* of them (i.e., of the essences having real being); [35] and aside from their substantiality Ideas were regarded as "simple, immovable, and without conflicting admixtures." [36] They are immanent in the mind of God (also occasionally in the mind of the angels), [37] and in accordance with Plotinus and the patristic writers they were called *exempla rerum in mente divina*. The human consciousness is capable of cognition only because "impressions" (Latin: *formulae*) of the Ideas are inherent to the human soul from its supraterrestrial pre-existence. [38] Like unto "sparks from the divine primordial light," these impressions "are almost extinguished" as a result of long inactivity, but they can be revived by "instruction" and can be caused to flash up again in the light of the Ideas "as the visual rays are by starlight":

> Addit in mentem denique sic affectam non paulatim quidem humano quodam amore, sed subito lumen veritatis accendi. Sed unde nam? Ab igne, id est a Deo, prosiliente sive scintillante. Per scintillas designat ideas . . . designat et formulas idearum nobis ingenitas, quae per desidiam olim consopitae excitantur ventilante doctrina, atque velut oculorum radii emicantes ideis velut stellarum radiis collustrantur. [39]

(Finally he [Plato] adds that in the mind thus affected the light of truth is lit not slowly in the manner of human love, but suddenly. But from where? From the fire, i.e. from God, which shoots forth and emits sparks. By sparks he designates the Ideas . . . and he also thus designates the impressions [*formulas*] of these Ideas innate in us, which, formerly benumbed by lack of use, are rekindled by the breeze of teaching, and they are brightened by the Ideas just as the rays emitted by the eyes [are] by starlight.)

What was true of cognition in general was true (and to an even higher degree) of the cognition of beauty in particular. The Idea of the beautiful is also impressed in our minds as a *formula*, and only by means of this inborn notion are we—that is, what is most spiritual in us—able to perceive visible beauty, since we relate it to an invisible beauty and enjoy the triumph of the εἶδος over matter thus revealed to our eyes. That earthly object is beautiful that most nearly agrees with the Idea of beauty (and at the same time with its own Idea), and we perceive this agreement by referring the sensory appearance back to its *formula* preserved within us.[40]

Alberti

Leone Battista Alberti assigned a completely different ethos to the Idea concept. In the middle of discussing the postulate of beauty, following the censure of the ancient realist Demetrius and immediately before the unavoidable story of Zeuxis and the Crotonian maidens, there appears, as though a warning against the other extreme, a sharp attack against those who believe that they can produce something beautiful without any study of nature:

Ma per non perdere studio e faticha, si vuole fuggire quella consuetudine d'alcuni sciocchi, i quali presuntuosi

di suo ingegnio, senza avere essemplo alcuno della natura, quale con occhi o mente sequano, studiano da se ad se acquistare lode di dipigniere. Questo non imparano dipigniere bene, ma assuefanno se a' suoi errori. *Fuggie l'ingegni non periti quella idea delle bellezze, quale i bene exercitatissimi appena discernono.*

Zeuxis prestantissimo . . . pictore, per fare una Tavola, qual publico pose nel Tempio di Lucina adpresso de' Crotoniati, non fidandosi pazzamente, quanto oggi ciascuno pictore, nel suo ingenio, ma perchè pensava non potere in uno solo corpo trovare, quante bellezze ricercava. . . .[41]

(But in order not to lose time and effort, one should avoid the custom of some fools who, boasting their own talent, seek to win a painter's fame by their own resources alone, completely without a natural model which they would follow with eye and mind. These never learn to paint well, but they habituate themselves to their own errors. *That idea of beauty, which even the most experienced mind can hardly perceive, escapes the inexperienced one.*

Zeuxis, a most excellent . . . painter, when he was going to make a painting to set up in public in the Temple of Lucina among the Crotonians, did not trust foolishly his own native talent, as every painter does today; but because he did not think he could find in a single body all the beauties he sought. . . .)

"That idea of beauty, which even the most experienced mind can hardly perceive, escapes the inexperienced one." Without doubt this statement proves that Alberti, too, was affected in some way by the Platonic movement, since the notion of an *idea delle bellezze* that appears to the mental eye of the painter or sculptor is utterly unmedieval. Yet it is understandable that those who see Alberti as a real "Neoplatonist" unanimously pass over this statement in silence. For the same Idea concept which Cicero and Plotinus used to demonstrate the unlimited power of artistic genius and its essential independence from any external experience, serves here to warn this artistic genius against overvaluing itself and to call it back to the contemplation of nature. "The idea of beauty, which even the most experienced mind can hardly perceive, escapes the inexperienced one." This means nothing else than that Renaissance theory, neither willing nor able to sacrifice its hard-won realistic creed to the Idea concept, had now altered this concept to such an extent that it could be reconciled with that realistic creed and could even be used to support it. Petrarch, a premature but genuine Neoplatonist, understood the ability to visualize beauty by means of color and line only in terms of a divine vision; [42] Alberti believed that the mental ability to perceive beauty could be attained only by experience and practice. And in fact, even though Cennini [43] and after him Leonardo [44] granted the artist the ability to emancipate himself from reality by varying and inventing, no Renaissance thinker would have dared to consider beauty the child of "phantasy," as Dion and Cicero had done.

Significantly it was a rather long time before Italian art theorists gave greater importance to the concept of Idea—and even longer before they became fully aware of the consequences. Alberti made only that one rather parenthetical statement about it. Leonardo, so far as I know, never used the term "idea" at all. And it is not uncharacteristic of the High Renaissance attitude to art that Castiglione, who in his *Cortigiano* defines and celebrates love in a thoroughly Platonic panegyric, bases the judgment of art on no other criterion than that of adequate imitation. [45]

Raphael

Only Raphael, in his world-famous letter to Castiglione written in 1516, took up the Idea concept; but he spoke his mind even less than Alberti had done about how we are to understand the relationship between "idea" and "experience." Indeed he expressly refused to discuss this question. He says in the letter: "In order to paint a beautiful woman I should have to see many beautiful women, and this under the condition that you were to help me with making a choice; but since there are so few beautiful women and so few sound judges, I make use of a certain idea that comes into my head. Whether it has any artistic value I am unable to say; I try very hard just to have it [the idea]."⁴⁶ These wonderful sentences, gracefully hiding artistic conviction behind a compliment to the great connoisseur of women, should not be subjected to the acid test of epistemological criticism. They prove that, on the one hand, Raphael was aware that he could form the image of perfect femininity only from an "inner notion" no longer dependent on the concrete single object, but that, on the other, he ascribed to this inner notion neither a normative validity nor a metaphysical origin. In fact, he could designate its nature only with the expression *certa idea*. Somehow it came into his mind, but whether it was of any value or correctness, he didn't know and did not care to know. If he had been asked whence it came to him, he probably would not have denied that the sum of sensory experiences had in some way been transformed into an inner mental image, in a similar way as Dürer spoke of a *versammlet heimlichen Schatz des Herzen* (secret collected treasure of the heart) which comes into existence only if the artist has *durch viel Abmachens sein Gemüt voll gefasst* (filled his mind by much drawing from life) and out of whose fullness he can create in his heart a *neue Kreatur in der Gestalt eins Dings* (new being in the shape of a thing).⁴⁷ But Raphael's final answer would have been: *Io non so.*

Vasari

Vasari, influenced to a certain extent by the new Mannerist theory of art though on the whole rather retrospective in his art-theoretical attitude, expressed himself somewhat more fully in the second edition of his *Lives*. He still did not go beyond stating the situation and refrained from providing a philosophic analysis of this situation as well as from drawing theoretical conclusions therefrom.[48] Alberti—for Raphael, we recall, did not commit himself with regard to this question—had thought that the *idea delle bellezze*, which for him had still preserved something of its metaphysical nimbus, was dependent on "experience"; but he had not as yet said that it originated in "experience." He thought that it abides in a mind familiar with nature in preference to a mind that dispenses with concrete observation; but this does not mean that it is, to use Kant's terminology, "abstracted" from natural objects. Vasari said:

Perchè il disegno, padre delle tre arti nostre [49] . . . cava di molte cose un giudizio universale, simile a una forma overo idea di tutte le cose della natura, la quale è singolarissima [read: *regolarissima*] nelle sue misure—di qui è, che non solo nei corpi umani e degli animali, ma nelle piante ancora e nelle fabbriche e sculture e pitture conosce la proporzione, che ha il tutto con le parti e che hanno le parti infra loro e col tutto insieme; e perchè da questa cognizione nasce un certo giudizio, che si forma nella mente quella tal cosa, che poi espressa con le mani si chiama disegno, si può conchiudere, che esse disegno altro non sia, che una apparente espressione e dichiarazione del concetto, che si ha nell' animo, e di quello, che altri si è nella mente imaginato e fabbricato nell' idea. . . ."[50]

(Design, the father of our three arts [49] . . . derives a general judgment from many things: a form or idea of all the things in nature, as it were, which in its proportions is exceedingly regular. So it is that design recognizes, not only in human and animal bodies but also in plants, buildings, sculptures, and paintings, the proportion of the whole in relation to its parts as well as the proportion of the parts to one another and to the whole. And since from this recognition there arises a certain judgment, that forms in the mind the thing which later, formed by the hand, is called a design, one may conclude that this design is nothing but a visual expression and clarification of that concept which one has in the intellect, and that which one imagines in the mind and builds up in the idea. . . .)

This says, then, that the Idea not just presupposes but actually originates in experience; not only can the idea be readily combined with observation of reality, it *is* observation of reality, only clarified and made more universally valid by the mental act of choosing the individual from the many and then combining the individual choices into a new whole. This interpretation amounts to a redefinition of "idea" both according to its nature—which presupposes and proves a complete misunderstanding of the Platonic, let alone the Plotinian, theory of Ideas [51]—and also according to its function. Since an idea is no longer present *a priori* in the mind of the artist (i.e., it does not precede experience) but is brought forth by him *a posteriori* (i.e., it is engendered on the basis of experience), its role is no longer that of a competitor with, much less that of an archetype for, the reality perceived by the senses, but rather that of a derivative of reality. For the same reasons an idea functions no longer as the given content or even as the transcendent object of human cognition, but as its product. This change is clearly recognizable even in purely semantic terms. From now on an idea no longer "dwells" or "pre-exists" in the soul of the artist, as Cicero [52] and Thomas Aquinas [53] had put it, and still less is it "innate" to him, as genuine Neoplatonism had expressed it.[54] Rather "it comes into his mind," [55] "arises," [56] is "derived" from reality,[57] "acquired," [58] nay, "formed and sculpted." [59] In the middle of the sixteenth century it even became customary to designate not only the content of artistic imagination but also the capacity for artistic imagination with the expression "idea," so that the term approximated the word *imagizione*.[60] Thus Vasari could say in the passage just quoted: *concetto che si ha fabbricato nell' idea;* [61] and elsewhere we encounter such phrases as: *le cose immaginate nell' Idea,* [62] *quella forma di corpo, che nell' Idea mi sono stabilita,* [63] *quella forma di corpo, che nell' Idea dello artefice è disegnata,* [64] etc.

Redefinition of Idea in High Renaissance Art Theory

It is clear from what has been said that the "subject-object problem" was now ripe for a basic clarification. For as soon as the "subject" is given the task of obtaining the laws of artistic production from reality by his own effort instead of being allowed to presuppose them above reality (and above himself), there necessarily arises the question of when and for what reasons he is justified in claiming to have these laws correct. Yet—and this is particularly significant—it was only the definitely "Mannerist" school of thought which first achieved a basic clarification of this problem, or at least consciously demanded it.

Renaissance thinkers could consider the "subject-object problem" to have been solved (by their modified theory of Ideas itself) even before it had been expressly stated. Since an "idea" engendered in the artist's mind and revealed in his design did not really originate within the artist himself but was taken from nature by way of a *giudizio universale*, the idea, even if actually recognized and realized by the "subject," seemed potentially prefigured in the "objects." Characteristically, Vasari based the possibility of arriving at an Idea on the reasoning that, because nature itself is so regular and consistent in its formations, one can recognize the whole of a thing in a single part of it (*ex ungue leonem*). This thought was not formulated in the Renaissance, as it was later, [65] nor was it necessary to do so. It seemed self-evident that the Idea, obtained by the artist from observation, at the same time revealed the actual purposes of nature "creating according to laws"—that "subject" and "object," mind and nature, did not stand in hostile or even opposite relation to each other but that the Idea, itself derived from experience, necessarily corresponded to experience, supplementing or even replacing it. Thus Raphael could say of himself— exactly as the classicistically oriented Guido Reni did a century later [66]—that because he lacked sufficiently beautiful models, he made use of a *certa idea*. And thus a later Spaniard, though thoroughly imbued with the spirit of classicism, could formulate the peculiar relationship of mutual supplementation between viewing nature and forming Ideas by stating that the good painter must "adjust" or "correct" his inner notions by observing nature, but that where this observation is lacking, he may make use of the "beautiful Ideas that he has acquired": "For perfection consists in passing from the Ideas to the natural model and from the natural model to the Ideas." [67]

In the High Renaissance, then, the art-theoretical doctrine of Ideas, insofar as it is concerned with the problem of beauty (and in being so concerned it essentially differs from the medieval doctrine of Ideas), seems almost like a more spiritualized form of the old selection theory— spiritualized in the sense that beauty is achieved not by an external combination of separate parts but by an inner vision that combines individual experiences into a new whole. [68] The classical thinkers themselves, even though the selection theory was a commonplace to them, had not identified the "Idea" with the παράδειγμα obtained by choosing from among the most beautiful things. They had conceived of Idea not as a compromise between the mind and nature but as that which guarantees the mind's independence of nature. But Renaissance thinkers understood the Idea concept in the light of a fundamentally novel attitude toward art which identified the world of ideas with a world of heightened realities. Even though this thought was not explicitly formulated before the rise of seventeenth-century classicism,[69] the concept of the "Idea" was already transformed into the concept of the "ideal" (*le beau idéal*) during the Renaissance. This stripped the Idea of its metaphysical nobility but at the same time brought it into a beautiful and almost organic conformity with nature: an Idea which is produced by the human mind but, far from being subjective and arbitrary, at the same time expresses the laws of nature embodied in each object, achieves basically the same thing by intuitive synthesis that Alberti, Leonardo, and Dürer had tried to achieve by discursive synthesis when they summarized and systematized a rich material, gained by observation and approved by expert judgment, into a theory of proportion: the perfection of the "natural" by means of art.

Vasari, in the passage quoted above, answered not so much the question of whether it is possible to realize beauty as the question of whether artistic representation as such is possible: the question of *disegno*. In the philosophy of the High Middle Ages, marked as it was by Aristotelianism, the term "idea"—or, more exactly, "quasi-idea"—was not connected with the concept of *idea delle bellezza* (which was first revived in Renaissance Platonism and later developed into the "ideal") but with "artistic conception pure and simple," no matter whether the content of this conception be "beautiful" or "unbeautiful." It is clear that Renaissance thinkers found themselves unable to abandon this wider meaning of "idea"; that is, they subsequently used the expression "idea" in about the same sense as *pensiero* or *concetto*. But it is also clear that they had to redefine "artistic conception pure and simple" as something no less functional and *a posteriori* than the "idea of beauty" in the narrower sense. What seemed to enable the artist to "devise" or "design" any work of art was the same *giudizio universale* that enabled him to visualize beauty (or, conversely, ugliness).[70] The possibility, guaranteed by the Idea, of *"enhancing* a form that originates in the observation of nature and yet surpasses the actual natural objects," corresponded to the possibility of *conceiving* a form that likewise originates in the observation of nature and yet is independent thereof.

The expression "idea," then, even if we disregard the loose usage according to which it could mean imaginative ability or power of conception (that is, not *forma* or *conceptus* but *mens* or *imaginatio*), had two essentially different art-theoretical meanings in the sixteenth century:

(1) As Alberti and Raphael used the word, "idea" meant the mental image of a beauty that surpasses nature, that is, about the same thing that "the ideal" was to denote at a later time.

(2) As Vasari and others used it, "idea" meant any image conceived in the artist's mind, that is, about the same thing as the expressions *pensiero* and *concetto*, which had been so used as early as the thirteenth and fourteenth centuries.[71] In this sense, which even came to be predominant in the late sixteenth century but tended to disappear in the seventeenth when the concept of "the ideal" was explicitly formulated, the expression "idea" designates every notion that, conceived in the artist's mind, precedes the actual depiction.[72] It can even designate what we customarily call "subject" or "theme." [73]

Often these two meanings were not kept clearly separated. And they could not be, since the second, as the broader of the two, could include the first one under given circumstances; it is for this reason that occasionally an adjective like *bella* or *hermosa* was added to the word "idea" when the word is used in the sense of definition number one.[74] Ultimately, after all, the two definitions agree in that in both spheres—in the realization of beauty as well as in artistic

6 6

representation as such—the relationship between subject and object is essentially analogous.

Insofar as the formation of ideas was connected in Renaissance art theory with observation of nature, it was placed into a realm that, while not yet that of individual psychology, was nevertheless no longer that of metaphysics. This was the first step toward recognizing that which today is called "genius." Early Renaissance thought had already presupposed an actual artistic "subject" as the counterpart of an actual artistic "object," just as the visible "thing" and the perceiving "eye" had been posited simultaneously by the discovery of central perspective. But as we have seen, laws were also believed to exist that, equally suprasubjective and supraobjective, seemed able to regulate the creative process almost as if handed down by a higher court. The acknowledgement of such suprasubjective and supraobjective rules was in basic contradiction to the notion of a creative artist freely following his own genius, and therefore their validity was gradually limited by the concept of the artistic Idea. It was assumed that the artistic mind was able intuitively to transform reality into an Idea, to effect an autonomous synthesis of the objective data, and such a mind no longer needed such regulations, valid *a priori* or empirically confirmed, as mathematical laws, the concurrence of public opinion, and the testimonials of ancient writers. Rather the artist's privilege and obligation is to acquire by his own efforts the *perfetta cognizione dell' obietto intelligibile*, as "idea" was described from this time on in the sixteenth and seventeenth centuries.[75] Giordano Bruno's almost Kantian statement according to which only the artist creates rules and true rules exist only insofar and only in such number as there are true artists,[76] can be wholly understood only in connection with the theory of ideas. But—and this is the important point—the Renaissance proper no more arrived at this explicit, almost polemical emphasis on artistic genius than it did at an express formulation of the concept of "the ideal." It knew no more of a conflict between genius and rule than of a conflict between genius and nature; and the compatibility of these two opposites, not as yet set apart from each other, was clearly expressed by the concept of Idea as reinterpreted in the Renaissance: this concept secured freedom to the artistic mind and at the same time limited this freedom vis-à-vis the claims of reality.

⌈5⌉

"MANNERISM"

[5]

THE UNPROBLEMATICAL and tranquil mood characteristic of Renaissance art theory corresponded to this
period's general tendency to harmonize the opposites. This
tendency gave way to a new mood in the art theory of the
second half of the sixteenth century, the time that used to be
called the "Early Baroque." It is admittedly difficult to iso-
late the distinctly new characteristics from the sum total of
this literature, and almost impossible to subsume them
under a single concept. For the cultural awareness of this
epoch is characterized precisely by the fact that it was simultaneously revolutionary and traditional, that it inclined both
to particularize and to unify all the existing artistic impulses.
Where Renaissance thinkers wanted to break unconditionally with the Middle Ages, the "Early Baroque" thinkers
wanted to surpass as well as to continue the Renaissance.
Where earlier there had been various "schools" that differed
in practical methods but agreed on theoretical goals, there
were now different "movements" that, although they developed out of those schools, began to attack each other in
didactic statements of principles. And yet these movements
were more similar to each other in certain basic presuppositions than the older schools had ever been. Likewise the
"laws" special to each of the individual "genres" such as
historical painting, portraiture, and landscape painting were
discovered, while at the same time these "genres" interpene-
trated in innumerable ways.

Thus within this epoch that prepared the High Baroque
as well as "Classicism" we are able to distinguish at least
three different stylistic currents, in many ways opposed to,

yet in many ways cross-fertilizing each other. There was a comparatively moderate trend which attempted to continue the classic style (represented in its purest form by Raphael) and to elaborate it only so as to keep abreast of the new developments. The other two trends were comparatively extreme: one, relying chiefly on Correggio and the other North Italians, worked with effects of color and light; the other—"Mannerism" in the narrower sense of the term—tried to outdo the classic style in an opposite way, namely, by modifying and regrouping the plastic forms as such.[1] This complicated state of affairs is in reality even more complicated, for the naturalistic trend, which ushered in the High Baroque and which, according to earlier art historians, suddenly burst forth in all purity in the works of Caravaggio, actually appeared neither pure nor unprepared.[2]

The art theory of the later Cinquecento, which summarized all the tendencies alive at this time, partly balancing them and partly playing them off against each other—but at the same time, as we can easily understand,[3] especially favoring the retrospective "late classic" movement—is a reflection, indeed the proper expression, of this situation. For one thing, the theoreticians of the second half of the century reiterated, in a form either unchanged or even more pointed, the same thoughts and demands that had already been expressed by Alberti and Leonardo. Indeed, those thoughts and demands still formed the foundation of the entire system of art theory. Thus we must carefully examine a sentence written in 1580 or 1590 before we can claim it to be a specific expression of contemporary artistic intention. To give only two examples, theory steadfastly demanded συμμετρία even though in practice it is precisely this postulate that was sacrificed to other ideals; and conversely, the precept that in the representation of a sad subject a weeping figure should face the viewer in order to move him to participation in grief—a precept that at first glance seems so genuinely baroque—can actually be traced back to Alberti.[4]

For another thing, the "painterly" Lombard-Venetian movement found its theoretical justification in a more or less outspoken protest against the Florentine and Roman fanatics of *disegno* (Paolo Pino, Lodovico Dolce, and to a certain extent Giovan Battista Armenini).[5] Finally, in a number of specific innovations the writing of the epoch reflects and, as it were, legitimizes the "mannerist" tendency in the narrower sense, as it is seen in the works of Parmigianino, Pontormo, Rosso, Bronzino, Allori, and Salviati, or—to name sculptors—Gianbologna, Danti, Rossi, and Cellini (apart from its more or less decisive influence on the art of Tintoretto or El Greco, even on that of Peruzzi or Siciolante da Sermoneta). And the most basic of these innovations was, perhaps, the systematic elaboration and rearrangement of the theory of Ideas, which for the theory of the Renaissance itself had not been so important.

Protest against Rules

The statement by Giordano Bruno, alluded to above, according to which there are only as many true rules as there are true artists, is only one symptom of a now general and almost passionate rebellion against all rigid rules, especially mathematical ones. The specifically "mannerist" art distorted and twisted the balanced and universally valid forms of the classic style in order to achieve a more intense expressivity, so that figures of ten or more head-lengths are not unusual and they writhe and bend as if they had neither bones nor joints. It abandoned the classic style's comfortingly clear rendering of space based on rational, perspective construction in favor of that peculiar, almost medieval manner of composition that pressed shapes into a single, often "unbearably crowded" plane[6] (*almost* medieval, for the plasticity of the single figure achieved during the Renaissance was by no means abandoned, so that it contrasted with the over-all planarity of the picture as a whole—a contrast foreign to the art of the Middle Ages which was dominated by this planarity from the outset).

Proceeding from Michelangelo's disparaging judgement of Dürer's theory of proportions,[7] the art theory after the middle of the century vigorously and consciously criticized the earlier attempts to place artistic representation on a scientific, especially mathematical basis. Leonardo had taken pains to determine the motions of the body according to the laws of strength and weight, even to fix numerically the changes of measurement induced by these movements;[8] Piero della Francesca and Dürer had sought to master "foreshortening" by geometrical construction; and all these theoreticians were agreed that the proportions of the human body at rest could and should be fixed with the aid of mathematics. But now the S-shaped *figura serpentinata*, proportioned and flexed irrationally and occasionally compared to an upward-licking flame,[9] became the ideal. And there was an express warning against overvaluing the theory of proportions, which the artist had to know but often had to disregard (with figures in movement it could not be used at all):

Le misure . . . è cosa necessaria à sapere; ma considerar si dee, che non sempre fa luogo l' osseruarle. Conciosiacosa che spesso si facciamo figure in atto di chinarsi, d' alzarsi, e di volgersi, nelle cui attitudini hora si distendono ed hora si raccolgono le braccie di maniera, che à voler dar gratia alle figure bisogna in qualche parte allungare ed in qualche altra parte ristringere le misure. La qual cosa non si può insegnare; ma bisogna che l' artefice con giudicio del naturale la imprenda.[10]

(As for measurements . . . , it is necessary to know them; but one must bear in mind that it is not always advisable to observe them. For often we make figures that bend, rise, or turn, in which attitudes the arms are now stretched out and now contracted; so that, in order to give the figures gracefulness, it is necessary to extend the measurements in some part and to shorten them in some other part. This cannot be taught; but the artist must judiciously learn it from nature.)

Mathematics, honored in the Renaissance as the firmest foundation of pictorial art, was now persecuted almost with hatred. For example, Federico Zuccari, the chief spokesman for that especially "mannerist" attitude:

Ma dico bene e so, che dico il vero, che l'arte della pittura non piglia i suoi principî, nè ha necessità alcuna di ricorrere alle mattematiche scienze, ad imparare regole e modi alcuni per l'arte sua, nè anco per poterne ragionare in speculazione; però non è di essa figliuola, ma bensì della Natura e del Disegno. L'una le mostra la forma; l'altra le insegna ad operare. Sicchè il pittore, oltre i primi principî ed ammaestramenti avuti da' suoi predecessori, oppure dalla Natura stessa, dal giudizio stesso naturale con buona diligenza ed osservazione del bello e buono diventa valent' uomo senz' altro ajuto o bisogno della mattematica.

Dirò anco, come è vero, che in tutti i corpi dalla Natura prodotti vi è proporzione e misura, come afferma il Sapiente: tuttavia chi volesse attender a considerar tutte le cose e conoscerle per speculazione di teorica mattematica, e conforme a quella operare, oltra il fastidio intollerabile sarebbe un perdimento di tempo senza sostanza di frutto alcuno buono; come ben mostrò uno de' nostri professori ben valent' uomo, che volle a proprio capriccio formar corpi umani con regola mattematica; a proprio capriccio, dico, non però da credere di poter insegnare a' professori operare per tal regola, che sarebbe stato vanità e pazzia

75

espressa, senza poterne mai cavare sostanza alcuna buona, anzi dannosa: perchè oltre gli scorci e forma del corpo sempre sferico, cotali regole non servono ne convengono alle nostre operazioni: che l'intelletto ha da essere non solo chiaro, ma libero, e l'ingegno sciolto, e non così ristretto in servitù meccanica di sì fatte regole, perocchè questa veramente nobilissima professione vuole il giudizio e la pratica buona, che le sia regola e norma al ben operare. Siccome a me già disse il mio dilettissimo fratello e predecessore nel mostrar mi le prime regole e misure della figura umana, che devono essere di tante teste, e non più, le perfette proporzioni e graziose. Ma conviene, disse egli, che tu ti facci sì familiari queste regole e misure nell' operare, che tu abbi nelli occhi il compasso e la squadra: e il giudizio e la pratica nelle mani. Sicchè coteste regole e termini matematici non sono, e non possono essere, nè utili nè buoni per modo di dovere con essi operare. Imperocchè in cambio di accrescere all' arte pratica, spirito e vivezza, tutto le torrebbe, poichè l'intelletto si avilirebbe, il giudizio si smorzerebbe, e torrebbe all' arte ogni grazia, ogni spirito e sapore.

Sicchè il Durero per quella fatica, che non fu poca, credo, che egli a scherzo, a passatempo e per dar trattenimento a quelli intelletti, che stanno più su la contemplazione, che su le operazioni, ciò facesse, e per mostrare, che il Disegno e lo spirito del pittore sa e può tutto ciò, che si presuppone fare. Parimente di poco frutto fu e di poca sostanza l'altra che lasciò disegnata con scritti alla rovescia un altro pur valent' uomo di professione, ma troppo sofistico anch' egli, in lasciare precetti pur matematici a movere e torcere la figura con linee perpendicolari, con squadra, e compassi: cose tutte d'ingegno sì, ma fantastico e senza frutto di sostanza: pur come altri se la intendano, ciascuno può a suo gusto operare. Dirò bene, che queste regole matematiche si devono lasciare a quelle scienze e professioni speculative della geometria, astronomia, arimmetica, e simili, che con le prove loro acquietano l'intelletto. Ma noi altri professori del Disegno non ab-

biamo bisogno d'altre regole, che quelle, che la Natura
stessa ne dà, per quella imitare. Sicchè vollendo pure noi,
che questa professione abbia ancor ella madre, come
hanno tutte l'altre scienze speculative e pratiche, diremo
per verità, che essa non ha altra genitrice, nudrice e balia,
che la Natura stessa, la quale va con tanta diligenza ed
osservazioni imitando per mostrarsi di essa figlia legit-
tima, cara e virtuosa, siccome similmente non ha altro
genitore di essa degno, che il Disegno interno e pratico
artificiale proprio, et particolare di essa, e da essa genito e
prodotto.[11]

(But I do say—and I know I speak the truth—that the art
of painting does not derive its principles from the mathematical sciences, indeed it need not even refer to them in
order to learn any rules or manners of procedure, or even
to be able to discuss them by way of speculation; for
painting is not their daughter, but the daughter of Nature
and Design. The first shows it form, the other teaches it to
work. Thus the painter, besides the basic principles and
instructions acquired from his predecessors, or also from
nature itself, becomes a skillful man through mere natural
judgment with proper care and observation of the beautiful and the good, without any aid from or need for mathematics.

I will also say, because it is true, that in all bodies
produced by Nature there is proportion and measure, as
the Sage [Aristotle] affirms: but if one wants to engage in
considering all things and understanding them by meditation on mathematical theory, and to work in conformance
to it, then besides the unbearable labor it would be a waste
of time with no useful result; as has been shown by one of
our profession [*scil*. Dürer], albeit a capable painter, who
wished to shape human bodies by mathematical rules after
his own whim. After his own whim, I say, not because he
believed to be able to teach artists to work by such rules,
which would have been vanity and outright madness, impossible of producing any good result, but rather a harm-

ful one. For apart from foreshortenings and the form of a completely spherical body, such rules neither serve nor suit our actions. The [artist's] intellect must be not only clear but also free, and his spirit unfettered, and not thus restrained in mechanical servitude to such rules, because this truly most noble profession wishes judgment and good practice to be the rule and norm of working well. As my most beloved brother and predecessor already told me when he showed me the basic rules and measures for the human figure, perfect and graceful proportions must be of so many heads and no more. But it is advisable, said he, that you make yourself so familiar with these rules and measures in working, that you have the compass and the square in your eyes, and judgement and practice in your hands. Therefore these rules and definitions of mathematics are not, and cannot be, either useful or good in such a way that one should work according to them. Because instead of increasing practical skill, spirit and liveliness, this kind of thing would take them all away: the mind would debase itself, the judgment extinguish itself, and all grace, all spirit and savor, would be taken away from art.

Thus Dürer did this work, which was not negligible, I think, as a joke, a pastime, and to give diversion to those minds that are inclined to contemplation rather than to action, and to show that the Design and spirit of the painter knows and can do all that he purposes to do. Equally of little profit and substance was the other work left sketched, with reverse writing, by another man of our profession [*scil.* Leonardo da Vinci], competent but also too sophistical, in leaving mere mathematical precepts for moving and turning the figure with perpendicular lines, with square and compasses: all things of genius, yes, but fantastic and without profit or substance: as others may understand it, each can work according to his liking. I will say that these mathematical rules should be left to those sciences and speculative professions of geometry, astronomy, arithmetic, and the like, that quiet the intellect with their proofs. But we, professors of Design, have no need of other rules than those which Nature herself gives for imitating her. Thus wishing that this profession may also have a mother, as all the other speculative and practical sciences have, we will say with certainty that it has no other mother, fosterer and nurse than Nature herself; let this [profession] imitate Nature with great care and observations in order to show itself to be a legitimate daughter, dear and virtuous, just as it has no other father worthy of itself than the internal, practical, artificial Design, proper and peculiar to it and created and produced by it.)

Dualism in Mannerist Thought

The most characteristic quality of "mannerist" art, however, is an internal dualism, an inner tension. Despite the apparent willfulness of its manner of composition, this style strives for strict control of the total image, and the contours of the figures are not loosened and blurred in a "painterly" way but firmly outlined and anatomically defined. In fact, "mannerist" artists sometimes emulated antiquity even more faithfully than the classic artists of the High Renaissance had done: [12] they rejected both the flowing freedom of baroque space and the lawful order and stability of Renaissance space, and created instead even severer restraints precisely by means of planarity. In a similar way the avowals of artistic freedom coexisted—not too peacefully—with the dogma that artistic creativity could be taught and learned, that is, that it could be systematized. Perhaps this dogma received very special stress precisely because it was feared that otherwise art might be threatened by subjective arbitrariness.

Thus the same age that so courageously defended artistic freedom against the tyranny of rules also made art into a rationally organized cosmos whose laws even the most talented had to learn and even the most untalented could learn. The same Vincenzo Danti, who rejected the mathematical schematization of the form and movement of the body,[13] nevertheless admitted that the anatomical method was unconditionally valid, since somehow a "scientific" way to art had to be found. He stated expressly that his *vera regola* would be useful to those born to art as well as to those not born to it—among which he counts himself.[14] Although a single proportion was now less often set forth as the norm of beauty than had been customary in the past (instead of which one tried to present a greater choice of types), yet even Zuccari, despite his distaste for *teorica matematica*, did not abstain from determining these types numerically and from defining the special application of each single one.[15] And Lomazzo, who championed the idea of the *figura serpentinata*, nevertheless repeated the much-maligned Dürer's detailed proportions. In fact, Lomazzo's doctrine of expressive movement, developed far beyond the degree usual up to his time, attempts, despite its far-reaching differentiation—or rather, because of this far-reaching differentiation—the rationalization of the unrationalizable.[16]

That which is fundamentally new in all this is not so much that such contradictions were present but rather that they came to be recognized—or at least clearly felt—to be contradictions. Art theorists consciously began to criticize endeavors that in earlier epochs were simply matters of course, and tried, albeit with questionable success, to find a way out of the aporias of which they had so suddenly become conscious. What was true of the problem of "genius and rule" was also true of the problem of "mind and nature" —both antitheses expressing the one great contrast between "subject" and "object." In itself it was nothing new that admonitions to beautify the reality perceived by the senses were accompanied by demands to deceive the eye with truth to nature; but it was new that these two postulates were recognized to be contradictions, so that the earlier "as-well-as" came to be transformed into an "either-or." Vincenzo Danti explicitly distinguished between two methods: *ritrarre*, which reproduces reality as we see it, and *imitare*, which reproduces reality as it ought to be seen; [17] he even tried to separate their respective areas of application, thereby stressing the opposition of both attitudes. In his opinion, *ritrarre* sufficed for representing things perfect in themselves; but when representing things in some way faulty, the painter had to call *imitare* to the rescue [18] (much as Mannerism admitted genre-painting as an independent "species," but under the condition that kitchen maids and butchers look like Michelangelesque heroes). The happy balance between subject and object, one might say, was irreparably destroyed. In the free but therefore unstable atmosphere created by the developments during the second half of the sixteenth century the artistic mind began to react to reality with simultaneous arrogance and insecurity.

The Question of the "Possibility" of Artistic Creation

On the one hand, arrogance is shown by a dissatisfaction with mere "reality." This is expressed in a contemptuous disdain that was foreign to the preceding epoch. For instance, Armenini wrote: "I laugh at those who consider everything natural to be good"; [19] and Lomazzo wrote about "errors" of nature that had to be "corrected." [20] How humble by comparison are the words of Dolce, written in 1550—and in Venice!

Deve il pittore procacciare non solo di imitare, ma di superare la natura. Dico superare la natura in una parte, che nel resto è miracoloso, non pur se si arriva, ma quando vi s' arriva. Questo è in dimostrare . . . in un corpo solo tutta quella perfezione di bellezza, che la natura non vuol dimostrare a pena in mille.[21]

(The painter must strive not only to copy nature but also to surpass it. I say surpass nature in one part, because on the whole it is miraculous, not only if he succeeds, but also when he succeeds, that is to say, to show . . . in a single body all that perfection of beauty, that nature hardly chooses to reveal in a thousand.)

Vasari, in this respect already preparing the ground for the Mannerist view, had defined *disegno* as a visible expression of the *concetto* formed in the mind; but he also said that the *concetto* itself arose from observing the visually "given." Later writers,[22] however, developed this still intermediate view into a strictly conceptualistic one which in certain respects reverts to the medieval notion of the nature of artistic production;[23] "design" was praised as the "living light" and the "inner eye" of the mind;[24] and the task of architecture, sculpture, and even painting was limited to an external, technical realization of the *disegno* directly engendered by the mind.[25] Even a portrait, whose very name expresses direct imitation (*ritratto-ritrarre*), is occasionally said to arise from an intellectual and universally valid *idea e forma*.[26]

On the other hand, however, the Mannerists considered it obvious that this "idea" or *concetto* could by no means be purely subjective or "psychological"; and the question arose, for the first time, how it was at all possible for the mind to form a notion of this kind—a notion that cannot simply be obtained from nature, yet must not originate in man alone. This question led eventually to the question of the possibility of artistic production as such. Precisely this self-reliant, conceptualistic way of thinking, which had dared to undermine the very foundations of Renaissance theory by doubting the unconditional validity of "rules" as well as the absolute authority of impressions from nature, which interpreted an artistic representation as the visible expression of a mental notion and wished even the *invenzione* of the picture's content to be derived not from biblical, poetic, or historical tradition but to be thought up by the artist himself,[27] and which nevertheless cried out for universal laws and standards for all artistic activity—precisely such a way of thinking was bound to realize that that which in the past had seemed unquestionable was thoroughly problematical: the relationship of the mind to reality as perceived by the senses.

The Turn Toward Speculative Thought in Art Theory

Before the eyes of art theorists there opened an abyss hidden until then, and they felt the need to close it by means of philosophical speculation. This gave a completely new character to the writings on art that appeared after the middle of the sixteenth century. Earlier art theory had tried to lay the practical foundations for artistic production; now it had to face the task of proving its theoretical legitimacy. Thought now took refuge, so to speak, in a metaphysics meant to justify the artist in claiming for his inner notions a suprasubjective validity as to both correctness and beauty.

It would be wrong to reproach the art theorists for this ever-increasing tendency toward the speculative. They saw themselves—this I hope to have proved—faced with problems that could not be solved by any other means, and the recognition of these problems necessarily led the theorists of pictorial art along the same paths which the founders of modern poetics, such as Scaliger and Castelvetro, were traveling at about the same time. From the viewpoint of intellectual history the ponderous treatises of Comanini, Danti, Lomazzo, Zuccari, and Scannelli, precisely in their withdrawal from the immediately useful and, if you will, from

"live" art, form an important, indeed indispensable link between the epoch of Alberti and Leonardo and that period in
the middle of which we ourselves still stand. For it was not
long after them that writing about art passed from the hands
of artists to those of antiquarians, *literati*, and philosophers,
who developed it into normative "aesthetics" and finally into
interpretative "art history" in the present sense; the path
from the practical to "pure" science and scholarship has more
than once passed through the "abstruse."

Thus we see the old questions "How does the artist
represent things correctly?" and "How does the artist represent the beautiful?" rivaled by the new one, "How is artistic
representation, and in particular the representation of the
beautiful, *at all possible?*" In order to answer the latter
question art theorists recalled everything in the way of metaphysical speculation that was at their disposal, that is, the
essentially Aristotelian system of medieval Scholasticism as
well as the Neoplatonism of the fifteenth century. In both
cases, however—and this is what is so illuminating for
us—it was the theory of Ideas that, recognized in its entire
consequences for the first time and therefore placed in the
center of art-theoretical thinking, fulfilled the double task,
first, of making the theory of art aware of a problem that had
not been acute before, and second, of indicating the way to
its solution. During the Renaissance the Idea concept, not
yet consistently reasoned out and not too important in art
theory, had helped conceal the gap between mind and nature. During the Mannerist period it served to reveal it: the
forceful stress on the artistic personality pointed directly to
the problem of "subject" and "object." But at the same time
the Idea concept made it possible to close up the gap by
reinterpreting "Idea" in its original, metaphysical meaning;
for this metaphysical meaning resolves the opposition of
"subject" and "object" in a higher, transcendental unity.

Zuccari: the Aristotelian-Thomistic Trend

The Aristotelian-Scholastic trend in the now speculative art theory already became important in the *Treatise on Painting* by the Milanese, Giovanni Paolo Lomazzo, published in 1584. And it reached its climax in 1607 in *L'Idea de' pittori, scultori ed architetti* by Federico Zuccari, whose passionate protest against mathematics has already been mentioned.[28] This voluminous work has been little appreciated and little understood by art historians;[29] but it deserves attention because it is the first book devoted entirely to investigating that purely speculative problem which, as I phrased it, amounts to the question of how an artistic representation is at all possible. Zuccari answered this question in the only way that he could answer it: he subjected that "inner Idea," which was presumably made visible in a work of art, to scrutiny as to its origin and its validity; and from this test the "inner Idea" emerged victorious.

The author, like a good High-Scholastic Aristotelian and quite in accord with his time, proceeds from the premise that that which is to be revealed in a work of art must first be present in the mind of the artist. This mental notion Zuccari designates as *disegno interno*, or *idea*, for according to his definition the *disegno interno* is nothing other than "a concept formed in our mind, that enables us explicitly and clearly to recognize any thing, whatever it may be, and to operate practically in conformance with the thing intended";[30] and he does not want to use the "theological" (!) expression "idea" throughout because he "speaks as a painter to painters, sculptors, and architects." The actual artistic representation, be it pictorial, plastic, or architectural, he designates as *disegno esterno*. On this basis the whole treatise is divided into two books: the first discusses the Idea as a *forma spirituale* devised and used by the intellect to apprehend all natural things clearly and distinctly (and not only in their individuality but also in their class characteristics); the second discusses the expression of this *forma spirituale* in colors, wood, stone, or any other material.[31]

The "inner design" (or "idea") which precedes execution and actually is completely independent of it [32] can (and this is the basic difference from the Renaissance interpretation) be engendered by man in his mind only because God has given him the ability to do so, indeed because in the final analysis man's idea is only a spark of the divine mind, a *scintilla della divinità*.[33] Primarily Zuccari's "idea"—the interpretation of which he bases on "Plato" only nominally—agrees with the definition given in the well-known passage in Thomas's *Summa Theologiae*, I.1.15, which he quotes: [34] it is the original image immanent in God's intellect and according to which He created the world (thus God, as a creator, also "designs" internally and externally, so to speak). Secondarily, "idea" is the concept implanted by God in the angels so that these purely spiritual beings, who as such are incapable of sensory perception, possess within themselves the images of those earthly objects with which they must deal knowledgeably, especially as guardian angels of definite persons or places.[35] Only thirdly is "idea" a notion existing in the mind of man. As such it differs essentially from that present in God and that present in the angels, for in contrast to the former it is individual and in contrast to the latter it is not independent of sensory experience. But even the human "idea" is evidence for the Godlike nature of man, since it enables him "to bring forth a new intelligible cosmos" and "to compete with Nature":

Dico adunque, che siccome Iddio ottimo, massimo e suprema causa d'ogni cosa per operare al di fuori necessa-

riamente mira e risguarda l'interno Disegno, nel quale
conosce tutte le cose fatte, che fa, che farà, e che può fare
con un solo sguardo, e questo concetto, entro al quale
intende, è l'istesso in sostanza con lui, posciachè in lui non
è, nè può essere accidente, essendo atto purissimo; così
avendo per sua bontà, e per mostrare in picciolo ritratto
l'eccellenza dell'arte sua divina, creato l'uomo ad imagine
e similitudine sua, quanto all' anima, dandogli sostanza
immateriale, incorruttibile, e le potenze dell' intelletto e
della volontà, con le quali superasse e signoreggiasse tutte
le altre creature del Mondo eccetto l'Angelo e fosse quasi
un secondo Dio, volle anco darli facoltà di formare in se
medesimo un Disegno interno intellettivo, acciocchè col
mezzo di questo conoscesse tutte le creature e formasse in
se stesso un nuovo Mondo, e internamente in essere spirituale avesse e godesse quello che esternamente in essere
naturale gode e domina; ed inoltre acciocchè con questo
Disegno, quasi imitando Dio ed emulando la Natura, potesse produrre infinite cose artificiali simili alle naturali, e
col mezzo della pittura e della scultura farci vedere in
Terra nuovi Paradisi. Ma l'uomo nel formare questo Disegno interno è molto differente da Dio, perchè ove Iddio
ha un sol Disegno, quanto alla sostanza compitissimo, com-
prensivo di tutte le cose, il quale non è differente da lui,
perchè tutto ciò, che è in Dio è Dio, l'uomo in se stesso
forma varî disegni, secondo che sono distinte le cose da lui
intese, e però il suo Disegno è accidente; oltre il che ha
l'origine sua bassa, cioè dai sensi, come diremo poi.[36]

(I say, therefore, that God, all-bountiful and almighty, and
first cause of everything, in order to act externally necessarily looks at and regards the internal Design in which
He perceives all things that He has made, is making, will
make, and can make with a single glance; and that this
concept by which He internally purposes, is of the same
substance as He, because in Him there is not nor can there
be any accident, He being the purest act. In a similar way,
because of His goodness and to show in a small replica the

excellence of His divine art, having created man in His image and likeness with respect to the soul, endowing it with an immaterial, incorruptible substance and the powers of thinking and willing, with which man could rise above and command all the other creatures of the World except the Angel and be almost a second God, He wished to grant him the ability to form in himself an inner intellectual Design; so that by means of it he could know all the creatures and could form in himself a new world, and internally could have and enjoy in a spiritual state that which externally he enjoys and commands in a natural state; and, moreover, so that with this Design, almost imitating God and vying with Nature, he could produce an infinite number of artificial things resembling natural ones, and by means of painting and sculpture make new Paradises visible on Earth. But in forming this internal Design man is very different from God: God has one single Design, most perfect in substance, containing all things, which is not different from Him, because all that which is in God is God; man, however, forms within himself various designs corresponding to the different things he conceives. Therefore his Design is an accident, and moreover it has a lower origin, namely in the senses, as we shall discuss in the following.)

At the end of his book Zuccari interprets the term *disegno interno* as an etymological symbol of man's similarity to God (*disegno = segno di dio in noi*),[37] and he celebrates it as the "second sun of the cosmos," the "second creating Nature," and the "second life-giving and life-sustaining world spirit." [38] But I must forgo describing how he attempts, in a thoroughly Scholastic but neither unimaginative nor uninteresting manner, to derive from this *disegno interno* all worthwhile accomplishments of the human intellect, *metaforicamente* even philosophy; [39] how he derives from it the activity of the *intellectus speculativus* (i.e., internal contemplation) as well as the activity of the *intellectus practicus* (i.e., internal action); and how he finally subdivides the *intellectus practicus* into a moral part and an artistic part.[40] Only the second subdivision of the *intellectus practicus*, viz., the *disegno interno humano, pratico, artificiale—interno* in opposition to *esterno, humano* to *divino* or *angelico, pratico* to *speculativo*, and *artificiale* to *morale*—is germane to the present discussion. And this is where Zuccari clearly answers the question of the possibility of artistic representation.

Since the human intellect, by virtue of its participation in God's ideational ability and its similarity to the divine mind as such, can produce in itself the *forme spirituali* of all created things and can transfer these *forme* to matter, there exists, as if by divine predestination, a necessary coincidence between man's procedures in producing a work of art and nature's procedures in producing reality—a predestination which permits the artist to be certain of an objective correspondence between his products and those of nature. Zuccari's explanation for this completely agrees with Aristotle and its verbal formulation depends on Thomas Aquinas, whose "general" theory of art is here applied to the special aims of a theory of the (designing) "arts" in the narrower sense.

> La ragione poi, perchè l'arte imiti la Natura è, perchè il Disegno interno artificiale e l'arte istessa si muovono ad operare nella produzione delle cose artificiali al modo, che opera la Natura istessa. *E se vogliamo anco sapere perchè la Natura sia imitabile, è perchè la Natura è ordinata da un principio intellettivo al suo proprio fine ed alle sue operazioni; onde l'opera sua è opera dell' intelligenza non errante,* come dicono i filosofi; *poichè per mezzi ordinarî e certi conseguisce il suo fine; e perchè questo stesso osserva l'arte nell' operare,* con l'ajuto principalmente di detto Disegno, *però e quella può essere da questa imitata, e questa può imitar quella.*[41]

(The reason, then, that art imitates Nature is that the inner artificial Design, and therefore art, proceeds to bring forth artificial objects in the manner that Nature itself proceeds. *And if we wish to know why Nature can be imitated, it is because Nature is guided toward its own goal and toward its own procedures by an intellective principle. Therefore her work is the work of unerring intelligence, as the philosophers say; for she reaches her goal by orderly and infallible means. And since art*, chiefly with the aid of the above-named design, *observes precisely the same* [*method*] *in its procedure, therefore Nature can be imitated by art, and art is able to imitate Nature.*)

Zuccari did not fail to appreciate that man, as a corporeal being and therefore dependent upon perception by corporeal organs, can form those inner notions only on the basis of sensory experience. He tried, however, clearly foreseeing the objections arising from this correlation between sensory and intellectual perception, explicitly to secure the genetic and systematic priority of the "idea" over the impressions of the senses: sensory perception does not induce the formation of ideas, but the latter (by means of the imagination) causes sensory perception to take place; the senses are only called upon, as it were, to assist in the clarification and enlivening of those inner notions.[42] The objection that such an intellectual and ideal notion, although it provides the original illumination and stimulation of the mind, yet cannot operate under its own power, since the intellect perceives only by means of the senses, was answered by Zuccari as follows.

E quì forse alcun bell' intelletto vorrà opporre con dire, che questo concetto ideale e questo Disegno intellettivo, sebbene è primo moto e prima luce all' intelletto, non opera però per se stesso, poichè l'intelletto per mezzo dei sensi è quello, che opera il tutto.

Sottile opposizione, ma vana e di nulla sostanza: perocchè siccome le cose communi a tutti sono proprie, e ciascuno se ne può liberamente servire, avendone parte, come beni di repubblica, nè niuno però se ne può fare assoluto padrone, se non il Principe stesso; in questo modo essendo l'intelletto e i sensi soggetti al Disegno e al concetto, potiamo dire, che esso Disegno, come Principe, rettore e governatore di essi, se ne serva come cosa sua propria.[43]

(Here perhaps some fine mind may want to object by saying that this ideal concept, this intellectual Design, although it provides the first impulse and the first light to the intellect, does not operate by itself, inasmuch as the intellect does everything by means of the senses.

A penetrating objection, but empty and of no substance: for as communal things are the property of all, and each may use them freely, possessing a part of them as the wealth of the republic, yet no one may become their absolute master except the Prince himself; in the same way we may say that, since the intellect and the senses are subjects to Design and concept, Design, as their Prince, ruler, and governor, uses them as his own property.)

To repeat: the symptomatic significance of this whole neo-Scholastic speculation about art—especially Zuccari's effusions, which are not easily accessible to modern thought—is not only that it injected medieval Scholastic trains of thought into the theory of art,[44] interesting though that is, but that here the very possibility of artistic representation became a problem for the first time. The reversion to Scholasticism is only a symptom; the really new element is a change of mental attitude that made this reversion both possible and necessary: the gulf between "subject" and "object" had now been clearly perceived, and an attempt was made to bridge it by a fundamental clarification of the relationship between ideation and sensory experience. Without contesting the necessity of sensory perception, the Idea was reinvested with its apriori and metaphysical character by deriving the ideational faculty of the human mind directly from divine knowledge. Thus the *disegno interno*, that can provide the mind with light, inspiration, and life and yet must be purified and perfected by sensory perceptions, appeared as a gift, even as an *afflatus*, of divine grace: the autocratic human mind, now conscious of its own spontaneity, believed that it could maintain this spontaneity in the face of sensory experience only by legitimizing the former *sub specie divinitatis;* the dignity of genius, now explicitly recognized and emphasized, is justified by its origin in God.

This metaphysical, even theological, justification of "artistic representation as such" is paralleled by a corresponding justification of the realization of beauty. This, however, we cannot expect to find in a book like Zuccari's. Zuccari, whose attitude—despite the "theory of ideas"—is essentially Peripatetic and Scholastic, could solve the "subject-object problem" only by means of an analogy between natural and artistic "creation"; and while he could ascribe to the artist the ability to *compete* with reality by representing all natural objects independently of models,[45] even by freely inventing the most manifold *capricci e cose varie e fantastiche*,[46] he could not credit him with the ability to *surpass* reality by "purification" or "intensification." For Zuccari the most essential aim of artistic representation—in accordance with the composition of man from *corpo, spirito*, and *anima* [47] the artist must strive for a painstaking definition of external forms, a bold, lively movement, and a certain grace and delicacy in line and color—remained imitation carried as far as possible. After telling numerous anecdotes about *trompe-l'œil*, he writes:

> Ecco il vero, il proprio ed universale fine della pittura, cioè l'essere imitatrice della Natura e di tutte le cose artificiali, *che illude e inganna gli occhi de' viventi e di più saputi.* Inoltre esprime nei gesti, nei moti, nei movimenti della vita, nelli occhi, nella bocca, nelle mani tanto al vivo e al vero, che scuopre le passioni interne, l'amore, l'odio, il

desiderio, la fuga, il diletto, il gaudio, la tristezza, il dolore, la speranza, la disperazione, il timore, l'audacia, l'ira,
lo speculare, l'insegnare, il disputare, il volere, il comandare, l'obbedire e insomma tutte le operazioni e effetti
[affetti?] umani.[48]

(Here is the true, proper, and universal aim of painting: to
be the imitator of Nature and of all artifacts, *so that it
deludes and tricks the eyes of men, even the greatest
experts*. In addition it expresses in gestures, motions, the
movements of life, eyes, mouth, and hands, so much of life
and truth that it discloses the inner passions: love, hate,
desire, flight, delight, joy, sadness, grief, hope, despair,
fear, boldness, anger, meditation, teaching, argument,
willing, commanding, obeying—in sum all human actions
and emotions[?].)

Connection with Neoplatonism

Thus Zuccari will not enlighten us about the Mannerist
solution of the problem of beauty: to him the specific
problem of beauty was necessarily secondary to the problem
of the formative process in general, as it is to all Aristotelians.[49] We shall find this enlightenment in those
authors who surrendered more or less completely to the
influence of Neoplatonism.[50] In their system the concept of
καλόν (overcoming as it did the metaphysical contrast
between εἶδος and ὕλη) occupied a central position from
classical antiquity; and in the Renaissance re-formation and
transformation of Neoplatonism the theories of the beautiful
were zealously developed. At first these "neo-Neoplatonic"
theories had left almost no trace in the theory of art, as we
have seen. But from the second half of the sixteenth century
they were eagerly adopted and imbued the art-theoretical
discussions of the problem of beauty with a unique character.

When the art theorists sought to define the mind's position in relation to nature, they felt the same need in relation to the problem of the realization of beauty that they had felt in relation to the problem of "representation as such": they found it necessary to legitimize the value and the meaning of the beautiful metaphysically. It no longer sufficed to know that the external attribute of the beautiful was that quantitative and qualitative "harmony" which was still acceptable with regard to its purely phenomenal aspect; [51] rather it seemed necessary to grasp that principle of which harmony is merely the visible expression. And this principle was found in the same place from which Zuccari had tried to derive man's capacity for artistic representation as such: in God. Sensory beauty was again, just as in Neoplatonism and the Middle Ages, valuable only because, and only insofar as, it represented a visible manifestation of the good [52] (thus a human being beautiful in body was necessarily "pure" and "simple" in spirit).[53] The definition of beauty most often repeated at this time was in complete agreement with the old analogy of light in the Pseudo-Dionysius's metaphysics that had been revised by Ficino and was passionately endorsed by men like Giordano Bruno and Patrizzi during the period now under discussion: beauty is a "reflection" or "ray" of the splendor radiating from the countenance of God.[54]

Correspondingly the negative phenomenon of ugliness was understood in a new sense. Art theorists of the Early and High Renaissance (and, as we can see now, also Zuccari) [55] were satisfied with the simple statement that nature very seldom or never brings forth anything perfectly beautiful; but now this fact was explained and justified metaphysically by the "resistance of matter." In the Aristotelianism of Zuccari matter had been a thoroughly suitable and unresistant substratum for both the divine and the human idea; [56] but the Neoplatonically oriented thinkers of this time considered it a principle of ugliness and evil. Henceforth it was the *prava disposizione della materia* that caused the faults or errors in a natural phenomenon,[57] and the artist, who according to the earlier view had only to choose and extract the beautiful from given appearances, now had the thoroughly metaphysical task of re-establishing and re-affirming the principles buried beneath the given appearance. As Carlo Ridolfi put it, the artist is a "steward of divine grace" who has to restore the things of nature to the original state intended for them by their eternal Creator; he himself is to give them a perfection and a beauty unattained [58] by themselves, creating in his mind the *perfetta forma intenzionale della natura*.[59] Thus the beautiful in art no longer results from a mere synthesis of a scattered yet somehow "given" multiplicity but from the intellectual grasp of an εἶδος that cannot be found in reality at all.

Lomazzo

With this the question arose, in which manner and under what conditions the artist can recognize and make visible this supraterrestrial beauty that surpasses all reality. The clearest answer to this question was given by the Milanese painter Giovanni Paolo Lomazzo. In his *Trattato dell'arte della pittura* his attitude seemed to be still essentially Peripatetic and High Scholastic, but six years later, in the *Idea del Tempio della pittura*, he became the chief spokesman of a Neoplatonic orientation in the metaphysics of art.[60] In this work [61] Lomazzo compared in a genuinely Mannerist way—for astrological and cosmological trains of thought also belong to the speculative elements that now entered into art theory [62]—the "temple" of art with the structure of the heavens; he installed seven painters as regents and treated art theory throughout according to the principle of the number seven. But he also devoted an entire chapter to "The

Way to Recognize and Determine the Proportions according to Beauty." [63]

Beauty—so it says in this exposition stuffed with cosmological and astrological notions—appears in many forms in nature and must thus be expressed in many forms in art; but according to its essence it is only one single thing: the living, spiritual *grazia* that radiates from the countenance of God and is reflected as though by three more or less pure mirrors. The divine radiance streams first into the angels, in whose consciousness it engenders perception of the heavenly bodies as pure archetypes or Ideas; next into the (human) soul, where it produces reason and thought; and finally into the corporeal world, in which it appears as image and form. Thus even in corporeal things the divine beauty comes into being by the influence of their Idea, but only under the condition that (and to the degree that) the material of those things is unresistant and ready to receive this influence. The material is made unresistant and ready by adapting itself, according to order, measure, and kind (*ordine, modo, specie*), to the nature of the Idea to be expressed, all of which depends on the "complexion" of the individual concerned. And since on its way to earth the radiance of the divine countenance must pass through the consciousness of the angels, where it is differentiated, so to speak, according to the nature of the heavenly bodies, there is a jovial, a saturnine, and a martial beauty,[64] each being of greater or lesser perfection than the others but all in their totality reflecting the one, absolute beauty. He who wishes to recognize these multiple forms and stages of beauty and even to reveal them in works of art needs other than corporeal organs. For since beauty—comparable to the light by which we perceive it—is itself essentially incorporeal (indeed so widely separated from the material world that it can be adequately expressed only under especially favorable conditions), it can be recognized only by means of an inner, intellectual sense and re-created only on the basis of an inner, intellectual image. This inner sense is reason, and this inner image is the imprint left on it ("sigil") by the eternal and divine archetypes: the *formulae idearum.*[65] By virtue of such endowments the painter can perceive the beauty of natural objects and, observing their exterior characteristics and conditions, reveal it in his handiwork.

Lomazzo's Idea *and Ficino's* Commentary on the Symposium

Everywhere in the chapter summarized above Lomazzo's trains of thought presuppose a peculiar interconnection of the heavenly and the earthly worlds, and just this makes them appear so odd. But usually only one sentence of the chapter is quoted and, ripped out of context, thoroughly misunderstood.[66] To one who knows a little about the philosophical literature of the Early Renaissance, however, Lomazzo's thoughts will seem remarkably familiar. And in fact his statements, aside from occasional omissions, interpolations, and editorial alterations, are nothing but an almost verbatim repetition of the theory of beauty expounded by Marsilio Ficino in his commentary on Plato's *Symposium,*[67] a theory which, employing such current art-theoretical categories as *proporzione, modo, ordine, specie,* had a special appeal for late sixteenth-century speculation.

Ficino's writings were concerned with beauty, but not with art, and up to then art theory was not concerned with Ficino. But now we are confronted with a notable fact of intellectual history: the mystical, pneumatological theory of beauty associated with Florentine Neoplatonism was resurrected, after the course of a whole century, as a Mannerist metaphysics of art. This was possible because art theory had by then been forced to turn speculative and because the

"subject-object problem"—which, as far as artistic representation was concerned, seemed to have been solved by the
Peripatetic and Scholastic theory of Ideas developed by Zuccari—demanded a corresponding solution with regard to the
problem of beauty. If Zuccari and Lomazzo seem to represent two opposing world views, it must be remembered that
never at any time during this epoch was this opposition
absolute. Both the Peripatetic and Scholastic view and the
Neoplatonic view agreed in that which most clearly distinguishes the Mannerist from the real Renaissance attitude
towards art—in the conviction that the visible world is only
a "likeness" of invisible, "spiritual" entities and that the
contradiction between "subject" and "object" which had now
become apparent to the intellect could be solved only by an
appeal to God. Just as the artists of this epoch often wished
to express in their works an allegorical or symbolical content
beyond the merely visual—never before or since was there
such wide use of emblem and allegory [68]—and so often
created their works in terms of allegory, so they also understood works of art from the past largely in terms of
allegory.[69] And just as the Mannerist transformation of the
compositional principles accepted by the Renaissance oper-
ated as a "spiritualization" of the representations themselves,[70] so the very faculty of artistic representation had to
be thought of as the expression of a higher principle that
could ennoble the inspired artist while rescuing him from
the threat of conflict and instability.

The artistic Idea in general and the Idea of beauty in
particular—both, after having been "empiricized" and
"aposteriorized" in the nature-happy and self-assured
thought of the Renaissance, regained for a short time their
apriori and metaphysical character in the art theory of Mannerism, the artistic Idea in general with the help of the
Peripatetic and Scholastic philosophy, the Idea of beauty in
particular with the help of the Neoplatonic philosophy. Both

Ideas were retransformed into thoughts or notions of supernatural Intelligences, and man could share in them only by
the direct intercession of divine grace. At odds with nature,
the human mind fled to God in that mood at once triumphant
and insecure which is reflected in the sad yet proud faces and
gestures of Mannerist portraits—and for which the Counter-
reformation, too, is only one expression among many.

⌈6⌋

CLASSICISM

IMITATIO
SAPIENS

[6]

SINCE THE MIDDLE of the seventeenth century Classicism became ever more important in the practice of art and almost completely sovereign in art theory.[1] For the "painterliness" that specifically characterizes the High Baroque and that also influenced the antibaroque movements more strongly than would ever have been admitted by their adherents, was acknowledged by art theorists only rarely and almost unwillingly, even when it was represented by a Bernini. Characteristically the relation of Classicism to Mannerism was understood in the same way that the relation of the Renaissance to the Middle Ages had been. Villani, Ghiberti, Manetti, and Vasari had conceived of the perfect art of antiquity as displaced by decadent Gothic or Byzantine art (divorced from nature and beauty) and as "revived" at the beginning of their own epoch as a result of a new relationship to antiquity and a new approach to nature.[2] Likewise the seventeenth-century historiographers understood the developments after the deaths of the great masters, above all the now idolized Raphael, as a terrible decline from which only the Carracci had been able to rescue art. Essentially the same complaints were made about this second "decadent" phase of art: the lack of a thorough study of nature, caused—or at any rate demonstrated—by the imitation of other masters as opposed to the direct contact with reality;[3] unrealistic production on the basis of mere "practice" instead of serious study; and the reliance on mere phantasy instead of concrete observation.

"Idealism" Opposed to Both "Mannerism" and "Naturalism"

In one respect, however, the position of classicistic art theory differed essentially from that of the Renaissance. Most Renaissance writers, given their own historical position, had found it necessary to combat only one form of artistic "degeneracy": the failure to study and observe nature.[4] Classicistic art theory, however, had to protest with the same vigor against both the *dipingere di maniera*[5] (in the derogatory usage still current today) and the artistic movement that seemed to be the opposite and equally ruinous extreme— Caravaggesque "naturalism." To be sure, attempts were made to comprehend the historical necessity of Caravaggio's art, in which the antinaturalistic elements were for the most part completely overlooked,[6] for "without doubt Caravaggio was good for art, since he appeared at a time when painters formed shapes on the basis of custom and manner only, with little concern for nature, and satisfied the sense of loveliness more than the sense of truth."[7] But the man who evaluated his fellow artists only according to their ability to reproduce natural objects,[8] and who declared the execution of a good flower painting to be just as difficult and worthwhile as the execution of a good historical picture,[9] seemed to have sinned even more unforgivably in the other direction. He was said to be uninventive, unintellectual,[10] completely subject to the natural model, and satisfied with the unselective reproduction of things as they appeared to the senses, no matter how faulty this appearance might be:[11] *un gran soggetto, ma non ideale.*[12]

Thus where Early Renaissance art theorists had had to combat primarily the estrangement from nature and in this respect were able to sanction the artistic practice of their own time, classicistic art theorists had to wage war on two fronts, so to speak. This brought them into opposition not only to their artistic heritage but also to their artistic environment,[13] and they were forced into a double defensive position. They had to prove that neither the Mannerists nor those who "glorified themselves with the name of Naturalists" [14] were on the right path: the true salvation of art had to be sought midway between these two equally ruinous extremes. The infallible measure of this *juste milieu* was obviously the art of antiquity, which was honored not as a "naturalistic" art but—precisely because of its limitation to a "purified" or "ennobled" reality—as a truly "natural" art.[15]

Bellori

In an academic lecture in 1664 an attempt was made to place this thesis on a firm, systematic basis. Later published by the author as an introduction to his great *Lives of the Painters*, this lecture was given by the most noted art scholar and archaeologist of his time—no longer a writing artist but an expertly trained "judge of art," to use the characteristic new term: Giovanni Pietro Bellori, important not only for Italian but also for French and German academicism.[16] But the chief support of his views—indeed their very foundation—is again the concept of Idea, which received from him its last and in a sense conclusive formulation.[17] The essay *L'Idea del pittore, dello scultore e del'architetto* [18] begins with a genuinely Neoplatonic introduction: in deep introspection the Supreme and Eternal Intellect establishes original and model images of all created things, the Ideas. But while the heavenly bodies, not subject to change, express these Ideas in eternal purity and beauty, terrestrial objects, because of the inequality of matter, appear only as clouded and distorted reflections of them; the beauty of human beings especially is only too often transformed into ugliness and deformity. Thus the artist is faced with the task posed by all Neoplatonic metaphysics: he, too, "in imitation of the highest Artist," must bear within himself a notion of that unclouded beauty according to whose image nature can be "improved."

Up to this point Bellori's discussions could have been written just as well by Lomazzo or any other Neoplatonic art theorist of the Mannerist period. But now there occurs a sudden break. The idea residing in the mind of the artist is not given a metaphysical origin or a metaphysical validity, for this would open the door to that disastrous opinion according to which the artist need look at sensory reality either not at all or only in order to clarify and to enliven his inner images. Instead, the artistic Idea itself is said to originate from sensory perception, except that in it sensory perception seems brought to a purer and higher form. "Superior to nature by selection from natural beauties," as the very title of the whole essay says, the Idea is reality in a higher and purer form—*originata dalla natura supera l'origine e fassi originale dell' arte* (born from nature, it overcomes its origin and becomes the model of art). Even one of Plato's statements was borrowed—in blatant contradiction with its real meaning[19]—in order to testify that the Idea is nothing but "a perfect notion of all things, starting with the observation of nature."

It is obvious that the Bellorian theory of Ideas, regardless of the Neoplatonic beginning, reverts to that interpretation according to which the idea is not inherent *a priori* in man but is won *a posteriori* from the observation of nature ("Idea is the result of experience," as Goethe once expressed it); and only on the basis of this new revision was it possible for the author to carry the battle into the camps of both his adversaries. Contemptible are the "Naturalists," who form themselves no Idea at all and, "swearing by the model," uncritically copy the deficiencies of natural objects.[20] But equally contemptible are those who, "without knowing the truth," pursue art on the strength of mere practice and, disdaining the study of nature, try to work *di maniera* or, as Bellori once says, from a mere "phantastical Idea." In his discussion of the Idea concept Bellori thus understandably referred not so much to the testimony of the genuine Platonists and Neoplatonists as to the statements of the nature-affirming Renaissance theorists like Raphael, Alberti, and even Leonardo da Vinci; and he had to fit Cicero's well-known statement in the *Orator* (still quite correctly interpreted by Melanchthon) into his altered interpretation by means of a few significant modifications. Where Cicero says (in Victorius's version of the text, which was Bellori's source) that visible *works of art* are referred to a *mentally* conceived inner image (*cuius ad excogitatam speciem referuntur ea, quae sub oculos cadunt*), Bellori's translation of this passage says that the visible *natural objects assimilate themselves* to an *imagined* inner image (*alla cui immaginata forma imitando si rassomigliano le cose, che cadono sotto la vista*). For Cicero the Idea excluded sensory perception; for Bellori the one merged with the other. For Cicero the visible *work of art* was referred to the Idea as to something superior; for Bellori the visible *natural object* was able to assimilate itself to the Idea as to something existing on the same level.

Idea as "Purified" Nature:
The "Beau Idéal"

Classicistic art can be defined as a classicism that has become conscious of its own nature after a past no longer classical and within an environment no longer classical; the same is true of classicistic art theory as formulated by Bellori. His demand for a balance between imitating nature and surpassing nature was not alien to Renaissance art theory; but he erected it into a consistent program. Similarly, his theory of Ideas is practically identical in content with that of the Renaissance; but confronted with Mannerist and naturalistic doctrines, he formulated it explicitly and attempted to demonstrate its validity by means of historical as well as philosophical reasoning. Late sixteenth-century metaphysics, which tried to find a solution for the opposition between "subject" and "object" in God, was again replaced by an interpretation that tried to harmonize the subject with the object and the mind with nature directly, re-emphasizing the perceptive faculty of man as opposed to divine omnipotence. But the original sin of knowledge could not be undone. Exactly like the art theorists of the Renaissance, the classicistic theorists maintained that the Idea was nothing else than the experience of nature "purified" by our mind. But while the Renaissance theorists, as we saw, had found this solution for the "subject-object problem" even before the problem as such had been explicitly posed, the classicistic theorists had to face the problem as it had become acute in the recent past. They had to bring the old solution *ex post facto* into a new and programmatic formula, to establish it systematically (hence the grand Neoplatonic-cosmological introduction!), and to defend it against the tenets of a tradition and an environment that thought otherwise.

Thus we can understand that the theory of Ideas, expressed so far only in occasional and more or less casual statements by Alberti, Raphael, and Vasari, was elevated to a "system" in the time of classicism. Bellori's essay, summarizing the views of a very large number of artists and art theorists and proclaiming itself as a programmatic manifesto by its physical bulk and its cumbersome philosophical and historical apparatus,[21] is nothing but a restatement of the Idea concept prevailing in the classic Renaissance. But it was Bellori who gave this concept the form in which it entered into French and German art criticism [22] and (disregarding the protests of the *Sturm und Drang* and the Romantic periods, and despite Rumohr's crushing criticism) survived until the beginning of our own epoch. *Originata dalla natura supera l'origine e fassi l'originale dell' arte*— with this the transformation of the Idea into the *beau idéal* [23] was officially proclaimed. "Down with the naturalists" and "Down with the Mannerists"—with this the program of "idealistic aesthetics" was determined as we understand it.

The Turn to Normative Aesthetics

The classicistic view of art was thus involved in a war on two fronts—against metaphysics and against empiricism —and this double opposition explains the peculiarly invective and normative character of classicistic theory. [24] It also explains the conviction—never stressed so much even in Mannerist theory—that art, though in need of nature as the substratum or material for the process of "purification" that it is to complete, is absolutely superior to a "vulgar" nature not yet subjected to this "purification," [25] and that the simple imitation of nature as she is must be considered inferior. Despite his Neoplatonic enthusiasm for beauty even Lomazzo, not to mention Zuccari or the earlier theoreticians, had always maintained respect for faithful imitation of nature. [26] But in classicistic art theory it became clear for the first time that idealism and naturalism, the study of antiquity and the study of models, are logically incompatible. For the first time the phrase "aping of nature" applied to art, assumed that absolutely derogatory meaning which it carried, for example, for Winckelmann. Bellori never tired of heaping up proofs for the fact that the human being represented in a painting or sculpture is more perfect—or at least can and should be more perfect—than the natural one. He cited the statements of all artists who claimed that in the world of reality they could find no example of the perfectly beautiful, and he quoted countless literary passages in which the highest beauty of a living being is expressed by a comparison with a picture or a statue. And it is delightful to hear him contest Homer's explanation of the origin of the Trojan War by pointing out that Helen, as a mere natural person, could not possibly have been beautiful enough to be the object of a ten-year struggle of nations: Homer assigned this part to the actual Helen only to ennoble the *soggetto* of the Trojan War and at the same time to flatter the Greeks with the alleged possession of a perfectly beautiful woman; actually the war was not waged because of the imperfect beauty of an actual woman but because of the perfect beauty of a statue abducted by Paris and brought to Troy. In antiquity, too, the myth of the Abduction of Helen was occasionally doubted; Dion Chrysostom, for example, said that she had been given to Paris for his legitimate wife.[7] But antique writers could hardly have dreamed that a time would come when this myth would be attacked on the ground that only a work of art, not an actual woman, could justify a ten-year struggle.

Summarizing, we may say, then, that classicistic theory was the first to develop the theory of Ideas into a normative, "law-giving" aesthetics: in the Renaissance the artistic practice was not so much paralleled by a normative philosophy about art as by a constructive theory for art; whereas the period of Mannerism produced neither but thrived on a speculative art metaphysics. One may feel tempted to carry these analogies further up to the most recent times. For quite consistently, alongside modern Impressionism there was an art theory that tried to establish on the one hand the physiology of artistic "vision," on the other the psychology of artistic "thinking." And Expressionism—in more than one respect related to Mannerism—was accompanied by a peculiar kind of speculation that, though often using such psychological terms as *Ausdruck* ("expression") or *Erlebnis* ("experience"), actually led back to the tracks followed by the art theorists of the late sixteenth century: the tracks of a metaphysics of art that seeks to derive the phenomenon of artistic creativity from a suprasensory and absolute—in today's language "cosmic"—principle.

MICHELANGELO

AND DÜRER

⌈7⌉

Aꜰᴛᴇʀ ᴛʜᴇ ɪɴᴠᴇsᴛɪɢᴀᴛɪᴏɴs of Ludwig von Scheffler,[1] Borinski,[2] and Thode[3] it is no longer necessary to demonstrate that the philosophy expressed in Michelangelo's poetry is essentially determined by Neoplatonic metaphysics. Michelangelo's thought was subject to this influence indirectly as well as directly: indirectly by his preoccupation with Dante and Petrarch, directly by the undeniable effect of the Florentine and Roman humanists. With his characteristic naïveté Condivi, to whom Plato was unknown, said he had heard many competent judges say that what Michelangelo said about love was nothing else than what was written in Plato;[4] and Francesco Berni wrote:

> Ho visto qualche sua composizione,
> Sono ignorante, e pur direi d'havelle
> Lette tutte nel mezzo di Platone.[5]

> (I have seen some of his compositions;
> I am not learned, nonetheless I would
>   say that I have
> Read them all in Plato's works.)

Both did not say too much. In a *canzone*[6] that was a model for Michelangelo even with respect to form, Petrarch described how he saw shining forth from Laura's eyes the light that showed him the way to heaven. Likewise, Michelangelo felt himself carried up toward God by the sight of his beloved.[7] He repeatedly proclaimed that terrestrial beauty is nothing more than the "mortal veil" through which we recognize divine grace, that we love and may love this beauty only because it reflects the divine[8] (and vice versa, that it is the only way in which we can attain to a vision of the divine),[9] and that the contemplation of bodily perfection leads the "healthy eye" up to heavenly heights.[10] The concept of ἀνάμνησις[11] was as familiar to him as the myths of the bestowal of wings to the soul [12] and metempsychosis,[13] and he expresses the opposition between soul-degrading sensual love and the true Platonic Eros in ever new turns of phrase.[14] It is not mere chance that it was Michelangelo who restored to the not specifically Neoplatonic notion that the work of sculpture comes into being through a "removal of the super-fluous" [15]—already a commonplace in art theory—the allegorical and moral meaning that it had had for Plotinus and the later Neoplatonists. With Michelangelo the emergence of the pure form from the crude mass of stone became again the symbol of a κάθαρσις, or rebirth [16]—a κάθαρσις, to be sure, that is no longer a self-purification, as it was for Plotinus, but rather a process that can be accomplished only by the gracious intervention of the *Donna* (a thoroughly unantique, indeed specifically Michelangelesque trait):

> Si come per levar, Donna, si pone
> In pietra alpestra e dura
> Una viva figura,
> Che là più cresce, u'più la pietra scema:
> Tal alcun'opre buone,
> Per l'alma, che pur trema,
> Cela il soverchio della propria carne
> Con l'inculta sua cruda e dura scorza.
> Tu pur dalle mie streme
> Parti puo' sol levarne,
> Ch' in me non è di me voler nè forza.[17]

> (Just as by taking away, Lady, one places
> in hard, alpine stone
> a living figure,
> that grows the more, the more the stone
>   diminishes:

so some good works are hidden
for the soul, that still trembles,
by the excess of its own flesh
with its rude, hard, and tough skin.
You alone can take away
from my outermost parts,
for in me there is no will nor strength of
    myself.)

In still another poem Michelangelo referred in the same allegoristic way to this notion of the figure hidden in the block (he occasionally said of his *Night* that he had not really made it but only freed it from the stone):

Non ha l'ottimo artista in se alcun concetto,
Ch'un marmo solo in se non circoscriva
Col suo soverchio; e solo a quello arriva
La man che ubbidisce all'intelletto.
Il mal ch'io fuggo, e'l ben ch'io mi prometto,
In te Donna leggiadra, altera e diva,
Tal si nasconde; e perch'io più non viva,
Contraria ho l'arte al disiato effetto.
Amor dunque non ha, nè tua beltate,
O durezza, o fortuna, o gran disdegno,
Del mio mal colpa, o mio destino o sorte,
Se dentro del tuo cor morte e pietate
Porti in un tempo, e che'l mio basso ingegno
Non sappia, ardendo, trarne altro che morte.[18]

(Not the best artist has in himself any concept
that a single marble does not enclose in itself
with its excess; and to this [idea] attains
    only
the hand that obeys the intellect.
The evil that I flee, and the good that I promise
    myself,
in you, gracious Lady, noble and divine,
are likewise hidden; and because I am no
    longer alive,

my art goes contrary to the desired effect.
Love, then, is not to blame for my misery, nor
    your beauty,
or hardness, or fortune, or great disdain;
a fault of mine, or my destiny or fate [is to
    blame],
if inside your heart you harbor death and
    compassion
at the same time, and my inferior talent
knows not, in its passion, to draw forth other
    than death.)

The train of thought in this sonnet is approximately this: potentially the block of stone contains any figure that the artist can think of, and it depends only on his skill as a sculptor what manner of figure comes into being; in a similar way, evil as well as the greatest bliss, death as well as compassion is potentially present in the beloved's heart,[19] and it is only due to the lover's poor skill in practicing the art of love if death instead of compassion is brought forth.

The notion that to the one who loves in a higher sense, the empirical reality of a beloved object is, so to speak, only the raw material or at most the stimulus of the inner vision in which the true object of his love (the erotic Idea, as it were) is created, again corresponds completely to the views of Neoplatonism.[20] And we are tempted to conclude that the conception of the nature of the artistic Idea, as expressed in this poem, be also interpreted in a purely Platonic sense. Here, however, the situation is somewhat more complicated. First of all, one might question whether the word *concetto*, used by Michelangelo here and elsewhere to designate the inner notion of the artist, does in fact agree with what in other sources is designated as "idea." This preliminary question can be answered affirmatively for two reasons. First, the equivalence of both expressions was completely usual in contemporary usage.[21] Second, Michelangelo himself, who seems to have avoided the expression "idea" on principle, consistently used the word *concetto* as an equivalent of "idea" and differentiated it sharply from the related word *immagine*.[22] In its proper and literal sense, already formulated by St. Augustine and Thomas Aquinas, *immagine* means that notion which *ex alio procedit*,[23] that is, which reproduces an already existing object.[24] *Concetto*, on the other hand, when it does not simply stand for "thought," "concept," or "plan," [25] means the free, creative notion that constitutes its own object, so that it in turn can become the model for external shaping: as the Scholastics put it, the *forma agens*, not the *forma acta*. Thus a smith shapes his beautiful handiwork according to the *buon concetto*,[26] and God's thoughts which must be venerated and cherished in His "works of art," the countenances of beautiful human beings, are called *divin concetti*.[27]

Michelangelo as an Aristotelian

Therefore we may unhesitatingly translate the expression *concetto* with "idea" in the above poem. How far, however, does the notion, which Michelangelo here and elsewhere connected with this expression, correspond to that of the Neoplatonists? Fortunately there exists an extensive commentary on the sonnet *Non ha l'ottimo artista in se alcun concetto* which was explicitly approved by Michelangelo himself.[28] Written by Benedetto Varchi,[29] a member of the Florentine Academy, this commentary first of all confirms what our examination of usage seemed to indicate:

In questo luogo si piglia Concetto del nostro Poeta per quello che dicemmo di sopra chiamarci da' Greci *idea*, da' Latini *exemplar*, da noi modello; cio è per quella forma o imagine, detta da alcuni intenzione, che avemo dentro nella fantasia di tutto quello, che intendiamo di volere o fare o dire; la quale se bene è spiritale . . . è però cagione efficiente di tutto quello, che si dice o fa. Onde diceva il Filosofo nel settimo libro della prima Filosofia: *Forma agens respectu lecti est in anima artificis.*[30]

(In this place our Poet's *Concetto* denotes that which, as we said above, is called in Greek *idea*, in Latin *exemplar*, us "model"; that is, that form or image, called by some people the intention, that we have within our imagination, of everything that we intend to will or to make or to say; which [form or image], although spiritual . . . is for that reason the efficient cause of everything that can be said or made. Wherefore the Philosopher [Aristotle] said in the Seventh Book of the First Philosophy [Metaphysics]: "The active form, as regards the bed, is in the soul of the artisan.")

But the curious thing is that Varchi, the great Platonist, interpreted the opinion about the nature of this ideal artistic *concetto* and its relationship to the actual work of art, as championed in Michelangelo's poem, in a purely Aristotelian sense. Not only does he mention the Seventh Book of Aristotle's *Metaphysics* in the passage quoted above; he even goes on to quote Averroës's commentary on this Seventh Book, from which he takes this formulation: *Ars nihil aliud est, quam forma rei artificialis, existens in anima artificis: quae est principium factivum formae arti- ficialis in materia* (Art is nothing but the form of an arti- ficial thing existing in the artist's soul; it is the operative principle of the artificial form in matter).[31] And there is nothing in Michelangelo's poem which, taken literally, would contradict such an explanation of the term *concetto*. In itself the thought that the "idea" of the work of art is present ἐνεργείᾳ in the artist, is just as Aristotelian as the notion that the work of art itself lies locked δυνάμει in the stone or wood. It would be "Platonic" (i.e., Neoplatonic) only if an unconditional supremacy of the Idea in relation to the realized work of art were maintained; but that is not the case here. Michelangelo thought it obvious that the work of art is created not by imitating an externally given object but by realizing an inner Idea; but he did not express the view that the latter's realization in matter is always and necessarily inferior to the ἔνδον εἶδος in the soul (although with regard to natural beauty he constantly stressed the immeasurable difference between heavenly and earthly beauty, internal and external vision). And though he would certainly have rejected—in contrast to the convictions of classical antiquity and modern classicism—a derivation of the artistic Idea from sensory experience,[32] he did not think it necessary explicitly to assert, as did the Mannerist metaphysics of art, that it originates in some supraterrestrial sphere.

Art, insofar as he did not reject it along with all other earthly things in the religious fervor of his old age, seems to have been for Michelangelo a perfectly valid method of bridging the gulf between Idea and reality. And probably it is not unintentional that he preferred the term *concetto* to "Idea," a term already somewhat worn out by other contemporary writers; for to him, who really knew Neoplatonism, "Idea" entailed of necessity a transcendent meaning. Michelangelo's artistic "thoughts" needed neither to boast about nor to seek justification in their divine origin and supernatural beauty.

Classic and Romantic Tendencies in Dürer

Entirely different but no less exceptional is the meaning which Dürer attached to the concept of the artistic Idea. In his mind the passionate desire to reduce art to rational rules, which had been aroused by his contact with Italian art theory, struggled with an almost romantic conviction that artistic "genius" is something individual and can be understood only as a wondrous gift. The same man who tried for half his lifetime to establish the suprasubjective "basis" (*Grund*) of artistic creation, who labored to find the universally binding laws of correctness and beauty, formulated on the other hand the opinion—which he himself said was "unusual" (*seltsam*) and understandable only to "powerful" artists—that one man can produce something more valuable in an unpretentious little drawing than another in a major painting that had occupied him for months and years; that one man can prove himself to be a greater artist by the representation of an ugly figure than another by the representation of a beautiful one:

> Dann es ist eine grosse Kunst, welcher in groben bäurischen Dingen ein rechten Gwalt und kunst kann anzeigen . . . und diese Gab ist wunderlich. Dann Gott giebt oft Einem Verstand, etwas Guts zu machen, desgleichen ihn zu seinen Zeiten keiner gleich erfunden wird und etwan lang keiner vor ihm gewest und nach ihm nit bald einer kummt.

> (For it is a great art that in crude, rustic things can show real power and art . . . and this gift is wondrous. For often God gives to one man the intellectual power [*Verstand*] to make something good, the equal of whom will not be found in his own time; and perhaps long before him there has been none and after him another will not come soon.)

With this inner dualism—for to follow the romantic-individualistic line of thought consistently would have reduced the whole art-theoretical effort of the Renaissance to absurdity—Dürer arrived earlier than the Italians at realizing the problematic nature of the relationship between law and reality, rule and genius, "object" and "subject." He recognized both the impossibility of establishing one universally valid norm of beauty and the impossibility of being satisfied with simply imitating that which was given to the senses. And finally he arrived at the conclusion that for the great artist both the mathematical method of investigating proportions and the empirical method of copying models could mean no more than a first step—admittedly very necessary—toward freely creative and yet "well-grounded" as well as "natural" production from the mind alone: he who has done much measuring will develop his own *Augenmass* (i.e., intuitive sense of proportion); he who "has filled his mind full" by much *Abmachen* (i.e., reproducing nature from life), will accumulate a "secret treasure of the heart," from which he can pour forth what he "has gathered in from the outside for a long time." [33]

With this Dürer had come very close to what contemporary Italian art theory understood by the concept "idea." And he himself did use the expression "idea"—in a few fragments that date as early as 1512—though in a very different and extremely personal sense:

Die gross Kunst der Molerei ist vor viel hundert Johren bei den mächtigen Künigen in grosser Achtbarkeit gewesen, dann sie machten die fürtrefflichen Künstner reich, hieltens wirdig, dann sie achteten solche Sinnreichigkeit ein geleichformig Geschopf noch Gott. *Dann ein guter Maler ist inwendig voller Figur, und obs müglich wär, dass er ewiglich lebte, so hätt er aus den inneren Ideen, dovan Plato schreibt, allweg etwas Neus durch die Werk auszugiessen.*[34]

(The great art of painting has been in great esteem with the powerful kings many hundred years ago, for they made the outstanding artists rich and honored them, considering such talent to be a creative thing like unto God. *For a good painter is inwardly full of figures, and if it*

*were possible that he live forever, he would have from the
inner ideas, of which Plato writes, always something new
to pour out in his works.*)

Primary Characteristic of Ideas for Dürer

Here, then, "idea" is not used, according to the Renaissance
view, to signify the final result of external experience
but—in much closer agreement with the views of the Middle
Ages and the Neoplatonism later adopted in Italy—to designate a completely internal notion, such as the soul's "inner
image" spoken of by Meister Eckhart. Still more important:
Ideas normally provide a guarantee of objective validity and
beauty in the work of art; with Dürer, however, their proper
function is to ensure originality and inexhaustibility in that
they enable the artist to pour forth "always something new"
from his mind. The theory of Ideas, which here almost take
on the character of inspirations, serves to support that romantic conception of genius that recognizes the mark of true
artistry not in correctness and beauty but in an unending
plenitude that always creates things unique and things that
never existed before.

The wording of Dürer's statement "For a good painter is
inwardly full of figures, and if it were possible that he live
forever, he would have from the inner ideas, of which Plato
writes, always something new to pour out in his works" is
influenced by two other pronouncements. On the one hand it,
like another oft-quoted statement from the same fragment,
sounds slightly like a remark by Ficino: *Unde divinis influxibus oraculisque ex alto repletus nova quaedam inusitataque
semper excogitat et futura praedicit* (Wherefore, filled with
divine influences and oracles from on high, he [the Saturnian
melancholic] always devises something new and unusual
and foretells the future).[35] On the other hand it seems to be

1 2 4

influenced by Seneca's well-known assertion: *Haec exemplaria rerum omnium deus intra se habet . . . plenus his figuris est, quas Plato ideas appellat* (God has within himself these models of all things . . . He is full of these figures, which Plato calls "ideas").[36] This blending of two such dissimilar sentences resulted, however, in a completely new thought. Whereas Seneca said that God is "inwardly full of figures" Dürer said the same thing of man. And whereas Ficino, basically not interested in representational art, aimed his statement about *divinis influxibus* only at the almost mantic ecstasy of philosophers (to him synonymous with theologians and seers), Dürer transferred it to the painter. Thus he combined the concept of "idea" with the concept of artistic inspiration, and gave an incomparably deep foundation to his statement, almost offensive to a pious sensibility, that artistic activity is a "creative thing like unto God." But this statement itself is an intrinsically humanistic one that was entirely common in Italian art theory: again and again it was proclaimed that the artist "in imitation of the highest Creator" actually "creates" his productions and that he himself is comparable to an *alter deus*.[37] In the Middle Ages it had been customary to compare God with the artist in order to explain the nature of divine creation; later the artist was compared with God in order to heroize artistic activity. This was the time when he came to be called *divino*.

The contrast between "theory of Ideas" and "theory of imitation" in art theory may be compared to the contrast between "representationism" and (in the broadest sense) "conceptualism" in epistemology. In both fields the relation of the "subject" to the "object" is explained now in terms of a purely reproductive portrayal, now in terms of a free construction that works from "innate ideas," and now in terms of an abstraction that chooses from that which is "given" and then combines the things chosen. In both fields the constant vacillation between these various possibilities and also the insoluble difficulty of proving the necessary correspondence between that which is "given" and the cognition of it without appealing to a transcendent authority, is based on the presupposition of a "thing in itself," with which the intellectual notion—be it mere reproduction or independent creation— can correspond, and must correspond, only if the necessity of this correspondence is guaranteed by a principle in one way or another divine. In epistemology the presupposition of this "thing in itself" was profoundly shaken by Kant; in art theory a similar view was proposed by Alois Riegl. We believe to have realized that artistic perception is no more faced with a "thing in itself" than is the process of cognition; that on the contrary the one as well as the other can be sure of the validity of its judgments precisely because it alone determines the rules of its world (i.e., it has no objects other than those that are constituted within itself).[38] Thus the opposition between "idealism" and "naturalism" that ruled the philosophy of art until the end of the nineteenth century and under multifarious disguises—Expressionism and Impressionism, Abstraction and Empathy—retained its place in the twentieth, must in the final analysis appear as a "dialectical antinomy." But just from this point of view we can understand how this opposition could affect arttheoretical thought for such a long time and force it again and again to search for new, more or less contradictory solutions. To recognize the diversity of these solutions and to understand their historical presuppositions is worthwhile for history's sake, even though philosophy has come to realize that the problem underlying them is by its very nature insoluble.

APPENDICES

Translated by Victor A. Velen

APPENDIX I

G. P. Lomazzo's Chapter on Beautiful Proportions and Marsiglio Ficino's Commentary on the Symposium

Marsiglio Ficino [1]

[*Che la Belleza è cosa spiritvale.* CAPI. III.

. . . Sono alcuni, che anno oppenione, la pulcritudine essere una certa posizione di tutti i membri o veramente commensurazione e proporzione con qualche suavità di colori. L'oppenione de quali non ammettiamo. . . . *Aggiugnesi, che quella proporzione include tutti i membri del Corpo composto insieme,* [in modo che ella non è in alcuno de' membri di per se, ma in tutti insieme. Adunque qualunche de' Membri in se non sarà bello,] *ma la proporzione di tutto il composto nasce pure dalle parti;* [onde ne resulta una absurdità. . . .] [2]

Che la Belleza è lo Splendore del Volto di Dio, CAPI. IIII.

La Divina Potenzia supereminente allo Vniverso, agli Angeli e agli animi da lei creati clementemente infonde, si come a suoi figliuoli, quel suo raggio, [nel quale è virtù feconda a qualunche cosa creare. Questo raggio divino in questi, come più propinqui a Dio, dipinge lo ordine di tutto il mondo molto più espressamente che nella materia mondana; per laqualcosa questa

G. P. Lomazzo's Chapter on Beautiful Proportions and Marsiglio Ficino's Commentary on the Symposium

Marsiglio Ficino [1]

[*That Beauty Is a Spiritual Thing.* CHAPTER III

. . . Some are of the opinion that beauty is a certain arrangement of all the limbs, or indeed commensurateness and proportion with some pleasantness of colors. We do not agree. . . .] *Further, that this proportion includes all the limbs of the body taken as a whole,* [in such a way that it exists in no one of the limbs alone but in all together. Thus any one of the limbs by itself will not be beautiful] *but the proportion of the entire combination comes about precisely from its parts;* [hence an absurdity results. . . .] [2]

That Beauty Is the Splendor of God's Visage.
CHAPTER IV

The Divine Power, being supreme over the universe, mercifully infuses with his ray, as though His sons, the Angels and spirits created by Him. [This divine ray, in which there is the fecund energy of creation, depicts the order of the entire world in the Angels and spirits, as more akin to God, much more clearly than in worldly matter. Hence this picture of the world is

pittura del mondo, la quale noi veggiamo tutta, negli Angeli e negli animi è più espressa, che innanzi a gli occhi.] *In quelli è la figura di qualunque spera, del Sole, Luna e Stelle, delli elementi, pietre, arbori e animali. Queste pitture si chiamano nelli Angeli esemplari e idee, nelli animi ragioni e notizie, nella materia del mondo immagini e forme. Queste pitture son chiare nel mondo, più chiare nell' animo e chiarissime sono nell' Angelo. Adunque un' medesimo volto di Dio riluce in tre specchi posti per ordine, nell' Angelo, nell' animo e nel corpo mondano: Nel primo, come più propinquo, in modo chiarissimo; nel secondo, come più remoto . . . men' chiaro: nel terzo, come remotissimo, molto oscuro. Dipoi la santa mente dello Angelo, perchè non è da ministerio di corpo impedita, in se medesima si riflette, dove vede quel' volto di Dio nel suo seno scolpito,* [et veggendolo si maraviglia, e maravigliandosi con grande avidità a quello sempre si unisce. Et noi chiamiamo Belleza quella grazia del volto divino, et lo Amore chiamiamo la avidità dello Angelo, per laquale si invischia in tutto al volto divino. Iddio volessi, amici miei, che sto ancora avvenisse a noi.] *Ma l' animo nostro, creato con questa condizione, che si circunda da corpo terreno, al ministerio corporale declina, dalla quale inclinazione gravato mette in oblio il tesoro, che nel suo petto è nascoso. Dipoi che nel corpo terreno è involto, lungo tempo all' uso del corpo serve e a questa opera sempre accomoda il senso e accommodavi ancora la ragione più spesso che è non debbe. Diquì avviene, che l' animo non riguarda la luce del volto divino che in lui sempre splende, prima che il corpo sia già adulto e la ragione sia desta, con laquale consideri il volto di Dio, che manifestamente alli occhi nella macchina del mondo riluce.* [Per laquale considerazione si inalza a risguardare quel volto di Dio, che dentro allo animo risplende. Et perchè il volto del padre a' figliuoli è grato, è necessario, che il volto del Padre Iddio alli animi sia gratissimo. Lo splendore e la grazia di questo volto, o nello Angelo o nello animo o nella materia mondana che si sia, si debbe chiamare universal' Belleza, e lo appetito, che si volge inverso quella, è universal Amore.] *Et noi non dubitiamo questa Belleza essere incorporale, perchè nello Angelo e nello animo questa non essere*

better expressed in the former than in what we see before our eyes] *In the latter is found the shape of any of the spheres, the sun, the moon, the stars, the elements, rocks, trees, and animals. In the Angels these images are called Ideas and prototypes; in the spirits, reasons and knowledge; and in worldly matter, appearances and forms. These images are clear in the world, more clear in the spirit, and clearest in the Angel. Hence one and the same visage of God is reflected in three mirrors in order, in the Angel, in the clearest way; in the second as more remote, less clear; in the third as the most remote, the most obscure. Thus the holy mind of the Angel, unimpeded by a body, reflects itself in itself, where it sees God's visage sculpted in its breast* [and seeing it, marvels, and marveling at it rapturously, unites with it forever. And we call this grace from God's visage Beauty, and the rapture of the Angel, with which it attaches itself completely to God's visage, we call Love. God would like us, my friends, to do as the Angels.] *But our spirit, created in this condition, surrounded by an earthly body, stoops from its corporeal ministry and, weighed down by this propensity, tends to forget the treasure buried in its breast. And since it is enveloped in an earthly body, it serves that body for a long time, adjusting reason and the senses to this service much more than it should. Consequently, the spirit does not always see the light of the divine visage that radiates within it, before the body is adult and reason is awake enough to consider God's visage as it manifestly illumines the entire world.* [It then raises itself up to contemplate the visage of God that shines within the spirit. And because the face of the father is pleasing to the sons, it follows that the face of God would be most pleasing to the spirits. The splendor and grace of this visage, in the Angel, in the spirit, or in worldly matter, whichever it might be, must be called universal Beauty, and the desire, which is attracted to it, universal Love.] *We do not doubt that this Beauty is incorporeal, since it is manifestly incorporeal in the Angel and the spirit, and we have shown above that it is incorporeal in the bodies. From this then we can understand that the eye does not see else but the light of the sun, because the shapes and colors of the bodies are*

corpo è manifesto, e ne' corpi ancora questa essere incorporale mostrammo disopra; e al presente diquì lo possiamo intendere, che lo occhio non vede altro, che lume di Sole, perchè le figure e li colori de' corpi non si veggono mai, se non da lume illustrati; et essi non vengono con la loro materia a lo occhio. Et pur necessario pare questi dovere essere negli occhi, acciochè dagli occhi sieno veduti. Vno adunque lume di sole, dipinto di colori e figure di tutti i corpi, in che percuote, si rappresenta agli occhi; li occhi per lo aiuto d' un' lor certo raggio naturale pigliano il lume del Sole così dipinto, e poichè l' anno preso, veggono esso lume e tutte le dipinture che in esso sono. Il perchè tutto questo ordine del mondo, che si vede, si piglia da gli occhi, non in quel modo, che egli è nella materia de' corpi, ma in quel modo, che egli è nella luce, laquale è negli occhi infusa. Et perchè egli è in quella luce, separato già da la materia, necessariamente è senza corpo. [Et questo diquì manifestamente si vede, perchè esso lume non può essere corpo, conciosia che in un momento di oriente in occidente quasi tutto il mondo riempie, e penetra da ogni parte il corpo della aria e della acqua senza offensione alcuna, et spandendosi sopra cose putride non si macchia. Queste condizioni alla natura del corpo non si convengono, perchè il corpo non in momento, ma in tempo si muove, e un corpo non penetra lo altro senza dissipazione dell' uno o dell' altro o di amenduoi; et duoi corpi, insieme misti, con iscambievole contagione si turbano. Et questo veggiamo nella confusione della acqua e del vino, del fuoco e della terra.] *Conciosia adunque, che il lume del Sole sia incorporale, cio ch' egli riceve, riceve secondo il modo suo. Et però i colori e le figure de' corpi, in modo spiritale riceve, et nel modo medesimo lui ricevuto da gl' occhi si vede. Onde nasce, che tutto l' ornamento di questo mondo, che è il terzo volto di Dio, per la luce del Sole incorporale offerisce se incorporale agli occhi.*

[*Come nasce lo Amore et l'Odio, et che fa Belleza è spirituale.* CAPI. V.

Di tutte queste cose seguita, che ogni grazia del volto divino, che si chiama la universal' pulcritudine, non solamente nello

*never seen unless illuminated by light, and they do not appear
with their matter to the eye. Yet it seems necessary to have them
in the eye, so that they may be seen by the eye. Hence one and
the same light of the sun, painted with the colors and shapes of
all the bodies it strikes, presents itself to the eyes. The eyes
through their own natural rays receive the light of the sun so
painted, and once they have received it, they see the light and all
the paintings that are in it. That is why the entire order of the
world, which is visible, is perceived with the eyes, not in the
matter of the bodies, but in the light which flows into the eyes.
And because this order is in the light, separated from matter, it
is necessarily incorporeal.* [And this is manifest, because the
light itself cannot be body, since it fills in one moment nearly the
whole world from east to west, and everywhere penetrates air
and water without the least difficulty, and although it embraces
vile things, it does not stain itself. These phenomena cannot be
attributed to the nature of the body, because the body does not
move in a moment but in time, and a body does not penetrate
another body without the dissolution of one, the other or both,
and the two bodies, mixed together, stain each other in the
process of combining. This we see in the mixture of water and
wine, of fire and earth.] *Therefore, since the light of the sun is
incorporeal, what it receives, it receives in its own way. Hence
the colors and the shapes of the bodies it receives in a spiritual
fashion, and in this same fashion it is received by the eyes. The
result is that all of the embellishment of this world, which is the
third face of God, is transmitted through the incorporeal light of
the sun and is presented incorporeal to the eyes.*

[*How Love and Hate Are Born, and What Makes
Beauty Spiritual.* CHAPTER V

It follows from all this that any grace received from the
divine visage, which is called universal Beauty, is incorporeal,
not only in the Angel and the spirit, but also in the sight of the
eyes. We love this visage not only as a whole, but also, being
moved by admiration, in its parts, from whence a special Love is

Angelo e nello animo sia incorporale, ma eziandio nello aspetto delli occhi. Non solamente questa faccia tutta insieme, ma eziandio le parti sue da ammirazione conmossi amiamo, dove nasce particulare Amore a particulare Belleza. Così ponghiamo affezione a qualche uomo, come membro dello ordine mondano, massime quando in quello la scintilla dell' ornamento divino manifestamente risplende. Questa affezione da due cagioni depende: si perchè la immagine del volto paterno ci piace, si eziandio perchè la spezie e figura dell' uomo attamente composta attissimamente si confà con quel sigillo o vero ragione della generazione umana, laquale l' anima nostra prese da l'Autore del tutto e in se ritiene. Onde la immagine dell' uomo esteriore presa per i sensi passando nello animo, s' ella discorda da la figura dell' uomo, laquale lo animo da la sua origine possiede, subito dispiace e come brutta odio genera; se ella si concorda, di fatto piace et come bella s' ama. Perlaqualcosa accade, che alcuni scontrandosi in noi subito ci piacciono o vero dispiacciono, benchè noi non sappiamo la cagione di tale effetto, perchè l' animo impedito nel ministerio del corpo non risguarda le forme, che sono per natura dentro a lui, ma per la naturale e occulta disconvenienza o convenienza seguita, che la forma della cosa esteriore con la immagine sua pulsando la forma della cosa medesima, che è dipinta nell' animo, dissuona o vero consuona, e da questa occulta offensione o vero allettamento lo animo commosso la detta cosa odia o ama. Quel raggio divino, di che sopra parlammo, infuse nell' Angelo e nell' animo la vera figura nell uomo, che si debbe generare intera; ma la composizione dell' uomo nella materia del mondo, laquale è da(1) divino artefice remotissima, degenera da quella sua figura intera:] *nella materia melio disposta resulta più simile, nell' altra meno. Quella che resulta più simile, come ella si confà con la forza di Dio e con la Idea dello Angelo, così si confà ancora alla ragione e sigillo che è nello animo; lo animo appruova questa convenienza del confarsi, e in questa convenienza consiste la Belleza,* [et nella approvazione consiste lo affetto di Amore, et perchè la Idea e la ragione o vero sigillo sono alieni da la materia del corpo, però la compositione dell' uomo si giudica simile a quelli, non per la materia o per la quantità, ma per qualche altra parte incorporale. Et secondo che

born of a special Beauty. In the same way we have affection for some man, as a member of the worldly order, all the more if the spark of divine ornament manifestly radiates in him. This admiration is inspired for two reasons: because the resemblance to the paternal visage pleases us, and because the appearance and the form of man, aptly composed, most aptly conforms with that stamp or true reason of human generation, which our soul has taken completely from its author and maintains within itself. Therefore if the image of the exterior man received through the senses by way of the spirit is discordant with the shape of the man, which the spirit possesses from the beginning, it immediately displeases and, being ugly, engenders hatred; if it conforms, it pleases for that reason and, being beautiful, is loved. Hence it happens that when we meet someone, we like or dislike him immediately, although we do not know the reason, because the spirit, impeded by the bodily function, does not consider the forms that by nature are within it. But from a natural and hidden capacity or incapacity it happens that the form of the exterior thing, as it pulsates with the image of the thing itself, which is revealed in the spirit, harmonizes or is truly discordant, and the spirit reacts to this hidden displeasure or true pleasure by hating or loving this particular thing. That divine ray, of which we have spoken, infused into the Angel and the spirit the true shape of man, which must be taken as a whole. But the composition of man within worldly matter, which is farthest removed from the divine maker, degenerates from this his integral shape:] *in better proportioned matter, it emerges more nearly similar, in other matter, less so. It emerges most similar as it conforms with the power of God and with the Idea of the Angel, in such a way that it also conforms with reason and the stamp which is its spirit. The spirit approves of this affinity of conformations, and Beauty consists of this affinity,* [and the desire to love consists in the approval. Because Idea and reason or the true stamp are alien to the matter of the body, the composition of man is therefore judged similar to these, not because of the matter or the quantity, but because of some other incorporeal part. And if it resembles, it is in harmony with them, and according to this harmony, it is beautiful. The body

è simile, si conviene con quegli, e secondo che si conviene, è bella, et però il corpo e la Belleza sono diversi. Se alcuno dimanda, in che modo la forma del corpo possa essere simile alla forma e ragione dell' anima e dell' Angelo, prego quel tale che consideri lo edificio dello Architettore. Da principio lo Architettore la ragione e quasi [3] Idea dello edificio nello animo suo concepe; dipoi fabrica la casa (secondo che e' può) tale, quale nel pensiero dispose. Chi negherà la casa essere corpo? Et questa essere molto simile alla incorporale Idea dello artefice, a la cui similitudine fù fatta? Certamente per un certo ordine incorporale più tosto che per la materia simile si debbe giudicare. Sforzati un poco a trarne la materia, se tu puoi: tu la puoi trarre col pensiero. Orsù trai a lo edificio la materia e lascia sospeso lo ordine: non ti resterà di corpo materiale cosa alcuna, anzi tutto uno sarà l' ordine che venne da lo artefice e l' ordine che nello artefice rimase. Dhè, fà questo medesimo nel corpo di qualunche uomo, e così troverrai la forma di quello, che si confà col sugello dell' animo, essere semplice e senza materia.] [4]

Quante parti si richieggono a fare la cosa bella, et che la Belleza è dono spirituale. CAPI. VI.

Finalmente che cosa è la Belleza del corpo? Certamente è un certo atto, vivacità e grazia, che risplende nel corpo per lo influsso della sua Idea. Questo splendore non descende nella materia, s' ella non è prima attissimamente preparata. Et la preparazione del corpo vivente in tre cose s' adempie, ordine, mode e spezie. L' ordine significa le distanze delle parti; il modo significa la quantità; la spezie significa lineamenti e colori. Perchè inprima bisogna, che ciascuni membri del corpo abbino il sito naturale, e questo è, che li orecchi, li occhi e il naso e gli altri membri siano ne' luoghi loro, et che gli occhi amenduni egualmente siano propinqui al naso, et che gli orecchi amenduni egualmente siano discosto da gli occhi. Et questa parità di distanzie, che s' appartiene a l' ordine, ancora non basta, se non vi si aggiugne il modo delle parti, il quale attribuisca a qualunche membro la grandeza debita, attendendo a la proporzione di tutto

and Beauty are therefore different. If someone asks in what way the form of the body may be similar to the form and reason of the spirit and the Angel, I ask this person to consider the edifice of the Architect. From the beginning the Architect conceives in his spirit the reason and approximately [3] the Idea of the edifice; he then makes the house (according to his ability) in the way in which he has decided in his mind. Who will deny that the house is a body, and that it is very similar to the incorporeal Idea of the artisan, in whose image it has been made? It must certainly be judged for a certain incorporeal order rather than for its matter. Try for a moment to abstract the matter, if you can. Abstract it in your thought. Then abstract the matter from the building, and leave the order suspended (as it is). Nothing will remain of the material body; in fact it will all be but one order as it came from the creator and as it has remained in this same work. Then do the same with the body of any man, and you will find that the form of what concords with the stamp of the spirit is simple and free of matter.] [4]

What Components Are Needed to Make a Thing Beautiful, and That Beauty Is a Spiritual Gift. CHAPTER VI

Finally, what is the Beauty of the body? Surely it is a certain attitude, vivacity and grace, which radiate in the body from the infusion of its Idea. This splendor does not derive from the matter, if the latter has not been most aptly prepared for it. And the living body is prepared according to three particulars: order, mode and form. The order is the distance of the parts, the mode is the quantity, and the form is lines and color. In order that all parts of the body have their natural place, the ears, the eyes, the nose and the other parts must first be in their proper positions, the eyes at an equal distance from the nose and both ears equally spaced from the eyes. And this proportion of distances, which is part of the order, is still not enough if the mode of the parts is not added, attributing to each limb its proper length in accordance with the proportion of the whole body. [And this is when three noses placed lengthwise fill the length of a face, when the

il corpo. [Et questo è, che tre nasi posti per lungo adempino la lungheza d' un volto, et ancora li duoi mezi cerchi delli orechi insieme congiunti faccino il cerchio della bocca aperte, e se questo medesimo faccino le ciglia, se insieme si congiungono. La lungheza del naso ragguagli la lungheza del labbro e similmente dello orecchio, e i duoi tondi degli occhi raguaglino la apertura della bocca. Otto capi faccino la lungheza di tutto il corpo, et similmente le braccia distese per lato e le gambe distese faccino l' alteza del corpo.] [5] *Oltre a questo stimiamo necessaria la spezie, acciochè li artificiosi tratti delle linee e le crespe e lo splendore de gli occhi odornini l' ordine e il modo delle parti. Queste tre cose benchè nella materia siano, nientedimeno parte alcuna del corpo essere non possono. L' ordine de' membri non è membro alcuno, perchè lo ordine è in tutti i membri e nessuno membro in tutti i membri si ritruova. Aggiugnesi, che lo ordine non è altro che conveniente distanzia delle parti, et la distanzia è o nulla o vacuo o un tratto di linee. Ma chi dirà le linee essere corpo? Cinciosiachè manchino di latitudine e di profondità, che sono necessarie al corpo. Oltra questo il modo non è quantità, ma e termine di quantità. I termini sono superficie, linee e punti, lequali cose non avendo profondità non si debbono corpi chiamare. Collochiamo ancora la spezie non nella materia, ma nella gioconda concordia di lumi, ombre, e linee. Per questa ragione si mostra la Belleza essere da la materia corporale tanto discosto, che non si comunica a essa materia, se non è disposta con quelle tre preparazioni incorporali, lequali abbiamo narrate. Il fondamento di queste tre preparazioni è la temperata complessione de' quattro elementi, in modo che il corpo nostro sia molto simile al cielo, la sustanzia delquale è temperata, e non si rebelli de la formazione della anima per la esorbitanza di alcuno umore. Così il celeste splendore facilmente apparirà nel corpo simile al cielo. Et quella perfetta forma dell' uomo, laquale possiede l' animo, nella materia pacifica e obbediente resulterà più propia.* [Quasi in simil modo si dispongono le voci a ricevere la Belleza loro. L' ordine loro è il salire da la voce grave a la ottava e lo scendere da la ottava a la grave. Il modo è il discorrere debitamente per le terze, quarte, quinte e seste voci, tuoni e semituoni. La spezie è

half circles of the ears joined together form the circle of the open mouth, and when the same is done with the eyelids they are joined together. The length of the nose equals the length of the lip and likewise of the ear, and the two eyebrows equal the opening of the mouth. Eight heads make up the length of the whole body, and similarly the outstretched arms and legs equal the height of the body.] [5] *Furthermore, we consider the form necessary so that a graceful disposition of the line and curves, and the splendor of the eyes, will adorn the order and mode of the parts. Although these three particulars are in the matter, they nonetheless may not be any part of the body. The order of the limbs is not a limb by itself, because the order is in all of the limbs and in no one limb are all of the limbs present. In addition, the order is nothing more than a proper spacing of the parts, and the spacing is either nothing, a void or a linear characteristic. But who will say that the lines are the body? They lack the length and the depth necessary to the body. Moreover, the mode is not quantity, but the limit of quantity. The limits are the surfaces, lines and points which, not having depth, cannot be called bodies. We also do not put shapeliness into the matter but into the joyful harmony of the lights, shadows and lines. For this reason Beauty is so distant from corporeal matter that matter does not communicate with it unless the matter is prepared according to the three incorporeal conditions that we have mentioned. The basis of these three conditions is the harmonious constitution of the four elements in such a way that our body most resembles heaven, the substance of which is harmonious, and does not rebel against the formation of the soul due to an excess of some humor. In such a way the splendor of heaven easily appears in the body as similar to heaven. And this perfect form of man, which the spirit possesses, will be more integral in peaceful and obedient matter.* [In a somewhat similar fashion the voices are arranged to receive their Beauty. Their order is to rise from the lowest voice one octave and to fall an octave to the lowest. The mode is to run adroitly through thirds, fourths, fifths and sixths, tones and halftones. The form is the resonance of the clear voice. By means of these three conditions, as by

la risonanza della chiara voce. Per queste tre cose come per tre elementi i corpi di molti membri composti, come sono arbori, animali e ancora la congregazione di molte voci, a ricevere la Belleza si dispongono; e i corpi più semplici, come sono i quattro elementi e pietre e metalli et le semplici voci si preparano a essa Belleza suffizientemente per una certa temperata fecondità e chiarità di loro natura. Ma l' animo è di sua natura a essa accommodato, massimamente per questo, che egli è spirito e quasi specchio a Dio prossimo, nel quale, come disopra dicemmo, luce la immagine del volto divino.

Adunque como all oro niente bisogna aggiugnere a fare che paia bello, ma basta separarne le parti della terra, se da esse è offuscato:] *così lo animo non à bisogno, che se li aggiunga cosa alcuna a fare che egli apparisca bello. Ma bisogna por' giù la cura e sollecitudine del corpo tanto ansia e la perturbazione della cupidità e del timore, et subito la naturale pulcritudine dello animo si mostrerrà.* [Ma acciochè il nostro sermone non trapassi molto il proposito suo,] *conchiudiamo brevemente per le sopradette cose la Belleza essere una certa grazia vivace e spiritale, laquale per il raggio divino prima si infonde negli Angeli, poi nelle anime degli uomini, dopo questi nelle figure* [e voci] *corporali; e questa grazia per mezo della ragione e del vedere* [e dello udire] *muove e diletta lo animo nostro, e nel dilettare rapisce, e nel rapire d' ardente amore infiamma.*

G. P. Lomazzo [6]

[*Del modo di conoscere e* [7] *constituire le proporzioni secondo la bellezza.* Capi. xxvi.

Resta hora ch'io tratti delle generali vie di disponere con ragione tutte le parti in che l'arte s'è divisa, e primieramente della proporzione come di tutte prima, la quale per comun parere si tien essere quella cosa incorporale, che nei corpi include tutte le membra insiemte, e nasce in loro dalle parti. Questa sebben in potenza è una medesima, in molti modi si può conoscere ed

three elements, bodies composed of many limbs, such as trees, animals and even a choir of many voices, prepare themselves to receive Beauty; and the most simple bodies, such as the three elements, stones and metals and the simple voices prepare themselves adequately for this Beauty by a certain harmonious fecundity and clarity in their nature. But the spirit is by its nature accommodated to Beauty mainly because it is spirit and a close mirror of God in which, as we said above, the likeness of the divine visage radiates.

Just as it is not necessary to add anything to gold, for it to appear beautiful—it is enough to separate parts of earth from it if it is dulled by them:]—*so the spirit does not need anything added to it for it to appear beautiful. One must only erase care and solicitude from the body as well as the anguish and perturbation of cupidity and fear, and the natural beauty of the spirit will immediately be manifest.* [But so that our discourse not over-reach its topic,] *We conclude briefly from the above discussion that Beauty is a certain vital and spiritual grace, which is infused first into the Angel by the divine ray, then into the spirits of men, and following these, into corporeal forms* [and voices]; *and this grace by means of reason and sight* [and hearing] *moves and delights our spirit; and in delighting, enraptures, and in enrapturing, inspires ardent love.*

G. P. Lomazzo [6]

[*On the Method of Knowing and* [7] *Establishing the Proportions in Accordance with Beauty.* CHAPTER XXVI

It remains for me now to deal with the general ways of ordering rationally all the parts into which art is divided, and first of all proportion, as the most important. According to accepted opinion, proportion is considered to be that incorporeal aspect which embraces in the bodies all the limbs together and is born out of their parts. Although this potentially is one and the

instituire, risguardando la natura della bellezza, a ch'ella serve nelle pitture, per rappresentare il vero che si considera nei corpi. Il quale per molte vie si conseguisce secondo le diversità, che si trovano in loro, tanto per la bellezza dell' animo, quanto per la temperanza del corpo; siccome a pieno ne discorrono i Platonici.] *E prima abbiamo da sapere, che la bellezza non è altro che una certa grazia vivace e spiritale, la qual per il raggio divino prima s'infonde negl' Angeli, in cui si vedono le figure di qualunque sfera, che si chiamano in loro esemplari ed idee; poi passa negli animi, ove le figure si chiamano ragioni e notizie, e finalmente nella materia, ove si dicono immagini e forme,* [e quivi per il mezzo della ragione e del vedere diletta a tutti, ma più e meno secondo le ragioni che si diranno più basso]. *Questa bellezza risplende in un medesimo volto d' Iddio in tre specchj posti per ordine, nell' Angelo, nell' Animo e nel Corpo, nel primo come più propinquo in modo chiarissimo, nel secondo come remoto men chiaro, nel terzo come remotissimo molto oscuro. Ma l'Angelo, perchè non è dal corpo impedito, in se stesso si riflette e vede la sua bellezza in se medesimo scolpita. E l' Animo creato con questa condizione, che sia circondato dal corpo terreno, al ministerio corporale declina. Dalla quale inclinazione gravato, mette in obblio questa bellezza, che ha in se nascosta, e tutto da poi ch' è involto nel corpo terreno, s' impiega all' uso d' esso corpo, accommodandovi il senso, ed alle volte la ragione ancora. E di quì è, ch' egli non risguarda questa bellezza, che in lui di continuo risplende, infino che il corpo non è già cresciuto, e la ragione svegliata, con la quale considera quella, che agli occhi della macchina del mondo riluce e in essa soggiorna. Finalmente la bellezza del corpo non è altro, che un certo atto, vivacità e grazia, che in lui risplende per lo influsso della sua idea, il quale non discende nella materia se ella non è attissimamente preparata. E tal preparazione del corpo vivente in tre cose si compisce, che sono ordine, modo e spezie. L' ordine significa le differenze delle parti, il modo la quantità, e la specie i lineamenti ed i colori. Imperrochè bisogna primieramente, che ciascuno delle membra sia nel suo debito loco, e che gli occhi per esempio ugualmente siano propinqui al naso, e gl' orecchi ugualmente*

same, it may be understood and established in many ways, with
due regard for the nature of beauty, which it serves in painting
to represent what is felt to be true in the bodies. It may be
variously obtained, according to the diversity found in the bodies, and derives as much from the beauty of the spirit as from
the temperament of the body—as the Platonists amply discuss
it.] *First we must understand that beauty is nothing more than a
certain spiritual and lively grace, which by means of the divine
ray is first infused into the Angels, in whom the shapes of any
sphere may be seen; reflected in the Angels these are called
exemplars and Ideas. Then it passes on to the spirits, in whom
these shapes are called reasons and notions, and finally into
matter, where they are called images and forms,* [and there by
means of reason and sight it delights us all, but more or less for
the reasons that we will enumerate below]. *This beauty shines
from one and the same visage of God into three mirrors, arranged in order, in the Angel, in the Spirit, and in the Body. In
the first as the nearest, in the clearest way; in the second as more
remote, less clear; and in the third as most remote, very dimly.
But the Angel, unimpeded by a body, reflects himself in himself,
and sees his own beauty sculpted within. And the spirit, created
as it is, surrounded by an earthly body, stoops from its corporeal
ministry. Weighed down by this propensity, it forgets the beauty
that is hidden within it, and insofar as it is enveloped in a terrestrial body, it proceeds to use this body, accommodating to it
the senses and sometimes also reason. Hence it does not behold
this beauty which radiates within it, until the body has matured
and reason has awakened, with which it observes the beauty that
shines in the sight of the whole world and there abides. Finally,
the beauty of the body is nothing more than a certain demeanor,
vivacity and grace, which radiate within it from the infusion of
its Idea; and the latter does not descend into matter unless it is
most properly prepared. This preparation of the living body is
accomplished in three particulars, which are order, mode and
form. The order signifies the differences of the parts, the mode
the quantity, and the form the lines and colors. Accordingly,
each limb must first be in its own place, and the eyes for instance*

*lontane dagli occhi. Ma questa parità di distanze, che appartiene
all' ordine, non però anco basta, se non vi si aggiunge il modo
delle parti, il quale attribuisca a qualunque membro la grandezza debita attendendo alla proporzione di tutto il corpo, siccome più innanzi si dirà, ed oltre a questi la specie necessaria,
acciocchè gli artificiosi tratti delle linee e lo splendore degli occhi
adornino l' ordine ed il modo delle parti. Queste tre cose benchè
nella materia siano.* niente di meno parte alcuna del corpo essere
non possono, [siccome afferma il Ficino sopra il convivio di
Platone], *dicendo che l' ordine dei membri non è membro alcuno, perchè l' ordine è in tutti i membri, e nessuno membro in
tutti i membri si ritrova. Aggiungesi che l' ordine non è altro che
conveniente distanza delle parti, e la distanza è o nullo, o vacuo,
o un tratto di linee. Nè le linee possono esser corpo, conciosiachè
mancano di latitudine e di profondità, che sono necessarie al
corpo. Oltra di ciò il modo non è quantità, ma è termine di
quantità, ed i termini sono superficie, linee e punti, le quali cose
non avendo profondità non si debbono corpi chiamare. E finalmente la specie anch' ella non è collocata nella materia, ma nella
gioconda concordia dei lumi, ombre e linee. E per questa ragione
si prova la bellezza essere dalla materia corporale tanto discosta,
che non si comincia da essa materia, se non è disposta con queste
tre preparazioni dette incorporali. Il fondamento delle quali è la
temperata complessione di quattro elementi, in modo che il corpo
nostro è molto simile a Cielo, la sostanza di cui è temperata. E
quando non si ribella dalla formazione dell' anima per qualche
esorbitanza di umori, facilmente i celesti splendori appareranno
nel corpo simile al Cielo e a quella perfetta forma dell' uomo, la
qual possiede l' animo nella materia pacifica ed ubbidiente.* [Ma
venendo alla temperatura dei corpi ella si cava dalle qualità, per
le quali tutti i corpi nostri vengono ad essere tra se dissimili,
trasferendosi l'una al' altra più e meno, come appresso i matematici [*scil.* astrologers] distesamente si legge, e vediamo ancora
per esperienza. Ma non possono però essere se non quattro
principali maniere di dissimiglianza secondo il numero degli
elementi e la forza delle loro qualità, che i matematici affermano
essere come fondamenti di tutte le forme over maniere dei corpi

must be equally distant from the nose, and the ears equally distant from the eyes. But this parity of distances, which pertains to the order, is still not enough if we do not add the mode of the parts, which attributes to each limb its proper size, taking into consideration the proportions of the whole body, as will be explained further on. In addition to these the necessary form must be added, so that the artful disposition of the lines and the splendor of the eyes will adorn the order and the mode of the parts. Although these three particulars reside in the matter, they nevertheless cannot be any part of the body [as Ficino states in speaking of Plato's *Symposium*], *saying that the order of the limbs is not any one limb, since the order is in all the limbs, and no limb is present in all the limbs together. Besides, the order is nothing more than a harmonious spacing of the parts and the spacing is either nothing, a void or a linear characteristic. Nor can the lines be the body, because they lack the width and depth necessary to the body. Moreover, mode is not quantity, but a limit of quantity, and the limits are surfaces, lines and points, which, not having depth, should not be called bodies. Finally, the form is not situated in the matter, but in the pleasing concordance of the lights, shadows and lines. Thus beauty is so removed from corporeal matter that it does not take shape out of this matter unless prepared according to these three incorporeal conditions. The basis of these is the harmonious constitution of the four elements in such a way that our body is very similar to heaven, whose substance is harmonious. And when the body does not rebel against the formation of the soul from some excess of humor, the celestial splendors easily appear in the body as similar to heaven and to that perfect form of man, which the spirit possesses in peaceful and obedient matter.* [But when it comes to fashioning the bodies, beauty is taken from the qualities that make all our bodies dissimilar, changing from one to the other more or less, as may be read extensively among the mathematicians (*scil.* astrologers), and as we also see from experience. There can however be only four main types of dissimilarity, in accordance with the number of the elements and the strength of their qualities, which the mathematicians assert are

umani. E perchè il fuoco è di qualità principalmente calda e secca, delle quali la prima dilata e la seconda inasprisce, ne segue che li corpi Marziali sono di membri grandi, rilevati, aspri e pelosi. Perchè l' aria ha l'umido principale e dal fuoco prende il calido, il quale manco dilata dove quello fa molle e lungo, causa, che i corpi Gioviali vengono ad essere non grandi di membra, come i Marziali, ma temperati, dilicati al tatto e rilevati. Perchè l' acqua ha principalmente del freddo e nell' aria partecipa dell' umido, ed il freddo astringe e fa duro, e l' umido mollifica, fa sì, che i corpi Lunari sono minori dei Gioviali, ma sproporzionati, duri e deboli. Finalmente perciocchè la terra per sua natura principalmente è secca per participazion del fuoco, e fredda che piglia dall' acqua ed il secco, e il freddo è asprissimo, quindi è, che i corpi Saturnini sono principalmente asprissimi più che non sono i Marziali, e di membra strette e concave. E con queste quattro qualità nascono tutte le altre figure, cioè le Solari, le quali, secondo che tengono gl' Astrologi, per participar il Sole in alcune cose delle qualità di Saturno, non sono così aspre di membra come le Marziali, ma si bene più che le Gioviali e men grandi di quelle, e le Veneree per tender questo pianeta alla natura di Giove sono grandi e ben proporzionate, delicatissime e di membri bellissimi, per avere la natura temperata nell' umido e nel caldo. E così alle Mercuriali danno gl' Astrologi la sua forma secondo le qualità di Mercurio. Di quì si può comprender, che da queste qualità attive e passive principalmente dipende la bellezza; ed ha da essere espressa in opera con le sue proporzioni e membra tolte dall 'esempio naturale dell' animo, al quale la materia fu ben disposta in Saturno per gravità, in Giove per magnificenza ed allegrezza, in Marte per fortezza e valore, nel Sole per magnanimità e signoria, in Venere per piacevolezza, in Mercurio per intelligenza ed arguzia, e nella Luna per clemenza. Siccome all' incontro si corrompono, in Saturno per miseria, in Giove per avarizia, in Marte per crudeltà, nel Sole per vituperio e tirannide, in Venere per lascivia, in Mercurio per sceleragine e stregheria, e nella Luna per instabilità e leggerezza. Questa bellezza quando non piacerà per alcuno di simili termini perfettamente, da altro non verrà che della contrarietà di tali qualità.

the bases of all the forms or rather types of human bodies. And since fire is mainly of a hot and dry nature, of which the former expands and the latter dries, the result is that Martian types have large limbs, are filled out, dry and hairy. Because humidity, which renders things soft and long, is mainly in the air, and takes the warmth from fire, whose lack causes dilation, the result is that Jovian types do not have large limbs like the Martians, but are harmonious, delicate to the touch and full-bodied. Because water is mainly cold and participates in the humidity of the air, and because cold contracts and renders things hard, while humidity renders things soft, Lunar types are smaller than Jovians, but are disproportioned, brittle and weak. Finally, because the earth is mainly dry, due to the participation of fire, and cold, which comes from water and from the dryness, and the cold is very sharp, Saturnine types are for the most part more dry than Martians and have straight and concave limbs. All the other forms are born of these four qualities, that is, the Solar types, who, according to the astrologers, due to the participation of the sun in some of the qualities of Saturn, have limbs as sharp as the Martians and sharper than the Jovians and less large than the latter; and Venus types, because this planet tends toward Jove, are large and well-proportioned, with delicate and beautiful lines, since their nature is tempered by humidity and heat. Thus astrologers give Mercurial types the form in accordance with the qualities of Mercury. It may be understood from this that beauty depends mainly on three active and passive qualities, and has to be expressed in the work with its proportions and limbs derived from the natural example of the spirit, to which matter is well disposed, in Saturn through gravity, in Jupiter through magnificence and joy, in Mars through force and bravery, in the Sun through magnanimity and lordliness, in Venus through gentleness, in Mercury through intelligence and cleverness, and in the Moon through mercy. This is why, on the other hand, they are corrupted, in Saturn by misery, in Jupiter by avarice, in Mars by cruelty, in the Sun by infamy and tyranny, in Venus by lasciviousness, in Mercury by cunning and witchcraft and in the Moon by instability and levity. When such

Imperocchè sappiamo con tutte le ragioni, che in tutti i modi nei gesti, negl' atti, nei corpi, nelle voci, e nelle disposizioni delle membra e nei colori sono discordi ai Saturnini gli uomini Marziali e Venerei; ai Gioviali i Marziali; ai Marziali i Saturnini, Giovali, Solari, Mercuriali e Lunari; ai Solari i Marziali, Mercurali e Lunari; ai Venerei i Saturnini; ai Mercuriali i Marziali e Solari; ai Lunari i Marziali, Solari e Mercuriali. E per il contrario ai Saturnini si confanno gl' uomini, che tengono del Mercuriale, Gioviale, Solare e Lunare; ai Gioviali i Saturnini, Solari, Venerei, Mercuriali e Lunari; ai Marziali, i Venerei; ed alli Solari i Gioviali e Venerei; ai Venerei i Gioviali, Marziali, Solari, Mercuriali e Lunari; ai Mercuriali i Gioviali, Venerei e Saturnini; e finalmente ai Lunari si convengono i Gioviali, Venerei e Saturnini. E tanto più si vede questa conformità o discordanza nelle creature, quanto più propriamente sono conformi le disposizioni delle materie over discordi dagli animi, con le quali crescono insieme le materie. Donde procede, che ad uno il quale vedrà quattro o sei uomini o donne, più uno o una li piacerà, che un' altro o un' altra, e ad un' altro sarà in odio, ciò che a lui piacerà. E particolarmente questo si comprende nell' arti che uno abborre un' arte e l' altro l' aggradisce, e quindi avviene, che tutte le nature occupano tutte le arti. Ma ciò in niuna cosa si vede più espresso che nel giudicio o sia gusto della bellezza, che se ben una donna sarà veramente bella, nondimeno veduta da diversi uomini a tutti non parerà tale per una medesima via. Imperocchè a chi ella piacerà per gli occhi, ad altri per il naso, a chi per la bocca, a chi per la fronte, per li capelli, per la gola, per lo petto, per le mani, e a chi per una cosa, e a chi per un' altra. Sarà ancora a chi piacerà la grazia, a chi il costume, a chi la virtù, a chi il moto, e a chi lo sguardo. E così avvienne di tutti i corpi, che di loro una parte piace ed è tenuta bella, come gli occhi, e un' altra dispiace ed è riputata deforme come la fronte o la bocca. Però tutte queste cose debbono essere considerate attentamente per poter dar le proporzioni convenienti alla natura de' corpi ed esercizj, acciochè eglino perfettamente siano o piacevoli o spiacevoli. Onde in una istoria la bellezza d' un Rè Solare si porrà nella maestà e nell' atto del principe o di chi

beauty does not please perfectly for any of similar states, it will not be seen from anything else but the opposition of such qualities. Therefore, we know with all reason that in all ways, in gestures, in actions, in the bodies, in voices, and in the disposition of the limbs and in colors men with the qualities of Mars and Venus are discordant with those with the qualities of Saturn; Martian types with Jovian types; Saturnine, Jovian, Solar, Mercurial and Lunar types with the Martians; Martian, Mercurial and Lunar with Solar types; Saturnine with Venusian types; Martian and Solar with Mercurial types; and Martian, Solar and Mercurial with Lunar types. On the contrary, men with the qualities of Mercury, Jupiter, the Sun and the Moon are in harmony with those with the qualities of Saturn; Saturnine, Solar, Venusian, Mercurial and Lunar types with Jovian types; Venusian with Martian types; and Jovian and Venusian with Solar types; Jovian, Martian, Solar, Mercurial and Lunar types with Venusians; Jovian, Venusian and Saturnine with Mercurial types; and finally Jovian, Venusian and Saturnine with Lunar types. And this harmony or discordance in the creatures may be seen all the better when they conform more properly with the disposition of the matter or discordance of the spirits, together with which matter increases. From whence it follows that when one sees four or six men or women, he will like one more than the others, and someone else will dislike what pleased him. It is especially understandable with the skills that one may abhor a skill and another value it, and thus it happens that all skills make use of all temperaments. This is nowhere better expressed than in the judgment of or taste in beauty, for even though a woman may be truly beautiful, nevertheless, seen by several men, she will not appear beautiful to all in the same way. Some will find her eyes pleasing, another her mouth, still another her forehead, her hair, her throat, her breasts, her hands, or one thing or another. And there will be some who are pleased by her grace, her manners, her virtue, her gestures, and her glance. Thus it happens with all bodies that a part of them is pleasing and considered beautiful, such as the eyes, and another is disliked and considered deformed, as the forehead or the mouth.

comanda, d' un soldato Marziale nelle zuffe o contrasti e negli
ati offensivi o diffensivi; d' un Venereo nella grazia e delicatura
di chi parla o baccia o rende cortesia. E così dando a ciascun
corpo gli atti corrispondenti alla natura ed arte sua si verrà a
verificar il piacere, come al manigoldo lacci, manaie e ceppi; ai
fanciulli uccelli, cani, fiori ed altre bagatelle. E tutto questo il
pittore ritroverà nella concordanza dell' arte, il Filosofo nelle
rappresentazioni secondo la materia, l' Istorico ne' consigli, e gli
altri artefici nelle altre loro aderenze. Ed è cosa che si vede
chiarissimamente per esperienza, come lasciando di parlar delle
membra e delle loro proporzioni, una faccia ritratta al naturale,
in presenza del vivo da molti sarà giudicata in molti modi,
secondo la natura del loro vedere. Imperocchè ad uno ella parerà
di colore simile al vivo, ad un' altro parerà di color più bianco,
ad un' altro di più giallo, e ad un' altro di più rosso ovver di più
scuro. Il che avviene, perchè non risplendendo la luce nella
Pittura, come fa nel vivo, i raggi spargendosi dagli occhi, vengono naturalmente secondo la qualità loro, ma la materia non
dee risplendere nello spirto, al quale è forza accostarsi tanto o
quanto. E così si ha da vedere la imitazione diversa sì de' colori
come ho detto, quanto delle superficie, le quali ancora parranno
a chi più larghe, e a chi più strette o lunghe o corte. Onde
possiamo considerare, che l' artefice ha d' aver riguardo più alla
ragione, che al particolar piacere d' alcuno, perchè l' opera dee
essere universale e perfetta, ed altrimenti facendo si lavora al
bujo.] *Il che non è punto usato da quelli, che riconoscono l'*
animo loro non aver bisogno, che si gli aggiunga cosa alcuna per
far, che apparisca bello nell' opera, ma solo esser bisogno che si
ponga la cura e la solecitudine del corpo, e si scaccino le pertur-
bazioni della cupidità e del timore, per mostrar a noi nelle opere
sue la ragionevol bellezza naturale [dell' animo loro e di coloro,
che così disposti e purgati d' affetti si trovano, da quali essi sono
poi ed approvati e lodati, non curandosi delle chiacchiere di
quelli, che più attendono al piacer sensuale del corpo, che alla
ragione dello spirito, e però vivono come nel fango, privi d' ogni
lume di giudizio.] *Imperocchè la vera bellezza è solamente*
quella, che dalla ragione si gusta, e non da queste due finestre

All these things however should be considered carefully in order to be able to give the proportions proper to the nature and function of the bodies, so that they may either be perfectly pleasing or displeasing. In one tale the beauty of a Solar king will be shown in his majesty, or of a prince or someone who commands in his actions, of a Martian soldier in battles or disputes and in offensive or defensive action; of a man of Venus in the grace and delicacy of his speech, his kisses or courteousness. Thus each body being provided with the function that corresponds to its nature and skill, pleasure will be served, as the noose, hatchet and chains serve the hangman, and birds, dogs, flowers and other small things please children. All this the painter will find in the harmony of art, the philosopher in representations according to matter, the historian in deliberations, and other artificers in their professions. This is a thing that may be seen most clearly through experience, putting aside discussion of the limbs and their proportions. A face drawn naturally, in the presence of the live subject, will be judged by many in different ways, according to how they see it, so that for one it will seem to have a color similar to the live model, and to another it will seem whiter, to another, more yellow, and to still another, too red or even too dark. This is due to the fact that the light does not shine in the painting as it does in the live model, the rays radiating naturally from the eyes according to their quality; but matter should not shine in the spirit, to which it is perforce more or less related. This is the case with various imitations either of colors, as I have said, or of surfaces, which also appear larger to some or more narrow, and longer or shorter to others. Hence we can imagine that the artist has to take reason more into account than the particular pleasure of someone, since the work must be universal and perfect, and to do it otherwise would be to work in the dark.] *This is not done by those who realize that their spirit has no need of it, so that if something is added that appears beautiful in the work, they must take care and pains with the body if they are to dispel perturbations of cupidity and fear, in order to show us in their work the rational, natural beauty* [of their spirit and of those who, thus disposed

corporali. Il che facilmente si dimostra, perchè niun mette in dubbio, ch' ella non si ritrovi negli Angeli, nelle anime e nei corpi, e che l' occhio non può veder senza il lume. Imperocchè le figure e i colori dei corpi non si veggono, se non da lume illustrati, ed essi non vengono con la lor materia all' occhio, sebben par necessario, che debbano essere negli occhi, acciocchè da quelli possano esser veduti. E così il lume del Sole dipinto dei colori e delle figure di tutti i corpi, in che percuote, si rappresenta agli occhi per l' ajuto di un lor certo raggio naturale. E in questo modo pigliandolo noi così dipinto veniamo a vedere esso lume e tutte le dipinture che in lui sono. Perchè tutto questo ordine del mondo, che si vede, pigliasi dagli occhi, non in quel modo, ch' egli è nella materia dei corpi, ma in quel modo ch' egli è nella luce, che negli occhi è infusa. E perchè egli è in quella luce, separato già dalla materia necessaria e senza corpo, tutto l' ornamento di questo mondo per la luce s' offerisce. Adunque s' è incorporato negli occhi nostri e non nei corpi, tanto più la bellezza ci si rappresenta, quanto ella nella materia ben disposta risulta più simile alla vera figura infusa nell' Angelo e nell' animo dal raggio Divino. Dove la materia confacendosi con la forza d' Iddio e con la Idea dell' Angelo, si confà ancora alla ragione ed al sigillo, che è nell' animo, dove approva questa convenienza del confarsi, nella quale consiste la bellezza, la quale per tal disposizione di materia diversamente per tutti i corpi più e meno appare discordandosi ovver accordandosi alla figura, che l' animo dalla sua origine possiede. [Ora da questa bellezza infusa ne' corpi ed apparente più e meno in loro, secondo che si è detto, il diligente pittore ne ha da ritrarre le proporzioni e accomodarle all' opera sua secondo le qualità, ovver nature diverse sopraddette.]

and purged of emotions, are then approved and praised. They do not heed the gossip of others who pay more attention to the sensual pleasures of the body than to the reason of the mind, and therefore live as though in the mire, deprived of the light of judgment.] *True beauty is only that which may be truly understood through reason and not through these two corporeal windows. This may easily be demonstrated in that no one doubts that it can be found in the Angels, in the spirits and in the bodies, and that the eye cannot see without light. So that the shapes and colors of the bodies are not seen, if not illuminated by light, and they do not appear with their matter to the eye, although they must be in the eyes in order to be seen. And thus the light of the sun, painted with the colors and shapes of all the bodies that it strikes, is manifest to the eyes through the aid of a certain natural ray. Receiving it painted in this fashion, we come to see this light and all the paintings that are in it. Because the entire order of the world, which is visible, is taken from the eyes, not in the way that it is manifest in the matter of the bodies but in the way that it is in the light that is infused into the eyes, and because this order is in that light, already separated from the necessary matter and without body, the whole embellishment of this world is transmitted through light. Hence, since it is incorporated in our eyes, and not in the bodies, all the more beauty is manifest there, as in well-disposed matter it emerges more similar to the true shape infused into the Angel and the spirit by the divine ray. Where matter, conforming with the divine power and with the Idea of the Angel is also combined with reason and with the divine stamp, which is in the spirit, where it approves this facility of adaptability, in which beauty consists, the latter due to such diverse disposition of matter diversely in all bodies appears to be more or less discordant or in harmony with the shape which the spirit possesses from its origin.* [Now from this beauty infused into the bodies and more or less apparent in them, as has been stated, the diligent painter has only to draw the proportions and adjust them to his work, according to the qualities of their diverse natures, mentioned above.]

APPENDIX II

Gio. Pietro Bellori: "L' Idea del Pittore, Dello Schultore e Dell' Architetto, Scelta Delle Bellezze Naturali Superiore Alla Natura"[1]

Quel sommo ed eterno intelletto autore della natura nel fabbricare l' opere sue marauigliose, altamente in se stesso riguardando, costituì le prime forme chiamate Idee, in modo che ciascuna specie espressa fù da quella prima Idea, formandosene il mirabile contesto delle cose create. Ma li celesti corpi sopra la luna, non sottoposti a cangiamento, restarono per sempre belli e ordinati, qualmente dalle misurate sfere e dallo splendore degli aspetti loro veniamo a conoscerli perpetuamente giustissimi e vaghissimi. Al contrario auuiene de' corpi sublunari soggetti alle alterationi e alla bruttezza; e sebene la Natura intende sempre di produrre gli effetti suoi eccellenti, nulladimeno per l' inequalità della materia si alterano le forme, e particolarmente l' humana bellezza si confonde, come vediamo nell' infinite deformità e sproportioni, che sono in noi. Il perche li nobili Pittori e Scultori, quel primo fabbro imitando, si formano anch' essi nella mente vn esempio di bellezza superiore, e in esso riguardando emendano[2] la natura senza colpa di colore e di lineamento. Questa Idea, ouero Dea della Pittura e della Scoltura aperte le sacre cortine de gl' alti ingegni de i Dedali e de gli Apelli, si suela a noi e discende sopra i marmi e sopra le tele; originata dalla

APPENDIX II

Gio. Pietro Bellori's "The Idea of the Painter, Sculptor and Architect, Superior to Nature by Selection from Natural Beauties" [1]

The highest and eternal intellect, author of nature, in fashioning his marvelous works looked deeply into himself and constituted the first forms, called Ideas, in such a way that each species was expressed by that original Idea, giving form to the marvelous context of things created. But the celestial bodies above the moon, not subject to change, remained forever beautiful and well-ordered, so that we come to know them from their measured spheres and from the splendor of their aspects as being eternally most just and most beautiful. Sublunar bodies on the contrary are subject to change and deformity; and although nature always intends to produce excellent effects, nevertheless, because of the inequality of matter the forms change, and human beauty is especially disarranged, as we see from the infinite deformities and disproportions that are in us. For this reason the noble Painters and Sculptors, imitating that first maker, also form in their minds an example of superior beauty, and in beholding it they emend [2] nature with faultless color or line. This Idea, or truly the Goddess of Painting and Sculpture, when the sacred curtains of the lofty genius of a Daedalus or an Apelles are parted, is revealed to us and enters the marble and

1 5 5

natura supera l' origine e fassi originale dell' arte, misurata dal compasso dell' intelletto diuiene misura della mano, e animata dall' immaginatiua dà vita all' immagine. Sono certamente per sentenza de' maggiori filosofi le cause esemplari ne gli animi de gli Artefici, le quali risiedono senza incertezza perpetuamente bellissime e perfettissime. Idea del Pittore e dello Scultore è quel perfetto ed eccellente esempio della mente, alla cui immaginata forma imitando si rassomigliano le cose, che cadono sotto la vista: tale è la finitione de Cicerone nel libro dell' Oratore a Bruto. „Vt igitur in formis et figuris est aliquid perfectum et excellens, cuius ad excogitatam speciem imitando referuntur ea que sub oculis ipsa cadunt, sic perfectae eloquentiae speciem animo videmus, effigiem auribus quaerimus." [3] Così l' Idea costituisce il perfetto della bellezza naturale e vnisce il vero al verisimile delle cose sottoposte all' occhio, sempre aspirando all' ottimo ed al marauiglioso, onde non solo emula, ma superiore fassi alla natura, palesondoci l' opere sue eleganti e compite, quali essa non è solita dimostrarci perfette in ogni parte. Questo pregio conferma Proclo nel Timeo, dicendo: se tu prenderai vn huomo fatto dalla natura e vn altro formato dall' arte statuaria, il naturale sarà meno prestante, perche l' arte opera più accuratamente.[4] Ma Zeusi, che con la scelta di cinque vergini formò l' immagine di Elena tanto famosa [5] da Cicerone posta in esempio all' Oratore, insegna insieme al Pittore ed allo Scultore a contemplare l' Idea delle migliori forme naturali con farne scelta da vari corpi, eleggendo le più eleganti.

Imperoche non pensò egli di poter trouare in vn corpo solo tutte quelle perfettioni, che cercaua per la venustà di Helena, mentre la natura non fa perfetta cosa alcuna particolare in tutte le parti. „Neque enim putauit omnia, quae quaereret ad venustatem, vno in corpore se reperire posse, ideo quod nihil simplici in genere omnibus ex partibus natura expoliuit." [6] Vuole però Massimo Tirio, che l' immagine de' Pittori così presa da corpi diuersi partorisca vna bellezza, quale non si troua in corpo naturale alcuno, che alle belle statue si auuicini.[7] Lo stesso concedeua Parrasio a Socrate, che 'l Pittore, propostosi in ciascuna forma la bellezza naturale, debba prendere da

the canvases. Born from nature, it overcomes its origin and becomes the model of art; measured with the compass of the intellect it becomes the measure of the hand; and animated by fantasy it gives life to the image. Certainly, according to the statements of the major philosophers, the exemplary motives reside with assurance in the spirits of the artists forever most beautiful and most perfect. The Idea of the Painter and the Sculptor is that perfect and excellent example of the mind, to which imagined form, imitating, all things that come into sight assimilate themselves: such is Cicero's fiction in his book on the orator, dedicated to Brutus: "Ut igitur in formis et figuris est aliquid perfectum et excellens, cuius ad excogitatam speciem imitando referuntur ea que sub oculis ipsa cadunt, sic perfectae eloquentiae speciem animo videmus, effigiem auribus quaerimus." [3] Thus the Idea constitutes the perfection of natural beauty and unites the truth with the verisimilitude of what appears to the eye, always aspiring to the best and the most marvelous, thereby not emulating but making itself superior to nature, revealing to us its elegant and perfect works, which nature does not usually show us as perfect in every part. Proclos confirms this value in *Timaeus* when he says that if you take a man fashioned by nature and another formed by sculptural art, the natural one will be less excellent, because art fashions more accurately. [4] But Zeuxis, who formed with a choice of five virgins the most famous image of Helen,[5] given as an example by Cicero in the *Orator*, teaches both the Painter and Sculptor to contemplate the Idea of the best natural forms in making a choice among various bodies, selecting the most elegant.

Hence I do not believe that he could find in one body alone all these perfections that he sought for in the extraordinary beauty of Helen, since nature makes no particular thing perfect in all its parts. "Neque enim putavit omnia, quae quaereret ad venustatem, uno in corpore se reperire posse, ideo quod nihil simplici in genere omnibus ex partibus natura expoluit." [6] Thus Maximus Tyrius claims that the image of the Painters taken this way from different bodies produces a beauty such as may not be found in any natural body that approaches the beautiful statues.[7]

diuersi corpi vnitamente tuttociò che ciascuno a parte a parte
ottiene di più perfetto, essendo malageuole il trouarsene vn
solo in perfettione.[8] Anzi la natura per questa cagione è tanto
inferiore all' arte, che gli Artefici similitudinarij e del tutto
imitatori de' corpi, senza elettione e scelta dell' Idea, furono
ripresi: Demetrio riceue nota di esser troppo naturale,[9] Dionisio
fu biasimato per hauer dipinto gli huomini simili a noi, com-
munemente chiamato ἀνθρωπόγραφος [sic], cioè pittore di huomini.[10] Pausone [11] e Pirreico [12] furono condannati maggiormente,
per hauere imitato li peggiori e li più vili, come in questi nostri
tempi Michel Angelo da Carauaggio fù troppo naturale, dipinse
i simili, e'l Bamboccio i peggiori. Rimproueraua però Lisippo al
vulgo de gli Scultori, che da essi veniuano fatti gli huomini quali
si trouano in natura, e egli gloriauasi di formarli quali doueuano
essere,[13] vnico precetto dato da Aristotele così alli Poeti, come
alli Pittori.[14] Di questo fallo non venne altrimente imputato
Fidia, che indusse merauiglia ne' reguardanti con le forme de
gli Heroi e de gli Dei, per hauer imitato più tosto l' Idea, che la
Natura; e Cicerone di lui parlando afferma, che Fidia figurando
il Gioue e la Minerua non contemplaua oggetto alcuno, ond' egli
prendesse la simiglianza, ma consideraua nella mente sua vna
forma grande di bellezza, in cui fisso riguardando a quella
similitudine indirizzaua la mente e la mano. „Nec vero ille artifex
cum faceret Iouis formam aut Minerue, contemplabatur aliquem,
a quo similitudinem duceret, sed ipsius in mente insidebat species
pulchritudinis eximia quaedam, quam intuens in eaque defixus
ad illius similitudinem artem et manum dirigebat.“ [15] Onde a
Seneca, benche stoico e rigoroso giudice delle nostre arti, parue
gran cosa e egli si marauigliò, che questo Scultore, non hauendo
veduto nè Gioue nè Minerua, nulladimeno concepisse nell' animo
le forme loro diuine. „Non vidit Phidias Iouem, fecit tamen
velut tonantem, nec stetit ante oculos eius Minerua, dignus
tamen illa arte animus et concepit Deos et exhibuit.“ [16] Apollonio
Tianeo c' insegna il medesimo, che la fantasia rende più saggio
il Pittore, che l' imitatione; perche questa fa solamente le cose
che vede, quella fa ancora le cose che non vede, con la relatione
a quelle che vede.[17] Hora se con li precetti delli antichi Sapienti

Parrhasius conceded the same to Socrates, that the Painter who has placed before him natural beauty in each of its forms must take from various bodies together what each has most perfect in its individual parts, since it is impossible to find a perfect being by itself.[8] Thus nature is for this reason so inferior to art that the copyist artists and imitators of bodies in everything, without selectivity and the choice of an Idea, were criticized. Demetrius was told that he was too natural,[9] Dionysius was blamed for having painted men resembling us and was commonly called *anthropographos*, that is, painter of men.[10] Pausanias [11] and Peiraeikos [12] were condemned even more for having imitated the worst and the most vile, just as in our time Michel Angelo da Caravaggio was criticized for being too natural in painting likenesses, and Bamboccio was considered worse than Michel Angelo da Caravaggio. Thus Lysippus reproached the vulgarity of the Sculptors who made men as they are found in nature, and prided himself for forming them as they should be,[13] following the advice given by Aristotle to Poets as well as Painters.[14] This shortcoming was not attributed to Phidias, on the other hand, who made marvels of the forms of heroes and gods and imitated the Idea rather than nature. Cicero asserts that Phidias, in shaping Jupiter and Minerva, did not look at any object that he could have taken for a likeness, but conceived a form full of beauty, in whose fixed image he guided his mind and hand to achieve a likeness. "Nec vero ille artifex cum faceret Iovis formam aut Minerve, contemplabatur aliquem, a quo similitudinem duceret, sed ipsius in mente insidebat species pulchritudinis eximia quaedam, quam intuens in eaque defixus ad illius similitudinem artem et manum dirigebat." [15] Hence it appeared to Seneca, although he was a Stoic and a severe judge of our arts, to be a great thing, and he marveled at how this Sculptor, never having seen either Jupiter or Minerva, had nevertheless conceived their divine forms in his mind. "Non vidit Phidias Iovem, fecit tamen velut tonantem, nec stetit ante oculos eius Minerva, dignus tamen illa arte animus et concepit Deos et exhibuit." [16] Appolonius of Tyana teaches us the same thing, that fantasy makes the Painter wiser than imitation, because the latter cre-

rincontrar vogliamo ancora gli ottimi instituti de' nostri moderni, insegna Leon Battista Alberti, che si ami in tutte le cose non solo la simiglianza, ma principalmente la bellezza, e che si debba andar scegliendo da corpi bellissimi le più lodate parti.[18] Così Leonardo da Vinci instruisce il pittore a formarsi questa Idea, e a considerare ciò che esso vede e parlar seco, eleggendo le parti più eccellenti di qualunque cosa.[19] Rafaelle da Vrbino, il gran maestro di coloro che sanno, così scriue al Castiglione della sua Galatea: „Per dipingere vna bella mi bisognerebbe vedere più belle, ma per essere carestia di belle donne, io mi seruo di vna certa Idea, che mi viene in mente." [20] Guido Reni, che nella venustà ad ogni altro Artefice del nostro secolo preualse, inuiando a Roma il quadro di S. Michele Arcangelo per la Chiesa de' Cappuccini, scrisse ancora a Monsignor Massani Maestro di casa di Vrbano VII: „Vorrei hauer hauuto pennello Angelico o forme di Paradiso, per formare l' Arcangelo e vederlo in Cielo, ma io non hò potuto salir tant' alto, e in vano l' hò cercato in terra. Si che hò riguardato in quella forma, che nell' Idea mi sono stabilita. Si troua anche l' Idea della brut-tezza, ma questa lascio di spiegare nel Demonio, perche lo fuggo sin col pensiero, nè mi curo di tenerlo a mente." Vantauasi pero Guido dipingere la bellezza non quale gli si offeriua a gli occhi, ma simile a quella che vedeua nell' Idea; onde la sua bella Helena rapita al pari dell' antica di Zeusi fù celebrata. Ma non fù così bella costei, qual da loro si finse, poiche si trouarono in essa difetti e riprensioni; anzi si tiene ch' ella mai nauigasse a Troia, ma che in suo luogo vi fosse portata la sua statua, per la cui bellezza si guerreggiò dieci anni. Stimasi però, che Homero ne' suoi poemi adorasse vna donna, che non era diuina, per gratificare i Greci e per rendere più celebre il soggetto suo della guerra Troiana; nel modo ch' egli inalzò Achille e Vlisse nella fortezza e nel consiglio. Laonde Helena con la sua bellezza naturale non pareggiò le forme di Zeusi e Homero; nè donna alcuna fù, che ritenesse tanta venustà quanta la Venere Gnidia, o la Minerua Ateniese chiamata la bella forma, nè huomo in fortezza hoggi si troua, che pareggi l' Hercole Farnesiano di Glicone, o donna, che agguagli in venustà la Venere Medicea

ates only those things that are seen, while fantasy creates even those that are unseen.[17] Now if we want to confront the precepts of the sages of antiquity with the best methods of our modern teachers, Leone Battista Alberti maintains that we love in all things not only the likeness but mainly the beauty, and that we must select the most praiseworthy parts from the most beautiful bodies.[18] Thus Leonardo da Vinci taught the painter to form this Idea, to consider what he saw and to consult himself, choosing the most excellent parts of everything.[19] Raphael of Urbino, the great master among those who know, wrote thus to Castiglione of his Galatea: "In order to paint a beauty I would have to see several beauties, but since there is a scarcity of beautiful women, I use a certain Idea that comes to my mind." [20] Guido Reni, who surpasses all the other artists of our century in creating beauty, wrote to Monsignor Massani, housemaster for Urban VII, when he sent the painting of Saint Michael to Rome for the Church of the Capuchins: "I would have liked to have had the brush of an angel, or forms from Paradise, to fashion the Archangel and to see him in Heaven, but I could not ascend that high, and I searched for him in vain on earth. So I looked at the form whose Idea I myself established. An Idea of ugliness may also be found, but that I leave to the devil to explain, because I flee from it even in thought, nor do I care to keep it in my mind." Thus Guido also boasted that he painted beauty, not as it appeared to his eyes, but as he saw it in the Idea; hence his beautiful abducted Helen was esteemed as an equal of that by Zeuxis. But Helen was not as beautiful as they pretended, for she was found to have defects and shortcomings, so that it is believed that she never did sail for Troy but that her statue was taken there in her stead, for whose beauty the Greeks and the Trojans made war for ten years. It is thought therefore that Homer, in order to satisfy the Greeks and to make his subject of the Trojan War more celebrated, paid homage in his poem to a woman who was not divine, in the same way that he augmented the strength and intelligence of Achilles and Ulysses. Hence Helen with her natural beauty did not equal the forms of Zeuxis and Homer; nor was there ever a woman who had so much extraordinary beauty

di Cleomene. Per questa cagione gli ottimi Poeti e Oratori, volendo celebrare qualche soprhumana bellezza, ricorrono al paragone delle statue e delle pitture. Ouidio descriuendo Cillaro bellissimo Centauro lo celebra come prossimo alle statue più lodate:

> Gratus in ore vigor, ceruix, humerique, manusque
> Pectoraque Artificum laudatis proxima signis.[21]

Et in altro luogo altamente di Venere cantò, che se Apelle non l' hauesse dipinta, sin hora sommersa rimarebbe nel mare, oue nacque:

> Si Venerem Cois nunquam pinxisset Apelles
> Mersa sub aequoreis illa lateret aquis.[22]

Filostrato inalza la bellezza di Euforbo simile alle statue di Apolline,[23] e vuole che Achille di tanto superi la beltà di Neottolemo suo figluolo, quanto li belli sono dalle statue superati.[24] L' Ariosto nel fingere la bellezza di Angelica, quasi da mano di Artefice industre scolpita l' assomiglia legata allo scoglio:

> Creduto hauria, che fosse stata finta,
> O d' alabastro o d' altro marmo illustre,
> Ruggiero, o sia allo scoglio così auuinta
> Per artificio di scultore industre.[25]

Nelli quali versi l' Ariosto imitò Ouidio descriuendo la medesima Andromeda:

> Quam simul ad duras religatam bracchia cautes
> Vidit Abantiades, nisi quod leuis aura capillos
> Mouerat, et tepido manabant lumina fletu,
> Marmoreum ratus esset opus.[26]

Il Marino, celebrando la Madalena dipinta da Titiano, applaude con le medesime lodi alla pittura e porta l' Idea dell' Artefice sopra le cose naturali:

> Ma cede la Natura e cede il vero
> A quel che dotto Artefice ne finse,

as the Venus of Cnidos or the Athenian Minerva, known as the beautiful form; nor did a man exist of the strength of the Farnese Hercules by Glycon, nor any woman who equaled in beauty the Medicean Venus of Cleomenes. For this reason the best Poets and Orators, when they wanted to celebrate some sublime beauty, turned to a comparison of statues and paintings. Ovid, describing Cyllarus, the most beautiful Centaur, praises him as most like the most famous statues:

> Gratus in ore vigor, cervix, humerique, Manusque
> Pectoraque Artificum laudatis proxima signis.[21]

And elsewhere he wrote in high praise of Venus that if Apelles had not painted her, she would have remained until now submerged in the sea where she was born:

> Si Venerem Cois nunquam pinxisset Apelles
> Mersa sub aequoreis illa lateret aquis.[22]

Philostratus upholds the beauty of Euforbus as similar to statues of Apollo [23] and he claims that Achilles surpassed the beauty of Neoptolemus, his son, as beauties are surpassed by statues.[24] Ariosto, in creating the beauty of Angelica tied to the rock, likens her to something moulded by the hands of an artist:

> Creduto havria, che fosse stata finta,
> O d'alabastro o d'altro marmo illustre,
> Ruggiero, o sia allo scoglio cosi avvinta
> Per artificio di scultore industre.[25]

In these verses Ariosto imitated Ovid, describing the same Andromeda:

> Quam simul ad duras religatam bracchia cautes
> Vidit Abantiades, nisi quod levis aura capillos
> Moverat, et tepido manabant lumina fletu,
> Marmoreum ratus esset opus.[26]

Marino, in celebrating the Magdalena painted by Titian, hails the work in the same way and places the Idea of the artist above natural things:

Che qual l' hauea ne l' alma e nel pensiero,
Tal bella e viua ancor qui la dipinse.[27]

Dal che apparisce non essere giustamente ripreso Aristotele nella Tragedia dal Casteluetro, volendo questi, che la virtù della pittura non consista altrimente in far l'immagine bella e perfetta, ma simile al naturale, o bello o deforme; quasi l' eccesso della bellezza tolga la similitudine.[28] La qual ragione del Casteluetro si ristringe alli pittori icastici[29] e facitori de' ritratti, li quali non serbano Idea alcuna e sono soggetti alla bruttezza del volto e del corpo, non potendo essi aggiungere bellezza nè correggere le deformità naturali senza torre la similitudine, altrimente il ritratto sarebbe più bello e meno simile. Di questa imitatione icastica non intende il Filosofo, ma insegna al tragico li costumi de' migliori, con l' esempio de buoni Pittori e Facitori d' immagini perfette, li quali vsano l' Idea; e sono queste le parole: ,,Essendo la tragedia imitatione de' migliori, bisogna che noi imitiamo li buoni Pittori; perche quelli esprimendo la propria forma con farli simili, più belli li fingono, ἀποδιδόντες τὴν οἰκείαν μορφήν, ὑμοίους ποιοῦντες, καλλίους γράφουσιν.[30]

Il far però gli huomini più belli di quello che sono commune-mente e eleggere il perfetto, conuiene all' Idea. Ma non vna di questa bellezza è l'Idea; varie sono le sue forme, e forti, e magnanime, e gioconde, e delicate, di ogni età, e d'ogni sesso. Non però noi con Paride nel monte Ida delitioso lodiamo solo Venere molle, o ne' giardini di Nisa celebriamo il tenero Bacco; ma sù ne' gioghi faticosi di Menalo e di Delo ammiriamo Apol-line faretrato e l'arciera Diana. Altra certamente fù la bellezza di Gioue in Olimpia e di Giunone in Samo, altra di Hercole in Lindo e di Cupidine in Thespia: così a diuersi conuengonsi diuersi forme, per non essere altro la bellezza, se non quella, che fa le cose come sono nella loro propria e perfetta natura; la quale gli ottimi Pittori si eleggono, contemplando la forma di cia-scuno. Dobbiamo di più considerare, che, essendo la Pittura rappresentatione d'humana attione, deue insieme il Pittore rite-nere nella mente gli essempi de gli affetti, che cadono sotto esse

> Ma cede la Natura e cede il vero
> A quel che dotto Artefice nefinse,
> Che qual l'havea ne l'alma e nel pensiero,
> Tal bella e viva ancor qui la dipinse.[27]

It appears that Aristotle, on Tragedy, was unjustly criticized by Castelvetro, who maintains that the virtue of painting is not in creating a beautiful and perfect image, but in resembling the natural, either beautiful or deformed, for an excess of beauty lessens the likeness.[28] This argument of Castelvetro is limited to icastic painters [29] and portraitists who keep to no Idea and are subject to the ugliness of the face and body, unable to add beauty or correct natural deformities without violating the likeness. Otherwise the painting would be more beautiful and less accurate. The Philosopher does not mean such icastic imitation, but he teaches the tragedian the methods of the best, using the example of good Painters and Makers of perfect images, who rely on the Idea. These are his words: "Since tragedy is the imitation of the best, we should imitate the good painters, because, in expressing the form proper to their subjects, they create them more beautifully, ἀπο-διδόντες τὴν οἰκείαν μορθήν, ὁμοίους ποιοῦντες, καλλίους γράθουπιν.[30]

However, making men more beautiful than they ordinarily are and choosing the perfect conforms with the Idea. The Idea is not one beauty; its forms are various—strong, noble, joyful, delicate, of any age and both sexes. We do not, however, praise with Paris on lovely Mount Ida only soft Venus, or extol the tender Bacchus in the gardens of Nyssa, but we also admire in the wearying games of Maenalos and Delos the quiver-bearing Apollo and Diana the huntress. The beauty of Jupiter in Olympia and of Juno in Samos, as well as of Hercules in Lindos and Cupids in Thespiae, was certainly different again. Thus different forms conform with different people, as beauty is nothing else but what makes things as they are in their proper and perfect nature, which the best Painters choose, contemplating the form of each. In addition to which we must consider that Painting being at the same time the representation of human

attioni, nel modo che 'l Poeta conserua l'Idea dell' iracondo, del timido, del mesto, del lieto, e così del riso e del pianto, del timore e dell'·ardire. Li quali moti deono molto più restare impressi nell'animo dell' Artefice con la continua contemplatione della natura, essendo impossibile ch' egli li ritragga con la mano dal naturale, se prima non li hauerà formati nella fantasia; e a questo è necessaria grandissima attentione, poiche mai si veggono li moti dell' anima, se non per transito e per alcuni subiti momenti. Siche intraprendendo il Pittore e lo Scultore ad imitare le operationi dal modello, che si pone auanti, non ritenendo esso alcun affetto; che anzilanguisce con lo spirito e con le membra nell' atto, in cui si volge, e si ferma ad arbitrio altrui. É però necessario formarsene vn' immagine su la natura, osseruando le commotioni humane e accompagnando li moti del corpo con li moti dell' animo; in modo che gli vni da gli altri dipendino vicendeuolmente. In tanto, per non lasciare l'Architettura, seruesi anch' ella della sua perfettissima Idea: dice Filone,[31] che Dio, come buono Architetto, riguardando all' Idea e all' essempio propostosi, fabbricò il mondo sensibile dal mondo ideale e intelligibile. Siche dipendendo l'Architettura dalla cagione esemplare, fassi anch' ella superiore alla natura; così Ouidio, descriuendo l'antro di Diana, vuole che la Natura nel fabbricarlo prendesse ad imitar l'arte:

> Arte laboratum nulla, simulauerat artem
> Ingenio Natura suo,[32]

alche riguardò forse Torquato Tasso descriuendo il giardino di Armida:

> Di natura arte par, che per diletto
> L'imitatrice sua scherzando imiti.[33]

Egli è inoltre l'edificio tanto eccellente, che Aristotele argomenta: se la fabbrica fosse cosa naturale, non altrimente di quello si faccia Architettura, sarebbe eseguita dalla natura costretta ad vsare le medesime regole per darle perfettione,[34] come le stesse habitationi de gli Dei furono finte da' Poeti con l' industria de gli Architetti, ordinate con archi e colonne, qual-

action, the Painter must keep in mind the types of effects which correspond to these actions, in the same way that the Poet conserves the Idea of the angry, the timid, the sad, the happy, as well as of the laughing and crying, the fearful and the bold. These emotions must remain more firmly fixed in the Artist's mind through a continual contemplation of nature, since it would be impossible for him to draw them by hand from nature without first having formed them in his imagination; and for this the greatest care is necessary, since the emotions are only seen fleetingly in a sudden passing moment. So that when the Painter or Sculptor undertakes to reproduce feelings, he cannot find them in the model before him, whose spirit as well as limbs languish in the pose in which he is kept immobilized by another's will. It is therefore necessary to form an image of nature, observing human emotions and accompanying the movements of the body with moods, in such a way that each depends mutually upon the others. Moreover, in order not to exclude Architecture, it too uses its own most perfect Idea: Philo [31] says that God, as a good Architect, looking at the Idea and at the example he had conceived himself, made the visible, from the ideal and intelligible world. So that since Architecture depends upon the example of reason, it also elevates itself above nature. Thus Ovid, describing Diana's cave, envisages that nature, in creating it, took its example from art:

> Arte laboratum nulla, simulaverat artem
> Ingenio Natura suo; [32]

Torquato Tasso perhaps recalled this in describing the garden of Armida:

> Di natura arte par, che per diletto
> L'imitatrice sua scherzando imiti.[33]

Moreover, it is such an excellent edifice that Aristotle argues: if construction were a natural thing, no different from Architecture, it would be executed by nature, which would be compelled to use the same rules in order to give it perfection,[34]

mente descrissero la Reggia del Sole e d' Amore, portando l'
Architettura al cielo. Così questa Idea e deità della bellezza fù da
gli antichi Cultori della sapienza formata nelle menti loro, riguardando sempre alle più belle parti delle cost naturali, che
bruttissima e vilissima è quell' altra Idea che la più parte si
forma su la pratica, volendo Platone che l' Idea sia vna perfetta
cognitione della cosa, cominciata su la Natura.[35] Quintiliano c'
instruisce, come tutte le cose perfettionate dall' arte e dall'ingegno
humano hanno principio dalla Natura istessa,[36] da cui deriua la
vera Idea. Laonde quelli, che senza conoscere la verità il tutto
muouono con la pratica, fingono larue in vece di figure; ne
dissimili gli altri sono, che pigliano in prestanza l'ingegno e
copiano l' idee altrui, fanno l' opere non figliuole, ma bastarde
della Natura, e pare habbiano giurato nelle pennellate de' loro
maestri. Al qual male si aggiunge, che per l'inopia dell' ingegno
non sapendo essi eleggere le parti migliori, scelgono i difetti
de' loro precettori e si formano l' idea del peggiore. Al contrario quelli, che si gloriano del nome di Naturalisti, non si
propongono nella mente Idea alcuna; copiano i difetti de' corpi, e
si assuefanno alla bruttezza e a gli errori, giurando anch' essi nel
modello, come loro precettore; il quale tolto da gli occhi loro, si
parte insieme da essi tutta l'arte. Rassomiglia Platone quelli
primi Pittori alli Sofisti, che non si fondano nella verità, ma nelli
falsi fantasmi dell' opinione;[37] li secondi sono simili a Leucippo
e a Democrito, che con vanissimi atomi a caso compongono li
corpi. Così l'arte della Pittura da costoro viene condannata all
opinione e all' vso, come Critolao voleua, che l'eloquenza fosse
vna vsanza di dire e vna peritia di piacere, τριβή e κακοτεχνία,
o più tosto ἀτεχνία,[38] habito senz' arte e senza ragione, togliendo
l' vfficio alla mente e donando ogni cosa al senso. Onde quello,
che è somma intelligenza e Idea de gli ottimi Pittori, vogliono
essi più tosto, che sia vn vso di fare di ciascuno, per accomunare
con la sapienza l'ignoranza; ma gli spiriti eleuati, sublimando il
pensiero all' Idea del bello, da questa solo vengono rapiti e la
contemplano come cesa diuina. La doue il popolo riferisce il
tutto al senso dell' occhio; loda le cose dipinte dal naturale,
perche è solito verderne di si fatte, apprezza le belli colori, non le

just as the habitations of the gods themselves had been imagined by Poets with the diligence of Architects, arranged with arches and columns, as they described the Realm of the Sun and of Love, thereby raising Architecture to heaven. Hence this Idea and divinity of beauty was conceived in the minds of the ancient cultivators of wisdom, by observing always the most beautiful parts of natural things, because that other Idea, formed for the most part from experience, is ugly and base, according to Plato's concept that the Idea should be a perfect understanding of the thing, starting with nature.[35] Quintillian teaches us that all things perfected by art and human ingenuity have their origin in the same nature,[36] from which the true Idea springs. Hence those who without knowing the truth follow common practice in everything create spectres instead of shapes; nor are they dissimilar from those who borrow from the genius and copy the ideas of others, creating works that are not natural children but bastards of nature, so that it seems as though they are wedded to the paintbrushes of their masters. Added to this evil, arising from lack of genius or the inability to select the best parts, is the fact that they choose the defects of their teachers and form an idea of the worst. On the other hand, those who glory themselves with the name of Naturalists have no idea whatever in their minds; they copy the defects of the bodies and satisfy themselves with ugliness and errors, they, too, swearing by the model, as their teachers. If the model is taken from their sight, their whole art disappears with it. Plato likens these first Painters to the Sophists, who did not base themselves on truth but upon the false phantom of opinion; [37] they resemble Leucippus and Democritus, who compose bodies of the vainest atoms at random. Thus the art of Painting is degraded by these Painters in concept and practice, since, as Critolaos argues, eloquence should be a manner of speaking and an art of pleasing, *tribe* (in Greek, *tribe* and *kakotechnia* or *atechnia*),[38] a habit without skill and reason, taking function away from the mind and turning everything over to the senses. Hence what is supreme intelligence and the Idea of the best Painters, they would prefer to be common usage, equating ignorance with wisdom; but the high-

belle forme, che non intende; s' infastidisce dell' eleganza, approua la nouità; sprezza la ragione, segue l' opinione, e si allontana dalla verità dell' arte, sopra la quale come in propria base à dedicato dell' Idea il nobilissimo simolacro. Ci resterebbe il dire, che gli antichi Scultori hauendo vsato l' Idea merauigliosa, come habbiamo accennato, sia però neccessario lo studio dell' antiche sculture le più perfette, perche ci guidino alle bellezze emendate delle natura, e al medesimo fine dirizzar l' occhio alla contemplatione de gli altri eccellentissimi maestri; ma questa materia tralasciamo al suo proprio trattato dell' imitatione, sodisfacendo a coloro, che biasimano lo studio delle statue antiche. Quanto l' Architettura, diciamo, che l' Architetto deue concepire vna nobile Idea e stabilirsi vna mente, che gli serua di legge e di ragione, consistendo le sue inuentioni nell' ordine, nella dispositione, e nella misura ed euritmia del tutto e delle parti. Ma rispetto la decoratione e ornamenti de gli ordini, sia certo trouarsi l' Idea stabilita e confermata su gli essempi de gli Antichi, che con successo di longo studio diedero modo a quest' arte; quando li Greci le costituirono termini e proportioni le migliori, le quali confermate da i più dotti secoli e dal consenso e successione de' Sapienti, diuennero leggi di vna merauigliosa Idea e bellezza vltima, che, essendo vna sola in ciascuna specie, non si può alterare senza distruggerla. Onde pur troppo la deformano quelli, che con la nouità la trasmutano, mentre alla bellezza stà vicina la bruttezza, come li vitij toccano le virtù. Tanto male riconosciamo pur troppo nella caduta del Romano Imperio, col quale caddero tutte le buone Arti, e con esse più d' ogn' altra l'Architettura; perche quei barbari edificatori, dispregiando i modelli e l'Idee Greche e Romane e li più belli monumenti dell' antichità, per molti secoli freneticarono tante e si varie fantasie fantastiche d' ordini, che con bruttissimo disordine mostruosa la resero. Affaticaronsi Bramante, Rafaelle, Baldassarre, Giulio Romano e vltimamente Michel Angelo dall' heroiche ruine restituirla alla sua prima Idea e aspetto, scegliendo le forme più eleganti de gli edifici antichi. Ma hoggi, in vece di rendersi gratie a tali huomini sapientissimi, vengono essi con gli Antichi ingratamente velipesi, quasi senza laude d' ingegno e senza

170

minded spirits, elevating thought to the Idea of the beautiful, are enraptured by the latter alone and consider it a divine thing. Yet the common people refer everything they see to the visual sense. They praise things painted naturally, being used to such things; appreciate beautiful colors, not beautiful forms, which they do not understand; tire of elegance and approve of novelty; disdain reason, follow opinion, and walk away from the truth in art, on which, as on its own base, the most noble monument of the Idea is built. It remains to be said that since the Sculptors of antiquity used the marvelous Idea, as we have indicated, a study of the most perfect antique Sculptures is therefore necessary to guide us to the emended beauties of nature and with the same purpose direct our eyes to contemplate the other outstanding masters. But we will leave this matter to its own proper treatise on imitation, in order to satisfy those who find fault with the study of the statues of antiquity. So far as Architecture is concerned, we say that the Architect must conceive a noble Idea and establish it in his mind, so that it can serve as law and reason for him, placing his inventions in the order, in the disposition, and in the measure and just proportion of the whole and of its parts. But with regard to the decoration and ornamentation of the orders, he is certain to find the established and confirmed Idea in the examples of the Ancients, who established a successful method in this art after long study. When the Greeks set the best limits and proportions for it, which have been confirmed by the most educated centuries and by the consensus of a succession of learned men, they became the laws for a marvelous Idea and an ultimate beauty. There being one beauty only for each species, it cannot be changed without being destroyed. Hence, unfortunately, those who change it with innovations deform it, since ugliness is close to beauty, just as vice touches on virtue. We recognize such an evil in the fall of the Roman Empire, along with which fell all the five arts, and Architecture most of all, because the barbarian builders, having contempt for the Greek and Roman models and Ideas as well as for the most beautiful monuments of antiquity, adopted indiscriminately so many dif-

inuentione l' vno dall' altro habbia copiato. Ciascuno però si finge da se stesso in capo vna nuoua Idea e larua di Architettura a suo modo, esponendola in piazza e su le facciate: huomini certamente vuoti di ogni scienza, che si appartiene all' Architetto, di cui vanamente tengono il nome. Tanto che deformando gli edifici e le città e le memorie, freneticano angoli, spezzature e distorcimenti di linee, scompongono basi, capitelli e colonne, con frottole di stucchi, tritumi e sproportioni; e pure Vitruuio condanna simili nouità [39] e gli ottimi essempi ci propone. Ma li buoni Architetti serbano le più eccellenti forme de gli ordini; li Pittori e gli Scultori, scegliendo le più eleganti bellezze naturali, perfettionano l' Idea, l' opere loro vengono ad auanzarsi e restar superiori alla natura, che è l' vltimo pregio di queste arti, come habbiamo prouato. Quindi nasce l' ossequio e lo stupore de gli huomini verso le statue e le immagini, quindi il premio e gli honore [40] degli Artefici; questa fù la gloria di Timante, di Apelle, di Fidia, di Lisippo e di tanti altri celebrati dalla fama, li quali tutti, solleuati sopra le humane forme, portarono l' Idee e l' opere loro all' ammiratione. Ben può dunque chiamarsi questa Idea perfettione della Natura, miracolo dell' Arte, prouidenza dell' Intelletto, essempio della mente, luce della fantasia. Sole, che dall' Oriente inspira la statua di Mennone, fuoco, che scalda in vita il simolacro di Prometeo. Questa fa, che Venere, le Gratie e gli Amori, lasciando l' Idalio giardino e le piaggie di Cithera, venghino ad albergare nella durezza de' marmi e nel vano dell' ombre. In sua virtù le Muse nell' Eliconie riue temprano li colori all' immortalità; e per sua gloria dispregia Pallade Babiloniche tele e vanta pomposa Dedalei lini. Ma perche l' Idea dell' eloquenza cede tanto all' Idea della Pittura, quanto la vista e più efficace delle parole, io però qui manco nel dire e taccio.

Annibale Carracci

All' Hora la Pittura venne in grandissima ammiratione de gli huomini e parue discesa dal Cielo, quando il diuino Rafaelle con gli vltimi lineamenti dell' arte accrebbe al sommo la sua bel-

ferent fantastic caprices for orders that they made it monstrous with the most unsightly confusion. Bramante, Raphael, Baldassare, Guilio Romano and most recently Michelangelo have worked tirelessly to restore antiquity to her original Idea and aspect from the heroic ruins, choosing the most elegant forms from the ancient structures. But today, instead of giving thanks to these most learned men, the latter are ungratefully vilified along with the Ancients, almost as though one had copied from the other without esteem for genius or originality. Moreover, everyone conceives in his mind a new Idea and appearance of Architecture in his own way, displaying it in the square and on façades—men certainly devoid of any science that pertains to the Architect, whose name they vainly bear. Not content with deforming buildings, cities and memories, they adopt crazy angles, broken spaces and distorted lines, and discompose bases, capitals and columns with yokes of stuccoes, fragments and disproportions; and yet Vitruvius condemns similar novelties [39] and holds the best examples up to them. But the good Architects retain the most excellent forms of the orders. Painters and Sculptors, choosing the most elegant natural beauties, perfect the Idea, and their works exceed and remain superior to nature—which is the ultimate value of these arts, as we have shown. This is the origin of the veneration and awe of men with regard [40] to statues and paintings, and hence of the rewards and honors of the Artists; this was the glory of Timanthes, Apelles, Phidias, Lysippus, and of so many others whose fame is renowned, all those who, elevated above human forms, achieved with their Ideas and works an admirable perfection. This Idea may then well be called the perfection of Nature, miracle of art, foresight of the intellect, example of the mind, light of the imagination, the rising sun, which from the east inspires the statue of Menon, and fire, which in life warms the monument to Prometheus. This is what induces Venus, the Graces and the Cupids to leave the gardens of Idalus and the shores of Cythera and dwell in the hardness of marble and in the emptiness of shadows. In its honor the Muses by the banks of Helicon tem-

lezza, riponendola nell' antica maestà di tutte quelle gratie e di que' pregi arricchita, che già vn tempo la resero gloriosissima appresso de' Greci e de' Romani. Ma perche le cose giù in terra non serbano mai vno stato medesimo, e quelle, che sono giunte al sommo, è forza di nuovo tornino a cadere con perpetua vicissitudine, l'arte, che da Cimabue e da Giotto nel corso ben longo di anni ducento cinquanta erasi a poco a poco auanzata, tosto fù veduta declinare, e di regina diuenne humile e vulgare. Siche, mancato quel felice secolo, dileguossi in breue ogni sua forma; e gli Artefici, abbandonando lo studio della natura, vitiarono l'arte con la maniera, o vogliamo dire fantastica Idea, appoggiata alla pratica e non all' imitatione. Questo vitio distruttore della pittura cominciò da prima a germogliare in maestri di honorato grido, e si radicò nelle scuole, che seguirono poi: onde non è credibile a raccontare, quanto degenerassero non solo da Rafaelle, ma da gli altri, che alla maniera diedero cominciamento. Fiorenza, che si vanta di essere madre della pittura, e 'l paese tutto di Toscana per li suoi professori gloriosissimo, taceua già senza laude di pennello; e gli altri della scuola Romana, non alzando più gli occhi a tanti essempi antichi e nuoui, haueuano posto in dimenticanza ogni lodeuole profitto; e se bene in Venetia più ch' altroue durò la Pittura, non però quiui o per la Lombardia vdiuasi più quel chiaro grido de' colori, che tacque nel Tintoretto vltimo sin' hora de' Venetiani Pittori. Dirò di più quello, che parrà incredibile a raccontarsi: nè dentro nè fuori d' Italia si ritrouaua Pittore alcuno, non essendo gran tempo, che Pietro Paolo Rubens il primo riportò fuori d' Italia i colori; e Federico Barocci, che haurebbe potuto ristorare e dar soccorso all' arte, languiua in Vrbino, non le prestò aiuto alcuno. In questa lunga agitatione l' arte veniua combattuta da due contrari estremi: l' vno tutto soggetto al naturale, l' altro alla fantasia: gl' autori in Roma furono Michel Angelo da Carauaggio e Gioseppe di Arpino; il primo copiaua puramente li corpi, come appariscono a gli occhi, senza elettione, il secondo non riguardaua punto il naturale, seguitando la libertà dell' instinto; e l' vno e l' altro, nel fauore di chiarissima fama, era venuto al Mondo in ammiratione e in essempio. Così quando la Pittura volgeuasi al suo fine, si ri-

pered colors to immortality; and for its glory Pallas scorned Babylonian cloth and vainly boasted of Daedalian linens. But as the Idea of eloquence yields to the Idea of painting, just as a scene is more efficacious than words, speech therefore fails me and I am silent.

Annibale Carracci

Painting is now greatly admired and seems as though descended from heaven, when the divine Raphael by his supreme drawing has raised its beauty to the summit of art, restoring to it all the graces of its ancient majesty and enriching it by the attributes that had once rendered it glorious among the Greeks and Romans. But since things here on earth never remain in the same state, and those that have attained the summit perhaps then turn to fall again in a perpetual succession, art, which from the time of Cimabue and Giotto progressed gradually for two hundred and fifty years, was soon seen to decline, and from a queen, became humble and vulgar. So that, this fortunate century having passed, each of its forms were dissipated in a short time; and the artists, abandoning the study of nature, corrupted art with manner, or we would say with a fantastic Idea, drawing on custom and not on imitation. This destructive vice in painting began to germinate with masters of honorable reputation and became rooted in the schools that followed later. From then on it is hard to believe how much they degenerated not only from Raphael but also from the others as well who introduced manner. Florence, which prides itself in being the mother of painting, and the entire Toscan country, for its most illustrious teachers, were already silent, unhonored in painting. And the others of the Roman school, no longer raising their sights to the many antique and new examples, have forgotten their noteworthy place. And neither even in Venice, where painting lasted longer than elsewhere, nor in Lombardy, could that clear voice of colors be heard any longer, which had fallen silent after Tintoretto, the last of the Venetian painters. I will say more that will seem incredible: neither within nor outside of Italy could any painter

uolsero gli astri più benigni verso l' Italia, e piacque a Dio, che nella Città di Bologna, di scienze maestra e di studi, sorgesse vn eleuatissimo ingegno, e che con esso risorgesse l'Arte caduta e quasi estinta. Fù questi Annibale Carracci . . . . . .

be found, and it was not so long that Peter Paul Rubens was the first to carry the colors out of Italy; and Federico Barocci, who could have restored and given aid to art, was languishing at Urbino, not lending it any aid. In this long period of agitation art was contested by two opposing extremes, one entirely subject to the natural, the other to the imagination: the exponents in Rome were Michel Angelo da Caravaggio and Giuseppe d'Arpino; the former simply copied bodies, as they appear to the eyes, indiscriminately; the latter did not consider the natural at all, following the freedom of instinct; and both, enjoying great reputations, became admired and were examples to the world. So that when painting was going toward its end, Italy came under more favorable stars, for it pleased God that in the city of Bologna, master of sciences and studies, a most elevated genius should appear and with him the fallen and nearly extinct art rose again. He was Annibale Carracci. . . .

NOTES

to Text & Appendices

CHAPTER 1

1. On Plato's doctrine of the beautiful in art, cf. Ernst Cassirer, "Eidos und Eidolon: Das Problem des Schönen und der Kunst in Platos Dialogen," *Vorträge der Bibliothek Warburg*, II:1 (1922–23), 1–27.

2. *Republic*, VI.501.

3. Cf. the passage quoted below, p. 184, n. 17.

4. *Laws*, II.656DE.

5. *Letters*, VII.342–343.

6. It is apparent that the Platonic concept of εὕρεσις is an exact inversion of that which is usually understood by the word "invention": the Platonic εὕρεσις is not so much an "invention" of new and individual forms as it is a "discovery" of eternal and universally valid principles, particularly as they are revealed in mathematics. Quite logically, therefore, the highest rank in a Platonic hierarchy of the arts would have to be given to architecture and music. E. Wind is preparing a paper on these questions.

7. Cf. Proclus's discussions quoted pp. 189 ff., n. 47.

8. *Sophist*, 233 ff.; cf. esp. J. A. Jolles, *Vitruvs Aesthetik* (diss. Freiburg, 1906), pp. 51 ff. On the misunderstanding in the sixteenth and seventeenth centuries of the Platonic differentiation between μίμησις εἰκαστική and μίμησις φανταστική, cf. pp. 212–215, n. 51, and p. 242, n. 20.

9. *Republic*, X.602.

10. J. Overbeck, *Die antiken Schriftquellen zur Geschichte der bildenden Künste bei den Griechen* (1868), Nr. 772.

11. *Sophist*, 235E–236A.

12. Cf. Cassirer, op. cit.

13. *Ennaratio libri I. Ethicor. Arist.*, ch. 6 (*Corp. Ref.*, Vol. XVI, col. 290).

14. Melanchthon consciously refused to interpret the Ideas as metaphysical οὐσίαι, in order to equate them—presumably interpreting Plato's own meaning more correctly—with the *defi-*

nitiones or *denotationes* of Aristotle, referring here not without reason to Cicero's *Orator* (see p. 7 above): *Hanc absolutam et perfectam rei definitionem Plato vocat Ideam. . . . Et ex hoc loco Ciceronis judicari potest, ideas apud Platonem intelligendas esse non animas aut formas coelo delapsas, sed perfectam notitiam iuxta dialecticam* ("Scholia in Ciceronis oratorem," *Corp. Ref.*, Vol. XVI, col. 771 ff.). Significantly, the concept "art" (which he naturally understands in the sense of *ratio*, like Dürer and others) was already chiefly related by Melanchthon to the representational artist, whereas Thomas Aquinas, for example, though almost literally agreeing with Melanchthon's definition, related this concept to the geometrician:

Thomas Aquinas, *Summa Theologiae*, II.1.57.3 (in the edn. by Fretté and Maré, II, 362): *Respondeo dicendum, quod ars nihil aliud est, quam ratio recta aliquorum operum faciendorum.*	Melanchthon, *Initia doctr. phys.*, *Corp. Ref.*, Vol. XIII, col. 305: *Est autem ars recta ratio faciendorum operum, ut statuarius certam habet notitiam dirigentem manus, sculpentem imaginem in statua, id est partes statuae tantisper ordinantem, donec efficiatur similitudo eius archetypi, quem imitatur.*

15. Only secondarily does Melanchthon cite Archimedes, who bore within himself the *imago motuum* αὐτομάτων *coelestium*.

16. On Melanchthon's general indebtedness to Cicero, cf. W. Dilthey, *Gesammelte Schriften* (1914), II, 172 ff.

CHAPTER 2

1. Cf. W. Kroll, *M. Tulli Ciceronis Orator* (1913), introduction.

2. Viz., II.5: the portrait of Jalysos by Protogenes (at Rhodes, where Cicero himself had seen it), the portrait of Aphrodite by Apelles (at Kos), the *Zeus* by Phidias, and the *Doryphoros* by Polycletus; thus two paintings and two statues.

3. Thus, if the *non* (attested by the MS) before *cadunt* is retained. This appears entirely possible if *ea, quae sub oculos non cadunt* is taken to mean "divine beings to be represented"; for this interpretation I am indebted to Prof. Plasberg (Hamburg). Recently

the passage has been interpreted in this sense also by H. Sjögren (*Eranos*, XIX, 163 ff.). If in agreement with Vettori (Victorius, *Var. Lectiones*, XI.14) the *non* is deleted (a conjecture supported by W. Friedrich, *Jahrbuch für klassischen Philologie*, CXXIII [1881], 180 ff.), then "things accessible to the eyes" must be understood as "visible work of art," which would thus correspond to "audible speech"; thus explicitly Vettori, *loc. cit.* Naturally it is impossible to understand the *ea, quae* . . . as a "visible natural model": the speaker describes the work of precisely those artists who work without any sort of external observation. On Giov. Pietro Bellori's significant reinterpretation of this passage on just this point, cf. pp. 105 ff.

4. Cicero, *Orator ad Brutum*, II.7 ff. (ed. Kroll, pp. 24 ff.; partly repr. in Overbeck, Nr. 717).

5. On this cf. Jakob Burckhardt, "Die Griechen und ihre Künstler," in his *Vorträge*, ed. Dürr, 2d edn. (1918), pp. 202 ff. That the creative significance of artistic production at least with respect to painting was appreciated at an early time is shown by a verse of Empedocles, which, anticipating the later *topos* of *deus pictor, deus statuarius, deus artifex*, compares the making of the cosmos with that of a picture (H. Diels, *Die Fragmente der Vorsokratiker*, 4th edn. [1922], I, 234, Nr. 23):

ὡς δ'ὁπόταν γραφέες ἀναθήματα ποικίλλωσιν
ἀνέρες ἀμφὶ τέχνης ὑπὸ μήτιος εὖ δεδαῶτε,
οἵτ' ἐπεὶ οὖν μάρψωσι πολύχροα φάρμακα χερσίν,
ἁρμονίηι μείξαντε τὰ μὲν πλέω, ἄλλα δ'ἐλάσσω,
ἐκ τῶν εἴδεα πᾶσιν ἀλίγκια πορσύνουσι,
δένδρεά τε κτίζοντε καὶ ἀνέρας ἠδὲ γυναῖκας.
θῆράς τ'οἰωνούς τε καὶ ὑδατοθρέμμονας ἰχθῦς
καί τε θεοὺς δολιχαίωνας τιμῆισι φερίστους·
οὕτω μήσ' ἀπάτη φρένα καινύτω ἄλλοθεν εἶναι,
θνητῶν, ὅσσα γε δῆλα γεγάκασιν ἄσπετα, πηγήν,
ἀλλὰ τορῶς ταῦτ' ἴσθι, θεοῦ πάρα μῦθον ἀκούσας.

6. The same arguments that "Paideia" (i.e., Education) hurls against "Techne" (i.e., Sculpture) in Lucian's *Dream* are again advanced against the same art by Painting in the rich Renaissance literature disputing the precedence of the arts; cf. esp. the famous *Paragone* at the beginning of Leonardo's "Book on Painting."

7. Characteristic examples are the famous anecdotes about the relationship of Alexander the Great to Apelles (Overbeck, Nrs. 1834, 1836).

8. Pliny, *Nat. Hist.*, XXXV.77. The passage is quoted with a few alterations, meant to heighten its importance still further, in Romano Alberti, *Trattato della nobiltà della pittura* (Rome, 1585), p. 18.

9. Plato, *Republic*, 605 ff.

10. M. Herzfeld, *Leonardo da Vinci, der Denker, Forscher und Poet* (1911), p. 157 (from MS Ash., fol. 20ʳ): "as he who scorns painting loves neither philosophy nor nature."

11. Philostratus, ed. G. L. Kayser, 3rd edn. (1853), p. 379. The characteristic attitude of the Ciceronian period is shown by the very fact that Cicero in his *Orator* cites four works of art as examples without naming their authors: he speaks of the *Jalysos* as we speak of the *Night Watch*—certain that the artist's name is common knowledge to his readers.

12. Overbeck, Nrs. 1649 and 550 ff.

13. Overbeck, Nr. 968 (=Quintilian, *Inst. orat.*, XII.10.7).

14. Overbeck, Nr. 903 (=Quintilian, *Inst. orat.*, XII.10.9).

15. Overbeck, Nr. 1701 (Xenophon, Ἀπομνημ, III.10.1): Καὶ μὴν τά γε καλὰ εἴδη ἀφομοιοῦντες, ἐπειδὴ οὐ ῥάδιον ἑνὶ ἀνθρώπῳ περιτυχεῖν ἄμεμπτα πάντα ἔχοντι, ἐκ πολλῶν συνάγοντες τὰ ἐξ ἑκάστου κάλλιστα, οὕτως ὅλα τὰ σώματα καλὰ ποεῖτε φαίνεσθαι; ποιοῦμεν γάρ, ἔφα, οὕτως.

16. Overbeck, Nrs. 1667–1669 (=Pliny, *Nat. Hist.*, XXXV.64; Cicero, *De invent.*, II.1.1; Dionysius of Halicarnassus, *De priscis script. cens.*, 1).

17. Plato, *Republic*, 472: Οἴει ἂν οὖν ἧττόν τι ἀγαθὸν ζωγράφον εἶναι, ὃς ἂν γράψας παράδειγμα, οἷον ἂν εἴη ὁ κάλλιστος ἄνθρωπος, καὶ πάντα εἰς τὸ γράμμα ἱκανῶς ἀποδοὺς μὴ ἔχῃ ἀποδεῖξαι, ὡς καὶ δυνατὸν γενέσθαι τοιοῦτον ἄνδρα; Μὰ Δί' οὐκ ἔγωγε, ἔφη.

18. Aristotle, *Politics*, III.6.5 (1281b); insofar as a single part is concerned, however, reality can surpass the painter's ideal picture, just as an ordinary man can surpass a great one in a single skill. On this cf. also *Poetics*, XXV: τὸ γὰρ παράδειγμα δεῖ ὑπερέχειν τοιούτους δ'εἶναι, οἵους Ζεῦξις ἔγραψεν.

19. When comparing the statements of Dion and Philostratus with those of Cicero, Plotinus, Proclus, and Seneca the Elder (for Dion and Philostratus, see the following notes; for Cicero, p. 3 f.;

for Plotinus, p. 26; for Proclus, pp. 189 f., n. 47; for Seneca, pp. 158 and 159), one will agree with Kroll (op. cit., p. 25 n) that there was an old and widely held tradition behind the thesis that no models were employed for Phidias's portrayals of the gods, especially for his *Zeus*. Here the well-known epigram in the Greek Anthology (Overbeck, Nr. 716), which perhaps was the starting point for the whole speculation, must also be mentioned. According to this story, Phidias answered the question of which *paradeigma* he proposed to use for *Zeus* as follows: "The words of Homer, ἦ καὶ κυανέῃσιν ἐπ' ὀφρύσι νεῦσε Κρονίων' (Overbeck, Nr. 698).

20. Dion of Prusa, ed. Joh. de Arnim (1893–), II, 167. In line with this statement is the high opinion Dion had of the artist's profession: he is a μιμητὴς τῆς δαιμονίας φύσεως.

21. Philostratus, *Apollonius of Tyana*, VI.19 (ed. Kayser, p. 118): φαντασία ταῦτα εἰργάσατο σοφωτέρα μιμήσεως δημιουργός· μίμησις μὲν γὰρ δημιουργήσει ὃ εἶδεν, φαντασία δὲ καὶ ὃ υὴ εἶδεν, ὑποθήσεται γὰρ αὐτὸ πρὸς τὴν ἀναφορὰν τοῦ ὄντος, καὶ μίμησιν μὲν πολλάκις ἐκκρούει ἔκπληξις, φαντασίαν δὲ οὐδέν, χωρεῖ γὰρ ἀνέκπληκτος πρὸς ὃ αὐτὴ ὑπέθετο. The exegesis by Jul. Walter, *Geschichte der Aesthetik im Altertum* (1893), p. 794, is not confirmed by a literal reading of the text.

22. Cf. Joh. ab Arnim, *Stoicor. vet. fragmenta*, I (1905), 19, and II (1903), 28. Further, Plutarch, *De placit. philos.*, I.10, and Stobaeus, *Eclogues*, I.12.332 (ed. Meinecke [1860], p. 89).

23. Aristotle, *Metaphysics*, VII.8 (1034a).

24. Aristotle, *Metaphysics*, VII.7 (1032a). Besides the two basic categories ὕλη and μορφή (εἶδος, ἰδέα) Aristotle recognizes three more (αἰτία, τέλος, τὸ κινοῦν) which seem to be applicable to artistic production and were later adopted by Seneca in this sense (cf. pp. 19 ff. above and n. 25 below). But Scaliger already recognized quite correctly that only the first two could be spoken of as the really "substantial" ones: only ὕλη and μορφή are the (*a priori*) conditions for the existence of the work of art; τέλος and κινοῦν are merely the (empirical) conditions for producing it.

25. Seneca, *Epistolae*, LXV.2–10. The letter goes on to prove that all these "causes" of the work of art are in truth only secondary causes, including the *idea* (which here equals *exemplar*): *Exemplar quoque non est causa, sed instrumentum causae necessarium. Sic necessarium est exemplar artifici, quomodo scalprum, quomodo lima* (par. 13).

26. Seneca, *Epistolae*, LXVIII.16–21.

27. The formulation *Idea erat Vergilii facies*, at first glance so singular, made an impression during the Renaissance (significantly) on Jul. Caes. Scaliger, who gave the title "Idea" to the third book of his *Poetics*. He explains that he had first spoken about the purpose of poetry (*quare imitemur*), and then about its means (*quibus imitemur*); in the following book he would discuss its forms (*quomodo imitemur*), but in the present one (i.e., the book "Idea") he would discuss its subjects (*quid imitandum sit*): *Idcirco liber hic "Idea" est a nobis inscriptus . . . quia, res ipsae quales quantaeque sunt, talem tantamque . . . efficimus orationem. Sicut igitur est Idea picturae Socrates, sic Troja Homericae Iliados.* H. Brinkschulte, *Julius Caesar Scaligers kunsttheoretische Anschauungen*, in *Renaissance und Philosophie: Beiträge zur Geschichte der Philosophie*, ed. A. Dyroff, X (1914), p. 9, correctly recognized that Scaliger used the term "idea" here not in Plato's sense but in the sense of "subject"; but Brinkschulte overlooked the connection with Seneca and was therefore misled into maintaining that Scaliger here anticipated Descartes's conception of "idea." For the rest, Scaliger exactly followed Aristotle, the *imperator* and *dictator perpetuus* of philosophy: he equated "idea" with the Aristotelian εἶδος, adopted the doctrine that the work of art comes into being by a form entering into a material (the material of the sculptor is bronze, that of the flutist air), and even tried to bring Plato into agreement with Aristotle: *Est enim consentanea eo ipso Aristotelicae demonstrationi: qua intelligimus balnei speciem esse in animo architecti, antequam balneum aedificet;* cf. Brinkschulte, p. 34.

28. Plotinus, *Ennead*, V.8.1

29. Cf. O. Walzel, "Plotins Begriff der ästhetischen Form," *Vom Geistesleben alter und neuer Zeit* (1922), pp. 1 ff., for an explanation of Plotinus's conception of εἶδος, which doubtless denotes not something purely conceptual but, as Schelling would say, the object of an *"intellectuelle Anschauung"* (i.e., an artistic "vision"). Thus it could be used as synonymous with ἰδέα, but also as synonymous with μορφή. Therefore it can be demonstrated on purely terminological grounds that Plotinus's aesthetics can be understood only as a synthesis of Platonic and Aristotelian trains of thought.

30. Plotinus, *Ennead*, I.6.2: οὐκ ἀνασχομένης τῆς ὕλης τὸ πάντη κατὰ τὸ εἶδος μορφοῦσθαι.

31. Plotinus, *Ennead*, V.8.1.

32. Plotinus, *Ennead*, I.6.3: beauty is an εἶδος σμνδησάμενον καὶ κρατήσας τῆς φύσεως τῆς ἐναντίας ἀμόρφου οὔσας.

33. Cf. p. 17 and p. 185, nn. 23 and 24.

34. Aristotle, *Metaphysics*, VII.7–8 (1032b ff.); the example of the statue in 1033a. The example of the "house," also used by Philo and other late-classical authors, was constantly repeated during the Middle Ages (Thomas Aquinas, Bonaventure, Meister Eckhart, *et al.*); even in modern times (e.g., by Scaliger) it was occasionally picked up; cf. p. 186, n. 27, and also ch. III, nn. 20, 21, 25, and ch. IV, nn. 23 and 53 below.

35. Aristotle, *Metaphysics*, VII.8 (1035a): "Thus that which is a union of form and matter . . . can dissolve into material parts; but that which is not bound up with matter, cannot dissolve. And therefore the clay statue can dissolve into clay . . . and also the [*scil.* bronze] circle into the segments of a circle."

36. On this point cf. Clemens Baeumker, *Das Problem der Materie in der griechischen Philosophie* (1890), p. 263; the comparison of the relationship of form to matter with the relationship of the feminine to the masculine is found in Aristotle, *Physics*, I.9.192.

37. See p. 186, n. 30.

38. Cf. Baeumker, pp. 405 ff.

39. Aristotle, *Metaphysics*, XII.3 (1070a): Ἐπὶ μὲν οὖν τινῶν τὸ τόδε τι οὐκ ἔστι παρὰ τὴν συνθέτην οὐσίαν, οἷον οἰκίας τὸ εἶδος, εἰ μὴ ἡ τέχνη.

40. Plotinus, *Ennead*, I.6.3: πῶς δὲ τὴν ἔξω οἰκίαν τῷ ἔνδον οἰκίας εἴδει ὁ οἰκοδομικὸς συναρμόσας καλὴν εἶναι λέγει; ἢ ὅτι ἔστι τὸ ἔξω, εἰ χωρίσειας τοὺς λίθους, τὸ ἔνδον εἶδος, μερισθὲν τῷ ἔξω ὕλης ὄγκῳ, ἀμερὲς ὂν ἐν πολλοῖς φανταζόμενον.

41. Plotinus, *Ennead*, I.6.1: Τί οὖν ἔστιν, ὃ κινεῖ τὰς ὄψεις τῶν θεωμένων, καὶ ἐπιστρέφει πρὸς αὐτό, καὶ ἕλκει, καὶ εὐφραίνεσθαι τῇ θέᾳ ποιεῖ; . . . Λέγεται μὲν δὴ παρὰ πάντων, ὡς εἰπεῖν, ὡς συμμετρία τῶν μερῶν πρὸς ἄλληλα καὶ πρὸς τὸ ὅλον τό τε τῆς εὐχροίας προστεθέν τὸ πρὸς τὴν ὄψιν κάλλος ποιεῖ . . . οἷς ἁπλοῦν οὐδέν, μόνον δὲ τὸ σύνθετον ἐξ ἀνάγκης καλὸν ὑπάρξει, τό τε ὅλον ἔσται καλὸν αὐτοῖς. Τὰ δὲ μέρη ἕκαστα οὐχ ἕξει παρ' ἑαυτῶν τὸ καλὰ εἶναι, πρὸς δὲ τὸ ὅλον συντελοῦντα, ἵνα καλὸν ῃ. Καίτοι δεῖ, εἴπερ ὅλον, καὶ τὰ μέρη καλὰ εἶναι· οὐ γὰρ δὴ ἐξ αἰσχρῶν, ἀλλὰ πάντα κατειληφέναι τὸ κάλλος. Τά τε χρώματα αὐτοῖς τὰ καλά, οἷον καὶ τὸ τοῦ ἡλίου ψῶς, ἁπλᾶ ὄντα, καὶ οὐκ ἐκ συμμετρίας ἔχοντα τὸ κάλλοσ, ἔξω ἔσται τοῦ καλὰ εἶναι. . . . Ὅταν δὲ δή, καὶ τῆς αὐτῆς συμμετρίας μενού-

σης, ὁτὲ μὲν καλὸν τὸ αὐτὸ πρόσωπον, ὁτὲ δὲ μὴ φαίνεται, πῶς οὐκ ἄλλο δεῖ ἐπὶ τῷ συμμέτρῳ λέγειν τὸ καλὸν εἶναι, καὶ τὸ σύμμετρον καλὸν εἶναι δι' ἄλλο; It seems that the Stoa was the first school to frame the definition of beauty as συμμετρία in the formula quoted and attacked by Plotinus, and that the Stoa was the chief object of his attack; Creuzer, in his edition of the *Liber de pulchritudine* (1814), pp. 146 ff., quotes Cicero's *Tusc. Disp.*, IV.13: *Et ut corporis est quaedam apta figura membrorum cum coloris quadam suavitate eaque dicitur pulchritudo.* However the equation "beauty" = συμμετρία, or as Lucian once expressed it, "beauty" = τῶν μερων πρὸς τὸ ὅλον ἰσότης καὶ ἁρμονία, is not just *a* definition but rather *the* definition of beauty for classic Greek art. It dominated aesthetic thought almost exclusively from Xenophon until Late Antiquity and also guided the efforts of theorizing artists; cf. Aug. Kalkmann, *Die Proportionen des Gesichts in der griechischen Kunst* (Berliner Winckelmannsprogramm, Nr. 53 [1893]), pp. 4 ff.

42. Plotinus, *Ennead*, I.6.2.

43. Plotinus, *Ennead*, I.6.9: "Αναγε ἐπὶ σαυτὸν καὶ ἰδέ˙ κἂν μήπω σαυτὸν ἴδῃς καλόν, οἷά ποιητὴς ἀγάλματος, ὃ δεῖ καλὸν γενέσθαι, τὸ μὲν ἀφαιρεῖ, τὸ δὲ ἀπέξεσε, τὸ δὲ λεῖον, τὸ δὲ καθαρὸν ἐποίησεν, ἕως ἔδειξε καλὸν ἐπὶ τῷ ἀγάλματι πρόσωπον. Οὕτω καὶ σὺ ἀφαιρεῖ ὅσα περιττά, καὶ ἀπεύθυνε ὅσα σκολιά, ὅσα σκοτεινὰ καθα ίρων ἐργάζου εἶναι λαμπρά, καὶ μὴ παύσῃ τεκταίνων τὸ σὸν ἄγαλμα, ἕως ἂν ἐκλάμψειέ σοι τῆς ἀρετῆς ἡ θεωειδὴς ἀγλαΐα, ἕως ἂν ἴδῃς σωφροσύνην ἐν ἁγνῷ βεβῶσαν καθαρῷ. Thus Plotinus already interpreted the sculptural process moralistically, as a self-liberation and self-purification; and this thought was then adopted by such later Neoplatonists as Pseudo-Dionysius; cf. K. Borinski, *Die Antike in Poetik und Kunsttheorie* (1914), pp. 169–170. In itself the notion that the sculptural image comes about by means of ἀφαίρεσις and painting by means of "addition" is substantially older (cf. Dion Chrysostom, op. cit., p. 167, which says of sculpture: ἀφαιροῦσα τὸ περιττόν, ἕως ἂν καταλίπῃ τὸ φαινόμενον εἶδος), and its real root is presumably in the Aristotelian doctrine of δύναμις and ἐνέργεια: Λέγομεν δὲ δυνάμει, οἷον ἐν τῷ ξύλῳ ῾Ερμῆν (*Metaphysics*, IX.6.1048a), which is recalled in Thomas Aquinas, *Physics*, I.11 (Fretté-Maré, XXII, 327): *alia vero fiunt abstractione* [literally equals ἀφαίρεσις], *sicut ex lapide fit per sculptorem Mercurius.* But this view of sculpture, particularly popular in the Renaissance, was not really "rooted" in Neoplatonism, much less in Christian Neoplatonism. Here it was only

adopted and given an ethical interpretation with special enthusiasm; in fact the notion of the εἶδος freeing itself more and more from the block of marble must have had a particular appeal for the metaphysical convictions of Plotinus and his followers (he consistently referred to the sculptor, although the painter was still more esteemed socially). It is significant, however, that Renaissance thinkers— except for Michelangelo (cf. pp. 115 ff. and pp. 245 f., n. 17)!— completely ignored the ethical interpretation of ἀφαίρεσις and, on the contrary, failed to mention sculpture when they demanded that man "conquer the material component of his make-up" (Leonardo, *Trattato della pittura*, ed. H. Ludwig [1881], Nr. 119).

44. For Plotinus the "elective process" had another and narrower significance than the one attributed to it in the anecdotes mentioned above about Zeuxis and Parrhasius (and in countless corresponding statements found in the Renaissance theoreticians). For Plotinus it meant by no means the only possibility of producing a beautiful figure, but only one (and indeed far less preferable) or two possibilities. Statues of the gods were exclusively produced by way of inner contemplation, and the elective process was proper only where this pure inner contemplation could have no effect, viz., in the "representation of men." But where not even the elective process was adhered to, where we are faced with the "iconic" representation of a human individual, there Plotinus would have refused to speak of "art" at all: the "representation of just one object chosen at random" is expressly excluded from that which is defended here, and portraiture remains for him, too, an εἴδωλον εἰδώλου (cf. the well-known account by Porphyry according to which Plotinus would never allow his portrait to be painted; repr. Borinski, p. 272, n. to p. 92). Plotinus could approve only the artist who brings forth either the likeness of a god from a pure Idea or, if indeed the likeness of a man, a likeness which combines the best features of various individuals. Cf. also n. 47 below.

45. The expression ὁ ἐννοήσας is very characteristic of Plotinus's "heuretic" interpretation of art.

46. Plotinus, *Ennead*, I.6.1.

47. The view that the materially realized work necessarily falls short of the ideal conception must of course not be confused with a statement such as *Ennead*, IV.3.10: Τέχνη γὰρ ὑστέρα αὐτῆς [*scil.* φύσεως], καὶ μιμεῖται ἀμυδρὰ καὶ ἀσθενῆ ποιοῦσα μιμήματα, παίγνια ἄττα καὶ οὐ πολλοῦ ἄξια, μηχαναῖς πολλαῖς εἰς εἰδώλων φύσιν προσχρωμένη. For here, just as in Plotinus's refusal to have his portrait

painted (see p. 191, n. 44), art is not understood as εὕρεσις but as μίμησις. All this shows that Neoplatonism did adhere to Plato's differentiation between "heuretic" and "mimetic" art, only it shifted the emphasis; that is to say, the limits of what can be considered "heuretic" art were considerably extended because—and just this is the immortal contribution of Plotinus—the criterion of value for a work of art was no longer theoretical truth but beauty (even though beauty was metaphysically identical with truth). With exemplary clarity these facts are explained in a statement by Proclus (*Comm. in Tim.*, II.81c), which in a way can be considered a condensed summary of Neoplatonic aesthetics: καὶ εἰ μὲν καλόν ἐστι τὸ γιγνόμενον [*scil.* the work of art], πρὸς τὸ ἀεὶ ὂν παράδειγμα γέγονεν, εἰ δὲ υὴ καλόν, πρὸς τὸ γεγονός . . . τὸ πρὸς νοητὸν γεγονὸσ καλόν ἐστι, τὸ πρὸς γενητὸν γεγονὸς οὐ καλόν ἐστιν . . . ὁ γὰρ πρὸς τὸ νοητὸν ποιῶν ἢ ὁμοίως αὐτὸ μιμεῖται, ἢ ἀνομοίως. Εἰ μὲν δὴ ὁμοίως, καλὸν ποιήσει τὸ μιμηθέν· ἦν γὰρ ἐκεῖ τὸ πρώτως καλόν· εἰ δὲ ἀνομοίως, οὐ πρὸς τὸ νοητὸν ποιεῖ . . . καὶ ὁ πρὸς τὸ γεγονός τι ποιῶν, εἴπερ ὄντως ἀφυρᾳ πρὸς ἐκεῖνο, δῆλον ὡς οὐ καλὸν ποιεῖ· αὐτὸ γὰρ ἐκεῖνο πλῆρές ἐστιν ἀνομοιότητος, καὶ οὐκ ἔστι τὸ πρώτως καλόν . . . Ἐπεὶ καὶ ὁ φειδίας ὁ τὸν Δία ποιήσας οὐ πρὸς γεγονὸς ἀπέβλεψεν, ἀλλ᾽ εἰς ἔννοιαν ἀφίκετο τοῦ παρ᾽ Ὁμήρου Διός. . . . Thus either artistic representation is "mimetic" and chooses for its object a γεγονός, a "created thing" (i.e., something empirically real), in which case the result cannot be beautiful because the model is already marred by countless faults; or artistic representation is "heuretic" and chooses for its model "something nonexistent" (i.e., a νοητόν; Phidias's *Zeus* can again serve for an example of this possibility), in which case the result is necessarily beautiful, insofar as it is adequate to this νοητόν; and insofar as it is not adequate to the νοητόν, the νοητόν is no longer its object. From this point of view it is only logical that Plotinus, with his high esteem for art based on the νοητόν, rejected portraiture because it is satisfied with the reproduction of a γεγονός and therefore merely "mimetic" by definition. The patristic writers followed him in this but naturally gave a more Christian direction to the thought. And it is just as logical that, later on, the Mannerists and Classicists, who had returned to conceptualism (even though a modified form of it), while not exactly rejecting portraiture, nevertheless for the most part considered it to be inferior to other genres. "No great and exceptional painter has ever been a portraitist," wrote Vicente Carducho (d. 1638) in his *Dialogos de la Pintura* (according to Karl Justi, *Michel-*

angelo: Neue Beiträge [1909], p. 407; cf. also p. 242, n. 20 below). On the position taken by the patristic writers, cf. Max Dvořåk, *Idealismus und Naturalismus in der gotischen Skulptur und Malerei* (1920), p. 70: Paulinus of Nola refused to allow a portrait to be painted of himself and his wife on the grounds that the *homo caelestis* (who had by then replaced the Platonic νοητόν) cannot be represented and the *homo terrenus* should not be represented. Many other passages show how the Church Fathers tried to place the Platonic and Neoplatonic arguments against sense-deceiving μίμησις in the service of their Old-Testament, antimagical fight against image worship. A summary of the pertinent statements is in Hugo Koch's (quite biased, however, in its conclusions) *Die altchristliche Bilderfrage nach den literarischen Quellen* (1917).

48. Plotinus, *Ennead*, I.6.8.

49. Plotinus, *Ennead*, I.6.9.

50. Plotinus, *Ennead*, I.6.8. (On the alleged connection of this passage with a statement in L. B. Alberti's *De pictura*, cf. pp. 208–209, n. 32 below, where both are quoted.) In a similar manner the beautiful parable of Odysseus and Circe, immediately following, admonishes us to fly from sensory to intellectual beauty.

CHAPTER 3

1. Augustine, *Confessions*, X.34 (ed. Knöll, p. 227).

2. On patristic aesthetics (Aug. Berthaud, *Sancti Augustini doctrina de pulchro ingenuisque artibus* . . . [Poitiers, 1891], was unfortunately not available to me) and its continuation in the High Middle Ages, cf. esp. M. de Wulf in *Revue néoscolastique*, II (1895) and III (1896), passim, and XVI (1909), pp. 237 ff.; further, K. Eschweiler, *Die ästhetischen Elemente in der Religionsphilosophie des Heiligen Augustin* (diss. Munich, 1909), where there are also remarks about Origen, Gregory of Nyssa, etc. The mark of beauty—for the writings quoted hardly go into the question of art, which indeed did not exist as an independent problem in medieval philosophy—is everywhere said to be first (according to the Plotinian "Idea shining through matter") a peculiar "radiance" that is interpreted as an immediate emanation of the divinity, particularly in Pseudo-Dionysius's "light metaphysics"; and second (according to the classical notion of συμμετρία) the proportionality of parts and the pleasantness of color: *Ipsum vero superessentiale pulchrum pul-*

chritudo quidem dicitur propter illam, quam rebus pro suo cuiusque modo pulchritudinem tradit. Atque ut omnium concinnitatis nitorisque causa [εὐαρμοσίας καὶ ἀγλαίας] *luminis videtur instar, cunctis coruscans, fontani radii sui derivationes omnia passim pulchra reddentes et tamquam ad se omnia vocans, unde a "vocando"* [καλεῖν] *pulchritudo Graece "callos" cognominatur* (Pseudo-Dionysius, *De divin. nom.,* IV.7; quoted by Marsilio Ficino, *Opera* [Basel, 1576], II, 1060). There is no real contradiction in this duality, for εὐαρμοσία is required only of the external appearance of beauty; Plotinus, too, considered it necessary, insofar as a given beautiful thing might have parts. Thus it need not cause surprise that Augustine in one place (quoted pp. 35 f. above) considered beauty to be a divine emanation and in another (*De civ. Dei,* XXII.19) defined it, in a quite Ciceronian (and thus apparently anti-Plotinian) manner as follows: *Omnis corporis pulchritudo est partium congruentia cum quadam coloris suavitate.* Here, where only corporeal beauty is concerned, phenomenal description has taken the place of metaphysical interpretation. A reconciliation between the one and the other is perhaps effected by the famous category of *numerus* (= rhythm), for "number" meant to Augustine on the one hand a visible principle of beautiful form and motion, on the other a "most general metaphysical determinant of being" (Eschweiler, p. 12). — The definition of beauty as a phenomenal *concinnitas* enhanced by a metaphysical *splendor* or *claritas* lasted almost until the end of the Middle Ages. The treatise *De pulchro et bono,* long attributed to Thomas Aquinas but actually an excerpt from Albertus Magnus's *Comm. in Dionys.* (cf. de Wulf, in *Revue néoscolastique,* XVI), says very clearly: *Pulchrum in ratione sua plura concludit, scilicet splendorem formae substantialis vel accidentalis super partes materiae proportionatas et terminatas.* And Thomas Aquinas himself, although he was not an adherent of "light metaphysics"—in contrast to St. Bonaventure, on whom cf. E. Lut., "Die Aesthetik Bonaventuras," in *Beiträge zur Geschichte der Philosophie des Mitteelalters,* Suppl.-Bd. (1913), pp. 200 ff.—nevertheless considered beauty to be the fulfillment of both of these postulates, which he expressed as *debita proportio* and *claritas.* — On the "light metaphysics" in Christian Neoplatonism and its further effect in the Middle Ages and in the Italian Renaissance, cf. K. Borinski, *Die Rätsel Michelangelos* (1908), pp. 27 ff.; also Cl. Baeumker, *Der Platonismus im Mittelalter* (Festrede gehalten in der öffentlichen Sitzung der königlichen Bayrischen Akademie der Wissenschaften am 18. März 1916), pp. 18 ff.; and in this book, see pp. 199 ff., n. 27 (Dante), p. 207, n. 29 (Ficino), and pp. 93 ff. (Mannerism).

3. Cf. n. 7 below.

4. Dionysus, for instance, did not "create" the vine, he found it and taught mankind its use; the same was true of Athena and the olive tree.

5. According to Philo, God created the Ideas, since he saw that without beautiful prototypes nothing beautiful could be created (*De opificio mundi,* IV); but they are immanent in His mind, and in order to serve further the execution of His divine intention, they are endowed with the function of "incorporeal forces" (ἀσώματοι δυνάμεις). Cf. Zeller, *Philosophie der Griechen* (4th printing), III:2, 409; further, the quotation from Seneca's Epistle LXV on pp. 19–21 above: *Haec exemplaria omnium rerum Deus intra se habet.*

6. On the dispute between Plotinus and Longinus concerning this, cf. Zeller, p. 418, n. 4. It is significant that Florentine Neoplatonism passionately claimed Plato himself as an adherent of the immanence theory; see Marsilio Ficino, *Comm. in Tim.,* XV (*Opera,* II, 1444): *Dicit et saepe [scil.* Plato], *quod species sunt in archetypo . . . utpote qui intelligat ideas rerum non inter nubes, ut maledici quidem calumniantur, sed in mundani architecti mente consistere.*

7. Augustine, *Liber octoginta trium quaestionum,* qu. 46 (according to the Basel edn. of 1569, III, col. 548); cf. Cicero, *Topica,* VII: . . . *formae . . . quas Graeci* εἰδαίας *vocant, nostri, si qui haec forte tractant, species appellant . . . nolim, non, ne si latine quidem dici possit, speciem et speciebus dicere. . . . at formis e. formarum velim; cum autem utroque verbo idem significetur, commoditatem in dicendo non arbitror negligendam;* and *Orator,* II.9: *Has rerum formas appellat ideas . . . Plato easque* gigni negat et ait semper esse ac ratione et intelligentia contineri: *cetera nasci, occidere, fluere, labi nec diutius esse in eodem statu.* Thus St. Augustine only needed to add *divina* to Cicero's *intelligentia* in order to achieve a "Christian" definition of "Idea"—an addition which Renaissance thinkers (cf. Melanchthon and Dürer) struck out. That another statement by St. Augustine (*De vera religione,* 3; Basel edn., I, col. 701) is based on the same passage in Cicero's *Orator* has been stressed by Kroll, *M. Tulli Ciceronis Orator* (1913), p. 26 n., and others: . . . *sanandum esse animum ad intuendam incommutabilem rerum formam, et eodem modo semper se habentem, atque undique sui simile pulchritudinem, nec distentam locis nec tempore variatam, sed unum atque idem omni ex parte servantem, quam non crederent*

esse homines, cum ipsa vere summeque sit; cetera nasci, occidere, fluere, labi, *et tamen, in quantum* sunt, *et illo aeterno Deo per eius veritatem fabricate* consistere: *in quibus animae tantum rationali et intellectuali datum est, ut eius aeternitatis contemplatione perfruatur atque affiniatur, orneturque ex ea, aeternamque vitam possit mereri.*

8. Augustine, *Liber octoginta trium quaestionum,* qu. 46: *Quis audeat dicere, Deum irrationabiliter omnia condidisse? Quod si recte dici et credi non potest, restat, ut omnia* ratione *sint condita, nec eadem ratione homo, qua equus; hoc enim absurdum est existimare. Singula igitur* propriis *sunt creata rationibus. Has autem rationes, ubi arbitrandum est esse, nisi* in ipsa mente creatoris? Non enim extra se quicquam positum intuebatur, *ut secundum id constitueret, quod constituebat, nam hoc opinari sacrilegum est. Quod si hae rerum omnium creandarum creatarumve rationes in divina mente continentur, neque in divina mente quicquam nisi aeternum atque incommutabile potest esse, atque has rerum rationes principales appellat ideas Plato: non solum sunt ideae, sed ipsae verae sunt, quia aeternae sunt et eiusmodi atque incommutabiles manent; quarum participatione fit, ut sit, quicquid est, quoquo modo est. Sed anima rationalis inter eas res, quae sunt a Deo conditae, omnia superat et Deo proxima est, quando pura est; eique, in quantum charitate cohaeserit, in tantum ab eo lumini intellegibili perfusa quodammodo et illustrata cernit, non per corporeos oculos, sed per ipsius sui principale, quo excellit, id est per intellegentiam suam, istas rationes, quarum visione fit beatissima. Quas rationes, ut dictum est, sive ideas sive formas sive species sive rationes licet vocare, et multis appellare conceditur nominibus—sed paucissimus videre, quod verum est.*

9. G. von Hertling, "Augustinus-Zitate bei Thomas von Aquin," *Sitzung-Berichte der königlichen Bayrischen Akademie der Wissenschaften, Phil.-Hist. Klasse* (1904), p. 542, justly describes the transformation of the Ideas from "Plato's independent essences" into "God's thoughts" as a "redefinition of the theory of Ideas in the Christian sense." But it must be remembered that this transformation had already been accomplished essentially by Philo and Plotinus.

10. Pseudo-Dionysius, *De divin. nomin.,* VII; cf. also Bonaventure, *Liber Sententiarum,* I.35.1 (*Opera* [Mainz, 1609], IV, 277 ff.).

11. Cf. Thomas Aquinas, *De veritate,* qu. 3 (Fretté-Maré, XIV, 386 ff.).

12. Cf. Thomas Aquinas, *Summa Theologiae,* I.1.15 (Fretté-Maré, I, 122 ff.). Here again Aristotle could be addressed as the

chief witness for the Christian interpretation: *et sic etiam Aristoteles
. . . improbat opinionem Platonis, secundum quod ponebat eas
[scil. ideas] per se existentes, non in intellectu.* One might say that
the medieval interpretation of Ideas was subjectivistic—except that
the "subject" was the intellect of the Godhead.

13. Cf. de Wulf, in *Revue néoscolastique*, II and III. Thomas
Aquinas defined the relationship between the *pulchrum* and the
bonum in the following way: *in subiecto quidem* (we would say
"ontologically considered") *sunt idem, quia super laudem rem fun-
dantur, scilicet super formam, et propter hoc bonum laudatur ut pulchrum. Sed ratione* (we would say "methodologically considered")
*differunt, nam bonum proprie respicit appetitum; est enim bonum,
quod omnia appetunt, et ideo habet rationem finis. . . . Pulchrum
autem respicit vim cognoscitivam, pulchra enim dicuntur, quae visa
placent.* (*Summa Theol.*, I.1.5.4; Fretté-Maré, I, 38.)

14. Cf. the end of the quotation from Augustine on p. 194, n. 8;
somewhat earlier in the same work: *Anima vero negatur eas* [*scil.*
ideas] *intueri posse, nisi rationalis, ea sui parte, qua excellit, id est
ipsa mente atque ratione, quasi quidem facie vel oculo suo interiore
atque intelligibili. Et ea quidem* rationalis anima non omnis et quae-
libet, *sed quae* sancta *et* pura *fuerit, haec asseritur illi visioni esse
idonea.* For the later Middle Ages cf. Franciscan mysticism; on that,
Cl. Baeumker, in *Beiträge zur Geschichte der Renaissance und Re-
formation: Festgabe für J. Schlecht* (1917), p. 9; further, Jos.
Eberle, *Die Ideenlehre Bonaventuras* (diss. Strassburg, 1911), or
Nicholas Cusanus's doctrine of the *contemplatio idearum.* Naturally
all these notions basically hark back to Neoplatonism and ultimately
to Plato himself. — The Ideas are connected with purely rational
cognition (as also later with Marsilio Ficino and Zuccari; see p. 210,
n. 39, and p. 231, n. 42) only by the fact that they, in themselves
exemplaria intelligibilis locked in the mind of God, leave in our own
minds *similitudines intelligibilium impressas ab eisdem intellectui
nostro;* thus for example William of Auvergne, *De univ.*, II.1, in
Guilielmi Parisiensis Opera (1674), I, 821.

15. Cf. Fr. von Bezold, *Das Fortleben der antiken Götter im
mittelalterlichen Humanismus* (1922), p. 53.

16. The ability to "create" in the actual sense of the word is
expressly denied to "art" (which, naturally, must be understood to
include all the *artes*): the form that is built into the material is, after
the actual act of Creation, not a subsistent but only an inherent one,
that is, it perishes with the destruction of the material; therefore the

products of art—and also those of nature, insofar as it is understood as *natura naturata*—are mere alterations rather than creations (thus Thomas Aquinas, *Summa Theol.*, I.1.45.8; Fretté-Maré, I, 306).

17. Thus when he has had to decide whether the soul at the resurrection of the flesh assumes the same or another body (Thomas Aquinas, *Comm. in Sent.*, IV.44.1.2; Fretté-Maré, XI, 299). Here just the differentiation between a human being and a statue helps clarify the matter: the resurrected human being cannot be compared with a statue that is melted down and then recast, for the recast statue is identical with the one melted down only with regard to its material; in its form it is another statue entirely because the original form perished in the process of melting (cf. p. 195, n. 16). The form of a human being, however, is the soul; and as such it cannot perish at all. Another example was given by Anselm of Canterbury (publ. P. Deussen, *Die Philosophie des Mittelalters* [1915], p. 384) which clarifies the difference, so important for judging the ontological proof of God, between the "existence of something in our cognition" and the "cognition of the existence of something."

18. Cf. Bonaventure, *Liber sententiarum*, I.35.1, quoted p. 194, n. 10, or the statement by Meister Eckhart quoted on p. 42. Zuccari also (cf. p. 86 and pp. 229 f., n. 34) refers to Thomas Aquinas's exposition.

19. *De opif. mundi*, 5.

20. *Summa Theol.*, I.15.1 (Fretté-Maré, I, 122 ff.).

21. Thus Thomas Aquinas, *Quodlibeta*, IV.1.1 (Fretté-Maré, XV, 431): *hoc enim significat nomen ideae, ut sit scilicet quaedam forma intellecta ab agente, ad cuius similitudinem exterius opus producere intendit, sicut* aedificator in mente sua praeconcipit formam domus, quae est quasi idea domus in materia fiendae. On the point at hand, cf. also *Summa Theol.*, I.1.45.7 (Fretté-Maré, I, 305): . . . *secundum quod* forma artificiati est ex conceptione artificis . . . ; *Summa Theol.*, II.1.93.1 (Fretté-Maré, II, 570 f.): *Respondeo dicendum, quod, sicut* in quolibet artifice praeexistit ratio eorum, quae constituuntur per artem, *ita etiam in quolibet gubernante oportet, quod praeexistit ratio ordinis eorum, qui gubernationi subduntur.* . . . Deus *autem per suam sapientiam conditor est* universarum rerum, *ad quas comparatur sicut* artifex ad artificiata. — The ambiguous concept *forma* is discussed with exemplary clarity in St. Thomas's *De veritate*, III (Fretté-Maré, XIV, 386 ff.), where the *forma, a qua aliquid formatur*, the *forma, secundum quam aliquid formatur*, and finally the *forma, ad cuius similitudinem aliquid forma-*

tur are differentiated. Only the last corresponds to the concept "Idea."

22. Insofar as comparing works of art with reality was concerned, the comparison necessarily turned out variously, according to whether the author applied the standard of "beauty" or the standard of "truth," which last is in the final analysis Platonic and completely nonartistic. In the first case the work of art had to be favored precisely because art was not considered to be "realistic." Thus in medieval poetry (as in the phrase "pretty as a picture") human beauty is very often characterized with flourishes such as *kein schiltaere entwürfe in baz* (further examples in Borinski, op. cit., p. 92, and von Bezold, pp. 47–54); needless to say, such turns of phrase originate in antique poetry. But in the second case (where painting and sculpture seem to be placed on the same level as the other *artes*) the decision was necessarily in favor of the natural object, because the work of art lacks many characteristics of the corresponding natural object and is an "ungenuine," indeed "false" substitution for it (hence the remarkable derivation of the *artes mechanicae* from *moechus*)—in the same way that today we speak of "artificial" flowers and jewels. For example, in Geiler von Kaisersberg's words (publ. Borinski, op. cit., p. 91; other examples on p. 89): *Wiewol die kunst volgt der natur noch, nüt desterminder übertrift die natur alle kunst. Als Aristoteles spricht. Wann es ward nye kein meister so kostlich vnd kunstrych, dass er möcht der natur glichen in farben oder leblicheit vnd so schoen gryen oder fyol farb oder rot machen, als grass ist oder bluomen als dann ir natur vnd art gibt. . . . Der ist uff ertrich nitt, der das kann.* In a genuinely Renaissance way Dürer recoined this thought of the limitedness of man's artistic skill (on the phrase *ars simia naturae*, cf. pp. 202 ff., n. 2): *Dann Dein Vermügen ist kraftlas gegen Gottes Geschöff* (Lange and Fuhse, *Dürers schriftlicher Nachlass* [1893], p. 227, Nr. 3). In context this no longer means renunciation of the ambition to emulate nature (this possibility is taken for granted), but a renunciation of the ambition to improve on nature in an arbitrary manner. — All of this holds true only for statements about the nature of art in general. Descriptions of particular works, especially those by humanistically educated authors such as the intriguing "magister Gregorius" (cf. von Bezold, pp. 50 ff.), often resort to classical phrases praising the "deceptive aliveness" of the portrayal, the almost blood-suffused lips, etc. It is significant, however, that such complete "aliveness," especially where works of art from pagan antiquity were concerned, tended to be considered something magical and demonic; even the well-educated

Gregorius avers that a classical Venus, which he admired, attracted him again and again not so much by its beauty as by a *nescio quae magica persuasio*.

23. Cf. p. 197, n. 22, as well as pp. 202 ff., n. 2. Where in the late thirteenth century an author thought to see the first evidences of an exact "realism," he even tended to object; cf. Ottokar von Steier's well-known irony (*Österreichische Reimchronik*, V, 35, 125–35, 170, curiously taken seriously by Borinski, op cit., p. 90) concerning the tomb statue of Rudolf von Habsburg. It is also characteristic that a thirteenth-century artist such as Villard de Honnecourt, when he worked not according to an *exemplum* but according to a natural model (although it was not yet rendered in a "realistic" way), felt the need to emphasize this fact by such inscriptions as *et sacies bien, quil fu contrefais al vif*.

24. Cf. Dvořàk, passim. It may perhaps be worthwhile to revert, in another context, to the parallelism between artistic intentions and psychological theories about the relationship of the soul to the body.

25. Cf. A. Dyroff, "Zur allgemeinen Kunstlehre des Heiligen Thomas," in *Beiträge zur Geschichte der Philosophie des Mittelalters* (Festgabe zum 70. Geburtstage Clemens Bäumkers), Suppl.-Bd. II (1923), 200, where the pertinent passages are quoted. On the resumption of this doctrine in the late sixteenth century, cf. pp. 230 f., n. 41. On St. Augustine, cf. Eschweiler, p. 15.

26. Meister Eckhart, *Predigten*, Nr. 101, in *Deutsche Mystiker des XIV. Jahrhunderts*, ed. F. Pfeiffer, II (1857), 324. This is a discussion, closely following "Meister Thomas," of the well-known question concerning the *vorgêndiu bilde* in God, and the quotation here is supposed to clarify the difference between the "speculative" and the "practical" meaning of these *bilde*. The example of the architect is used first to explain the speculative function of the mind, then also to explain the practical: *Ouch ist etwenne ein vorgêndez bilde des werkes in der würkenden kraft* [= ἐνέργεια], *niht in natiurlîcher art, mêr: in vernünftikeit, als daz hûs in dem steine und in dem holze, daz hât sînen vorgênden bildener in des meisters würkender vernunft, der daz ûzer hûs gelîch machet dem bilde, als vil er kann. Sît nu got. . . ."* — The passage quoted by Dvořàk (p. 75) from Thomas Aquinas, *Summa Theol.*, I.1.35.1 (Fretté-Maré, I, 238), which defines the concept *imago* according to St. Augustine, has in my opinion nothing to do with the question of art's relationship to nature. It is meant only to clarify the fact that the concept of

"image" includes, besides the formal "similarity" between the image and the imaged, another relationship between these two, namely, that of the image's "being derived" from that which is imaged; otherwise, for example, one egg would be the "image" of another. *Respondeo dicendum quod de ratione imaginis est* similitudo. *Non tamen quaecumque similitudo sufficit ad rationem imaginis, sed similitudo, quae est in specie rei vel saltem in aliquo signo speciei* [namely, a similarity of "figure" and not just of color, as is shown by the continuation]. *Sed neque ipsa similitudo speciei sufficit vel figurae, sed requiritur ad rationem imaginis* origo, *quia, ut Augustinus dicit in lib. LXXXIII quaestionum, qu. 74: "unum ovum non est imago alterius, quia non est de illo expressum."* Ad hoc ergo quod *vere aliquid sit imago, requiritur, quod ex alio procedat simile ei in specie, vel saltem in signo speciei.* This *ex alio procedere* is therefore to be interpreted, in a purely ontological sense, as "being derived," not, in an art-theoretical sense, as a "being painted according to nature." The latter notion was apparently quite alien to Thomas Aquinas, for as Dvořák himself emphasized elsewhere (p. 43), he determined even the truth value of the work of art not according to its agreement with the natural object but according to its agreement with the notion fixed in the mind: *Et inde est, quod res artificiales dicuntur verae per ordinem ad intellectum nostrum: dicitur enim domus vera, quae assequitur similitudinem formae, quae est in mente artificis (Summa Theol.,* I.1.16.1; Fretté-Maré, I, 127). Theoretically, this "shifting of objectivity from the object to the subject" (perhaps better: from the visible to the knowable) expressed here, was already achieved in Aristotle: τέχνη δὲ γίγνεται, ὅσων τὸ εἶδος ἐν τῇ ψυχῇ. —When the Scholastics at all considered the dependence of art on a visible model, they had in mind, characteristically, less the imitation of a particular object in nature than the imitation of a work of art similar to the one about to be produced (to translate from the language of the Schools into the language of the studio: less the use of a "model" than the use of an *exemplum*): . . . *ut cum aliquis artifex ex artificio aliquo viso concipit formam, secundum quam operari intendit (De veritate,* III.3; Fretté-Maré, XIV, 394).

27. *De monarchia,* II.2; this statement, too, serves only as a comparison within a larger systematic context: *Sciendum est igitur, quod, quemadmodum ars in triplici gradu invenitur, in mente scilicet artificis, in organo et in materia formata per artem, sic et naturam in triplici gradu possumus intueri* [namely, in God as the Creator,

in heaven as in the tool, and in matter]. — It may be remarked that Dante, too, used the term "idea" in an exclusively metaphysical and theological sense. To him the idea was the archetype created by God, and he considered everything mortal and immortal (i.e., the corporeal world as well as human souls and angels) to be the image of this archetype, whose radiance, "as if mirrored," permeates all stages of the cosmos and—according to the greater or lesser "readiness of matter"—more or less "shines through" the material things:

> Ciò che non muore e ciò che può morire
> Non è se non splendor di quella Idea
> Che partorisce amando il nostro Sire;
> Che quella viva luce che si mea
> Dal suo lucente, che non si disuna
> Da lui, nè dall' amor, che in lor s' intrea,
> Per sua bontate il suo raggiare aduna,
> Quasi specchiato, in nuove subsistenze
> Eternamente rimanendosi una.
> Quindi discende all' ultime potenze
> Giù d' atto in atto, tanto divenendo,
> Che più non fa che brevi contingenze;
> E queste contingenze essere intendo
> Le cose generate, che produce
> Con seme e senza seme il ciel movendo.
> La cera di costoro, a chi la duce,
> Non stà d' un modo, e però sotto il segno
> Ideale poi più e men traluce.

Dante has Thomas Aquinas speak these thoroughly Neoplatonic words (*Divina Commedia, Paradiso*, XIII.52–69; see pp. 191 ff., n. 2), and he was justified in that Thomas's system indeed assimilated and preserved so many Neoplatonic elements that on the whole it can be characterized as a grandiose synthesis of Aristotelianism and Neoplatonism (cf. C. Baeumker, "Der Platonismus im Mittelalter," loc. cit., p. 26 ff.; ibid., p. 19, a reference to *Paradiso*, XXX.37 ff., and XXXIII.115 ff., which also belongs in this context). — Insofar as the conception of "idea" as such is concerned, Dante treated it more thoroughly in *Convito*, II.5, where he characterized the Ideas (almost in the sense of the Philonic ἀσώματοι δυνάμεις) as "Intelligences": they are the *movitori del terzo cielo*, that is, *sustanze separate da materia, cioè intelligenze, le quali la volgare gente chiama angeli*. Some philosophers, therefore, say there are only as many Ideas as there are heavenly movements, but others,

like Plato (*uomo eccellentissimo!*), as many *quante sono le spezie delle cose . . . siccome una spezie tutti gli huomini, e un' altra tutto l'oro . . . ; e vollero, che siccome le inteligenze de' cieli sono generatrici di quelli, ciascuna del suo, cosi queste fossero generatrici dell' altre cose ed* esempli ciascuna della sua spezie. *E chiamale Plato "idee," che tanto è a dire quanto* forme e nature universali. *Li gentili le chiamavano* Dei *o* Dee, *avvegnacchè non cosi filosoficamente intendessero quelle come Plato.* Thus here, still in the form of a historical retrospect, began the attempt to connect the word "idea" with *deus* or *dea*—an etymology which was then used ever more eagerly—and playfully; cf. Bellori's *questa Idea ovvero Dea della pittura et scoltura* and *questa Idea e deità della bellezze* (quoted pp. 154 and 168 above), or Landino's commentary on *Paradiso*, XIII, interesting also because of its passionate protest against Aristotle's objections to the theory of Ideas: *Idea è nome prodotto da Platone e impugnato da Aristotele non con uere argomentationi, perche al uero nessun uero contradice, ma con sofistice cauallationi* [!]. *A Platone assentiscono Cicerone, Seneca, Eustratio, Agostino, Boetio, Altiuidio, Calcidio e molti altri. È adunque essempio e forma nella diuina* mente, *alla cui similitudine la diuina sapientia produce tutte le cose uisibili e inuisibili. Scriue Platone e Mercurio trimegisto, che Iddio ab eterno ogni cosa conosce. Adunque nella diuina mente e sapientia pongono le cognitioni di tutte le cose, e queste Platone chiama Idee: ma non mi distenderò in tal materia, perche è molto più difficile, che non si conuiene a questo luogo. . . . Adunque bene disse* [*scil.* Dante] Idea, cioè Iddio, perche cio che è in Dio, è Iddio; e la Idea è in Dio.

CHAPTER 4

1. Cennino Cennini, *Trattato della pittura*, ed. H. Ilg (1871), ch. 88, p. 59: "If you want to sketch mountains well, so that they will look natural, take large stones, rough and unpolished, and lend them light and shadow, according to what your insight allows you"; cf. also ch. 28, where the study of nature is praised as the "most perfect leader" and "rudder and gate of triumph of design." Interestingly, Cennini's method was suggested again in the eighteenth century by, for instance, Pahlmann and Salomon Gessner (cf. the unpubl. work by Ludwig Münz, "Rembrandts Bedeutung für die deutsche Kunst des XVIII. Jahrhunderts"). Gessner's "Letter on landscape painting" (*Schriften*, V [1772], 245 ff.) tells how he, at

first unable to see more than details in nature, acquired the capability of "observing it like a painting" by studying the works of various masters. He then continues: . . . *wenn mein Auge gewöhnt ist, zu finden, so find' ich in einem sonst schlechten Baum eine einzelne Partie, ein paar schön geworfene Äste, eine schöne Masse von Laub, eine einzelne Stelle am Stamm, die, vernünftig angebracht, meinen Werken Wahrheit und Schönheit gibt. Ein Stein kann mir die schönste Masse eines Felsstückes vorstellen; ich hab' es in meiner Gewalt, ihn ins Sonnenlicht zu halten, und kann die schönsten Effekten von Schatten und Licht, und Halblicht und Wiederschein, darbey beobachten.* This announces a completely new interpretation of the old studio prescription—an interpretation that was to emerge in full clarity with Schiller and Goethe. A fieldstone not only becomes a rock, it becomes a "beautiful" rock; and this it becomes not because it is mechanically enlarged by the artist's pencil but because the mental vision of the artist, by virtue of aesthetic empathy and theoretical insight, enables him to realize in that which is small the same laws of nature that also determine the appearance of that which is large (*Müsset im Naturbetrachten/Immer Eins wie Alles achten*). Gessner gained this aesthetic insight, which enabled him not so much to enlarge the single form as to see it large, by studying such artists as Waterloo and Berchem; Schiller did so by studying classical poetry. When Goethe praised the verisimilitude of the whirlpool described in *Der Taucher*, Schiller answered that he had seen such a thing only in a millrace (the eddy of which is indeed as similar to an ocean whirlpool as Gessner's fieldstone is to a rock). "But," Schiller continued, "because I carefully studied Homer's description of Charybdis, this helped me perhaps to remain true to nature" (letter dated 6 Oct. 1797; cf. also H. Tietze, in *Repertorium für Kunstwissenschaft*, XXXIX [1916], 190 ff.).

2. Thus in Filippo Villani's *Chronicle;* cf. esp. J. von Schlosser, *Die Denkwürdigkeiten Lorenzo Ghibertis* (1912), Introduction; idem, in *Kunstgeschichtliches Jahrbuch der Zentralkommission*, IV (1910), 5 ff.; idem, *Materialien zur Quellenkunde der Kunstgeschichte* (1914–), II, 60 ff. In the mouth of a Villani, therefore, the stereotyped locution *ars simia naturae* was metamorphosed into exalting praise. It must be admitted (cf. Borinski, op. cit., pp. 89 and 271) that in the Middle Ages this comparison of art with an ape (for example, by Clemens Alexandrinus and especially clearly by Alanus ab Insulis, who despite his Platonic orientation characterized art as *sophisma*) had nothing to do with the concept of truth

to nature; it meant only that the products of the *artes* are not "genuine" products of nature and in merely "aping" nature fall short of it in many respects (cf. pp. 197 f., n. 22). Thus Dante spoke of Capocchio, an "alchemist," i.e., a counterfeiter of precious metals, as *di natura buona scimmia* (*Inferno*, XXIX.139). Also in Boccaccio's account of the transformation of the "statuary" Epimetheus into an ape there survives, to some extent, this medieval interpretation (on the illustration of the Prometheus legend on a *cassone* panel from the workshop of Piero di Cosimo and now in Munich, cf. G. Habich and K. Borinski, *Sitzung-Berichte der Bayrischen Akademie der Wissenschaften, Phil.-Hist. Kl.* [1920], Nrs. 1 and 12 respectively). But on the other hand Borinski's interpretation of Villani's well-known statement about Giotto's pupil Stephanus as a medieval denial of genuineness is completely mistaken and possible only by means of an artificial, even distorting exegesis of the text. Villani wrote: *Stefanus nature symia tanta eius imitatione valuit, ut etiam a physicis in figuratis per eum corporibus humanis arterie, vene, nervi quoque minutissima liniamenta colligantur et ita, ut ymaginibus suis sola aeris attraccio atque respiratio deficere videatur.* Without doubt he did not mean to emphasize here that the artist despite all his diligence had not achieved actual life (because the breath is lacking!); he rather meant exactly the reverse, and just this reversal is the illuminating thing: he praises the naturalness of a representation which, to use Dürer's words, allows the *allerkleinsten Runtzelein und Ertlein* to show forth in their individuality (*proprie*), so that even physicians could learn something from Stephanus's work. Thus in the Renaissance (on the continued use of *concetto* by Landino, Vasari, and Shakespeare, cf. Schlosser, in *Kunstgeschichtliches Jahrburch der Zentralkommission*, IV [1910], 132) the comparison of the artist with an ape was transformed from a reproachful reference to the (factual!) unreality of the work of art into an encomium on its (artistic!) truth. Classicistic writers also understood it to mean imitation completely true to nature; but in classicistic thought, which had come to reject this kind of truth in favor of an idealizing "selection" that broadmindedly passes over minor details, the ape analogy was used again as the harshest opprobrium. In Bellori's *Vite de' Pittori* there is a copper engraving (see p. 101 above) in which *Imitatio sapiens* tramples on an ape (symbolizing a foolish, mindless imitation that only "copies" the model); and Winckelmann's idealistic sensibility was insulted by nothing so much as the "apes of common nature" (K. Justi, *Winckelmann und seine Zeit-*

genossen, 2d edn. [1898], I, 357). This, then, is the history of the phrase *ars simia naturae*, which contains in a nutshell the history of artistic attitudes, and which in a sense shows a return to its starting point. For it seems obvious to me that originally (i.e., in classical antiquity) the ape simile was aimed at the mimetic art κατ᾽ ἐξοχήν, the art of the actor; and in this its original use it characterized exaggerated, aesthetically objectionable naturalism like that of the actor Kallipides who was mocked as ὁ πίθηκος (cf. Aristotle, *Poetics*, XXVI, and other writers). In the Middle Ages the phrase was transferred from the realm of theatrical art to the other arts and redefined to mean a representation that does not fully satisfy because it falls short of the "real thing" (thus, in an even more metaphorical sense, the devil was characterized as *simia Dei.*). In the Renaissance the ape simile was used to characterize a representation that fully satisfies because it is absolutely true to nature. In the Middle Ages, then, the aesthetic category of "naturalism" was thoroughly suppressed by the theoretical category of "aping, i.e. lack of genuineness, unreality"; in the modern era the aesthetic as opposed to the theoretical way of looking at art came again to the fore, but with this difference: in the Renaissance, especially the Early Renaissance, absolute naturalism seemed to be an aesthetic plus, but in the classicistic period it became an aesthetic minus that could not be compensated.

3. Cf. Vasari, *Lives of the Painters*, ed. Milanesi, I, 250: *La qual maniera scabrosa, goffa ed ordinaria avevano, non mediante lo studio, ma per una cotal usanza, insegnata l'uno a l'altro per' molti e molti anni i pittori di quei tempi.*

4. Leonardo, *Trattato della pittura*, ed. Ludwig (1881), Nr. 411.

5. Cf. E. Panofsky, *Dürers Kunsttheorie, vornehmlich in ihrem Verhältnis zur Kunsttheorie der Italiener* (1915), pp. 6 ff.

6. Alberti, *Della pittura*, in *L. B. Albertis kleinere kunsttheoretische Schriften*, ed. Janitschek (1877), p. 151; quoted by Panofsky, pp. 157–158, where the parallel passages from Dolce, Biondo, and Armenini are also given.

7. Leonardo, *Trattato*, Nr. 270 (quoted by Panofsky, p. 143) and Nr. 137.

8. Alberti, p. 151.

9. Thus Scheurl, for example (*Libellus de laudib. Germaniae*, in Schlosser, *Materialien zur Quellenkunde der Kunstgeschichte*, III, 71) maintained that Dürer's pet dog touched his master's self-

portrait with his muzzle *putatus hero applaudere*—a "first-hand" story whose credibility is not increased by the fact that exactly the same story, only with different names, appears in Leonardo's *Trattato*, Nr. 14, from which Scheurl probably took it. Other examples of this sort are in Federico Zuccari, *L'Idea de' Pittori, Scultori e Architetti* (1608; here quoted from the reprint in Bottari, *Raccolta di lettere sulla Pittura, Scultura ed Architettura*, VI [1768]), p. 131.

10. Ariosto, *Orlando furioso*, XI.71.

11. As early as *ca.* 1375 Giovanni Dondi told in a letter (Schlosser, in *Jahrbuch der Kunstsammlungen des Allerhöchsten Kaiserhauses*, XXIV [1903], 157) of a sculptor infatuated with antique statues, who said "that if those works did not lack life, they would be better than living beings, as though he wished to say that nature is not only imitated by the genius of the great artists, but has been surpassed." Conversely Boccaccio told (*Decamerone*, VI.5) how Giotto had so deceived men's eyes by his works that that which was merely painted was considered to be real.

12. In the Middle Ages the concept of "originality" played no great part even in the realm of philosophy; rather the authors strove to demonstrate the opposite—agreement of their own views with those of older authorities. See the interesting study by J. Hessen, *Thomistische und Augustinische Erkenntnistheorie* (1920).

13. Bellori, for instance, championing an idealizing naturalness, reproached copyists by saying that their works were "not daughters, but bastards" of nature, and, on the other hand, that they "borrowed genius in copying the ideas of others" (see Appendix II, p. 168).

14. Leonardo, *Trattato*, Nr. 81 (one is reminded of the well-known statement by Lysippus, who, when asked which artist he emulated, is supposed to have answered: "I imitate no artist, only nature"); see also Alberti, p. 155, who characteristically added that if a young painter really wants to copy the works of others, he should choose a mediocre piece of sculpture rather than a good picture, for then he would at least learn to discover and reproduce correct lighting (since the work of sculpture, being a three-dimensional figure, *is*, in a sense, a natural object!). Leonardo's warning referred naturally only to an *imittare la maniera dell' altro*, that is, to a fundamental lack of independence on the part of the artist. As a mere method of study, copying he not only allowed but recommended (*Trattato*, Nrs. 63, 82). — The derogatory judgment of imitation

can be based, therefore, on a naturalistic as well as on a conceptualistic interpretation of art (with Bellori, as we saw in n. 13 above, both ways of thinking coincide). But at first imitation did not at all disgrace the artist; it proved his poverty but it did not make him a "thief." For that which he took from others was not as yet considered their personal property: nature belonged to everyone, and the idea was looked upon as a notion that, despite its origin in the subject, was endowed with a suprasubjective, indeed a normative value. It was in the nineteenth century, when the work of art was considered to be the revelation of a thoroughly personal experience of nature or emotion, that the modern concept of "plagiarism" emerged.

15. Cf. Vasari, I, 250.

16. The Renaissance interpretation of art was marked, in contrast to that of the Middle Ages, by a novel externalization of the artistic "object" and concomitantly by a novel personalization of the artist as a "subject." This is true, *mutatis mutandis*, of the entire cultural awareness of the epoch, especially its relationship to "classical antiquity." Classical literature and art were known in the Middle Ages too, yet they were not so much "object" as nourishment and tools for mental activity; it was in the Renaissance that philology and archaeology were born, that classical poetics and rhetoric were rediscovered—with the same necessity that classical art theory was resurrected.

17.. It is characteristic that even this "beautiful invention" (namely, an interesting and charming fable) was credited less to the talent than to the erudition of a painter (Alberti, p. 145). This unequivocal statement simply emphasizes the aesthetic importance— probably never contested before Caravaggio—of content ("the beautiful invention is so effective that it already excites delight by itself, even without being painted"). It does not mean that the basically quite unphilosophic Alberti champions a "consciously held critical and idealistic point of view"—that he was an anticipative Neo-Kantian, if one may say so—who, as an aesthetician of "pure feeling," would have advised borrowing the *invenzione* from rhetoricians and poets only because to him it would have been "mere subject matter." Thus in W. Flemming, *Die Begründung der modernen Ästhetik und Kunstwissenschaft durch L. B. Alberti* (1916), pp. 52 f.

18. Cf. Alberti, p. 139, for example.

19. On this and the following, cf. Panofsky, *Dürers Kunst-*

theorie, pp. 78 ff., and idem, in *Monatshefte für Kunstwissenschaft*, XV (1921), 188 ff.

20. On the exceptional position of Dürer, cf. Panofsky, *Dürers Kunsttheorie*, passim.

21. Leonardo, *Trattato*, Nr. 137.

22. Alberti, pp. 199–201 (*"De statua"*).

23. See pp. 42 f. and ch. II, nn. 27 and 34, ch. III, nn. 20, 21, and 25, and p. 216, n. 53.

24. One cannot more completely misunderstand the essence of Renaissance Platonism than by maintaining that in the Renaissance Plato "was reborn as a critical philosopher" and accordingly demanding a "sharp distinction between mystical Neoplatonism and Plato" in the historical treatment of this epoch in philosophical history (as does Flemming, p. 91). M. Meier, "Gott und Geist bei Marsilio Ficino," in *Beiträge zur Geschichte der Renaissance und Reformation: Festgabe für J. Schlecht* (1917), pp. 236 ff., has rightly said: "For him [Ficino] Plato is indeed the theologian who, in contrast to the natural scientist Aristotle, knows how to lead us to God, the true home of our souls."

25. Ficino, *Opera*, II, 1576 (quoted p. 210, n. 40).

26. Alberti, p. 125: *Qualunque cosa si muove da luogo, può fare sette vie: in su, uno; in giu, l'altro; in destra, il terzo; in sinistra, il quarto; colà lunge movendosi di qui o di là movendo in quà; et il settimo andando atorno.* This division of motion is also found in the *Timaeus* as well as in Quintilian (cf. K. Borinski, *Die Rätsel Michelangelos* [1908], p. 179); but it is characteristic of Alberti that he refrained from a symbolic interpretation of or even an aesthetic comment on the various possibilities; he confined himself to the division, pure and simple. The threefold division of "motion in general" into quantitative, qualitative, and local, which overlaps the sevenfold division of "local" motion, is, as Janitschek has shown, Aristotelian (cf. *Metaphysics*, XI.12.1068a).

27. Thus Ficino, *Opera*, II, 1115, and in greater detail 1063; but cf. Borinski, pp. 177 ff.

28. Ficino, *Opera*, II, 1576: *Pulchritudo in corporibus est expressior ideae similitudo;* ibid., p. 1575 (quoted p. 210, n. 40).

29. Ficino, II, 1336 ff. (Symposium Commentary); quoted extensively in Appendix I (pp. 129 ff.) according to the Italian translation published in 1544. On older parallels to this Christian-Neoplatonic theory of beauty, cf. ch. III, nn. 2 and 27; on its

resurrection in Mannerist art theory, see pp. 93 ff. Significantly, Ficino completely accepts the etymology "κάλλος from καλέω" explained and advocated by Pseudo-Dionysius: *Proprium vero pulchritudinis est, allicere simul et rapere. Unde graece Calon quasi provocans appellatur* (*Opera*, II, 1574).

30. Alberti, *De re aedif.*, IX.5. See also the more famous definition in VI.2: *nos tamen brevitatis gratia sic diffiniemus: ut sit pulchritudo quidem certa cum ratione concinnitas universarum partium in eo, cuius sint, ita ut addi aut diminui aut immutari possit nihil, quin improbabilius reddatur.* This latter definition was already recognized as Aristotelian by Irene Behn, *L. B. Alberti als Kunstphilosoph* (1911), p. 25.

31. Alberti, *Della pittura*, p. 111; quoted *inter alios* by Panofsky, *Dürers Kunsttheorie*, p. 143.

32. Usually cited as Platonisms and Plotinisms in Alberti's thought are the following: (a) *De re aedif.*, IX.5: *ex his patere arbitror pulchritudinem quasi suum atque innatum toto esse perfusum corpore quod pulchrum sit.* As Behn translates it (p. 24): "what is in the entire body, and yet is not localized, but is in itself, that we call ideal with Plotinus and later Idealists." The continuation of the sentence, however (*ornamentum autem afficti et compacti naturam sapere magis, quam innati*), shows that Alberti intended only to clarify the difference between "beauty" as an inherent value and "decoration" as an accessory one, since he then (similar to Cicero, *De natura deorum*, I.79) recommends to youths who are in themselves not handsome the use of "ornaments" for hiding their defects and accentuating their strong points. (b) The alleged claim that in art "form" and "matter" must be in union (Behn, p. 22; Flemming, p. 21). Here there is a gross confusion. Alberti wrote (*De re aedif.*, Prooemium): *nam aedificium, quod corpus quoddam esse animadvertimus, quod lineamentis, veluti alia corpora, constaret et materia, quorum alterum istic ab ingenio produceretur, alterum a natura susciperetur. Huic mentem cogitationemque, huic alteri parationem selectionemque adhibendam, sed utrorumque per se neutrum ad rem valere intelleximus, ni et periti artificis manus, quae lineamentis materiam conformaret, accesserit.* These sentences are by no means an aesthetic demand according to the thesis (neither Platonic nor Plotinian) that there be union of form and matter; rather they are an ontological definition of existence according to the (Aristotelian!) view that every corporeal structure, whether work of art or product of nature, cannot come into being except by a certain material being

shaped into a certain form. Therefore Alberti says expressly that this definition holds true for the work of art not insofar as it is a "work of art" but as it is a "body." He does not *demand* a union of form and matter (the contrary—discrepancy between form and matter— would have been inconceivable to him) but *demonstrates* this union by pointing out that the work of art comes into being only by the *conformatio* of matter by means of *lineamenta* (= form). If Alberti, which Irene Behn actually deplores, failed to define beauty as a "perfect union of form and matter," this omission is not surprising, but absolutely necessary: the step from a statement about the conditions of existence for a work of art as a corporeal object to a definition of beauty as an aesthetic value would not have been "tiny" but impossible. (c) The reference to the myth of Narcissus, which Flemming (pp. 103 ff.) calls a "direct quotation" from Plotinus. In truth the two passages, when juxtaposed, read as follows:

Alberti (p. 91 f.): *Però usai di dire tra i miei amici secondo la sentenzia de' poeti quel Narcisso convertito in fiore essere della pictura stato inventore. Che gia ove sia la pictura fiore d' ogni arte ivi tutta la storia di Narcisso viene a proposito. Che dirai tu essere dipigniere altra cosa che simile abracciare con arte quella ivi superficie del fonte?*

Plotinus (*Ennead*, I.6.8): Εἰ γάρ τις ἐπιδράμοι, λαβεῖν βουλόμενος ὡς ἀληθινόν, οἷα εἰδώλου καλοῦ ἐφ' ὕδατος ὀχουμένου, οὐ λαβεῖν βουληθείς, ὥς που τὶς μῦθος δοκῶ μοι αἰνίττεται, δὺς εἰ ϛὸ κάτω τοῦ ῥεύματος ἀφανὴς ἐγένετο· τὸν αὐτὸν δὴ τρόπον ὁ ἐχόμενος τῶν καλῶν σωμάτων καὶ μὴ ἀφιείς, οὐ τῷ σώματι, τῇ δὲ ψυχῇ καταδύσεται εἰς σκοτεινὰ καὶ ἀτερπῆ τῷ νῷ βάθη, ἔνθα τυφλὸς ἐν ᾅδου μένων καὶ ἐνταῦθα κἀκεῖ σκιαῖς συνέσται.

Plotinus, then, referred to the myth to warn against "losing oneself" in mere visible beauty; Alberti (basing himself on Ovid; cf. Janitschek, p. 233) used it to show that painting originated from love of the beautiful, and he compared painting with embracing an image (not just a phantom!). Thus one can hardly maintain that Plotinus and Alberti understood the parable "quite in the same sense."

33. Alberti, *Della pittura*, p. 95; cf. Overbeck, *Die antiken Schriftquellen zur Geschichte der bildenden Künste bei den Griechen* (1868), Nrs. 1951, 1952. We should not have too high an opinion of Alberti's knowledge of Greek: R. Förster, in *Jahrbuch der Königlichen Preussischen Kunstsammlungen*, VIII (1887), 34,

has shown that he used Lucian, for example, only in a Latin translation.

34. On the passage by Leonardo, *Trattato*, Nr. 108.2 (similarly Nrs. 109, 499), which is based on Platonic premises but completely un-Platonic in its conclusions, see Panofsky, *Dürers Kunsttheorie*, pp. 192 ff.

35. Ficino, *In Parmenidem* (*Opera*, II, 1142): *Et Plato in Timaeo septimoque de Republica manifeste declarat substantias quidem veras existere, res vero nostras rerum verarum, id est idearum, imagines esse.* This and all the passages quoted in the following notes represent countless others that sound more or less alike.

36. Ficino, *Argum. in VII. Epistul.* (*Opera*, II, 1535): *Docetque interea ideam a reliquis longe differre quatuor praecipue modis: quia scilicet idea substantia est, simplex, immobilis, contrario non permixta.*

37. See Federico Zuccari as cited pp. 86 f.

38. Ficino, *Comm. in Phaedrum*, esp. *Opera.* II, 1177 ff.

39. Ficino, *Comm. in Phaedrum;* a series of further examples in Meier, "Gott und Geist bei Marsilio Ficino"; especially characteristic is *Theologia Platonica*, XI.3 (*Opera*, I, 241): *Quemadmodum pars vivifica per* insita semina *alterat, generat, nutrit et augit, ita* interior sensus et mens *per formulas innatas* quidem et ab extrinsecis excitata omnia iudicant. Thus sense impressions serve only as "motivation" in the act of perception.

40. Ficino, *Comm. in Plotin. Ennead, I.6* (*Opera*, II, 1574): *Pulchritudo vero, ubicumque nobis occurrat . . . placet atque probatur, quoniam ideae pulchritudinis nobis ingenitae respondet et undique convenit;* cf. the quotation on p. 207, n. 28, and its continuation: *Praeterea rationalis anima proxime pendet ex mente divina et pulchritudinis ideam sibi illinc impressam servat intus;* or p. 1576: *Quisnam pulcher homo? aut leo pulcher? aut pulcher equus? Certe praecipue ita formatus, ita natus est, ut et* divina mens *instituit per ipsius* ideam, *et* natura *inde* universalis *seminaria virtute* concepit. *Iam vero illius ideae formulam* anima nostra in mente habet *ingenitam, habet et in natura propria seminalem similiter rationem, igitur naturali quodam iudicio de homine vel leone vel equo ceterisque iudicare solet hunc quidem pulchrum non esse, illum vero pulchrum, quia videlicet hic prorsus* a formula et ratione dissentit, *ille vero* consentit; *atque inter pulchros hunc illo pulchriorem esse, quia hic cum formula rationeque magis consentit. . . . Dum vero de pulchritudine iudicamus, id prae ceteris pulcherrimum approbamus, quod*

animatum est atque rationale atque ita formatum, ut et per animum *satisfaciat formulae pulchritudinis, quam habemus in* mente, *et per* corpus *rationi pulchritudinis seminali respondeat, quam in* natura *secundaque anima possidemus.* Forma *vero in corpore formoso ita* suae similis est ideae, *sicut et figura aedificii in materia similis exemplari in architecti mente . . . itaque si homini materiam quidem detraxeris, formam vero reliqueris, haec ipsa quae tibi reliqua est forma, illa ipsa est idea, ad quam est homo formatus. . . .* Naturally corporeal beauty falls far short of intellectual beauty (Ficino would not have been the *pater Platonicae familiae* had he not indefatigably emphasized this with all his might, esp. well in *Comm. in Plotin. Ennead, I.6.4: Memento si delectaris . . . (Opera,* II, 1576), and in closing, *Librum denique totum sic conclude . . .* (p. 1578). But corporeal beauty is nevertheless the *imperium formae super subjectum (Comm. in Ennead, I.6.3 [Opera,* II, 1576]) and remains *divinum et imperiosum aliquid, quia et imperium regnantis formae significat et artis rationisque divinae victoriam refert super materiam, et ipsam perspicue repraesentat ideam (Comm. in Ennead, I.6.2 [Opera,* II, 1575]).

41. Alberti, *Della pittura,* p. 151.

42. Petrarch, Sonnet LVII:

> Ma certo il mio Simon fù in paradiso,
> Onde questa gentil Donna si parte;
> Ivi la vide e la ridusse in carte
> Per far fede quaggiù del suo bel viso.

43. Cennini, *Trattato della pittura,* ch. I; repr. by J. von Schlosser, in *Kunstgeschichtliches Jahrbuch der Zentral-Kommission,* IV (1910), p. 131.

44. Leonardo, *Trattato,* Nr. 28: *Et in questo supera [l'occhio] la natura, che li semplici naturali sono finiti, e le opere che' l'occhio comanda alle mani, sono infinite, come dimostra il pittore nelle finitioni d'infinite forme di animali et erbe, pianti e siti.*

45. Baldassare Castiglione, *Il Cortigiano,* IV, 50 ff. Here there is an especially noteworthy reconciliation of the Neoplatonic metaphysical interpretation of beauty with the classic-phenomenal interpretation: the essential origin of beauty is an *influsso della bontà divina* (so that external beauty is necessarily an expression of internal goodness); but external beauty can become visible only if this divine influx (poured out *sopra* tutte *le cose create*) becomes

active in a body which is (in good Ciceronian and Albertian terms) *ben misurato e composto con una certa gioconda concordia di colori distinti* [συμμετρία . . . τό τε τῆς εὐχροίας προστεθέν!], *siutati dai lumi e dall' ombre e da una ordinata distanza e termini di linee.* Castiglione gives a purely imitative definition of representational art in I, 50 (one of the usual *paragoni* between painting and sculpture).

46. Repr., e.g., in Passavant, *Raphael von Urbino* (1839), I, 533. Mario Equicola's interpretation is entirely superficial; misleadingly referring to Cicero, he understands "idea" to be only the "form" whose agreement in several individuals we call "similarity": *I Platonici dicono esser necessario la cognitione e conuenientia dell' Idea, del Genio e della stella al principio d'amore. Per l'Idea intendiamo la forma, secondo Tullio: questa* [*scil,* conuenientia *dell' Idea*] *non è altro che similitudine. Non uoglio dire delle Idee di Platone disputare, da lui in più luoghi scritte, massimamente nel Parmenide, da Aristotele nella Ethica e Metafisica riprouate, e da Agostino dette ragioni eterne e cosi laudate: basti in questo luogo, che la similitudine delle forme, dell' aspetto, de' membri e de' lineamenti può causare beniuolentia . . .* (*Di natura d'amore*, ch. IV; in the Venice edition of 1583, pp. 180 f.).

47. Lange and Fuhse, p. 227.4.

48. On this see pp. 107 ff.

49. "The design" (*il disegno*) is masculine in Italian. The "mother" of the arts is (*la*) *invenzione* (Vasari, II, 11), occasionally also *la natura* (Vasari, VII, 183). On this cf. W. von. Obernitz, *Vasaris allgemeine Kunstanschauung auf dem Gebiet der Malerei* (1897), p. 9.

50. Vasari, I, 168. The whole passage first appeared in the 2d edition in 1568. The draft for it (repr. in Karl Frey's annotated edition of Vasari [1911], p. 104) enables us to correct *singolarissima* into *regolarissima*, which also agrees far better with the following interpretation of the phrase *ex ungue leonem* (the absolute validity of the laws of nature permits us to draw conclusions about the whole from the tiniest part).

51. Apparently the only art theorist who tried to come to terms with the original Platonic doctrine of ideas was Gregorio Comanini, an author not lacking acumen and originality but standing quite outside the general development. He was not a practicing artist but a highly educated churchman, and in his dialogue *Il Figino* (Mantua, 1591) the most manifold problems (some of them not taken up again until very much later, e.g., the relationships of play

and art, pictorial and poetic phantasy, etc.) are treated in a very interesting way. First the arts are divided into the well-known Platonic categories (pp. 14 ff.): the *arti usanti*, such as warfare, navigation, lute playing, which merely use implements; the *arti operanti*, such as architecture, smithing, etc., which produce the implements employed by the *arti usanti* and other useful objects; and finally the *arti imitanti*, which only imitate the products of the producing arts. These *arti imitanti* are then treated, in thorough Platonic fashion, in accordance with the viewpoints set forth in *Republic*, X, as follows:

Guazzo: . . . L' arte imitante è poi quella, che imita le cose fabbricate dall' arte operante, ouero dalla soggetta: quale apunto è la pittura, la quale va co' suoi colori imitando l' arme fabbricate dal fabbro, e la naue formata dal legnaiuolo, e le viuole lavorate dal maestro de musicali istromenti. Ouero quale ancora è l' arte poetica, la quale imita e esprime con le parole quel medesimo, che dall' arte operante vien fabbricato: e perciò Platone ha detto di quest' arte imitante. che ella forma vna cosa terza dal vero, e che ciascuno imitatore è 'l terzo dalla verità.

Figino: Io non intendo questo passo compiutamente. Vorrei, che voi lo mi dichiaraste con più limpidezza di sentimento.

Guazzo: Volontieri. Consideriamo tre freni. Il primo secondo l' arte vsante *nella mente del caualiere:* il secondo fabbricato dall' arte operante, che sarà la frenaria: e'l terzo finto dall' arte imitante, che sara quella della pittura. Il freno nella mente del caualiere, secondo Platone, terrà il primo grado di verità, perchè il caualiere saprà meglio render conto del freno e della sua forma, che non saprà fare il fabbro, che l' ha formato: essendo, che all' arte vsante conuien comandare, e all' operante vbidire. Il freno fatto dalla frenaria, la quale è l' arte operante e soggetta all' architettonica, occuperà il secondo grado, come quello che segue immediatamente il freno, ch' è nella mente dell' artefice comandante. Il freno poi lineato dalla pittura, la quale è l' arte imitante, per conseguente ritrouerassi nel terzo grado della verità, come terzo dal freno imaginario dell' arte vsante. *Non ho voluto darui l' essempio di Platone nel decimo della Republica* de tre letti, vno nella mente di Dio, vno formato dall' arte soggetta, e vno figurato dall' imitatrice; accioche voi Martinengo non vi pensaste, che io forse mi credessi darsi secondo' i Platonici l' idea delle cose artificiate. Perche io sò molto bene, che tutto quello è detto dal gran

maestro dell' academia solamente per *vna cotal maniera d'*
essempio e non altrimenti. Conchiude adunque questo Filosofo
per le ragioni da lui allegate, che l' imitatore è terzo della verità,
e perciò vie più d' ogn' altro artefice lontano dal vero. Ma non mi
tirate più oltre in questo ragionamento, o Figino, perciochè non
poco vi spiacerebbe.

It is significant that all the participants do not admit the under-
valuation of the imitative arts that results from this; but the rebuttal
is put off until another day:

Martinengo: Vuol dire in somma, che Platone con questo suo
fondamento, che l' imitatore faccia vna cosa terza dalla verità, la
pittura e la poesia auuilisce, come due arti, le cui opere sono imi-
tationi non di verità, ma d'apparenti imagini: e passa à pungere
Homero infin sù l' ossa, e lo rimprouera vi sò dire di mala maniera: e che per questo voi Figino, che siete cosi dotto in questa, e
tanto suiscerato amatore di quella, non potreste sofferire con
patienza cotali maledicenze. Vedete modestia di forastiero, che
non ardisce d' offenderui in casa vostra. Non sò poi come se la
facesse di fuori.

Guazzo: Arme e caualli metterò per la difesa d'ambedue
queste nobilissime arti, e per ogni luogo campion singolare ne sarò
sempre.

Martinengo: Buone parole in casa d' altrui.

Guazzo: Migliori fatti, quando io ne sarò partito.

Figino: Così mi gioua di credere, che esser debba: se non per
altro, almeno per difesa di voi medesimo, il quale pur poetate
alcuna volta, e con tanta dolcezza e purità, che io hò sentito dire
da valent' huomini, che chi vi chiamasse il Toscano Flacco, non
errerebbe.

Summarizing, again in a genuinely Platonic manner, the *freno
intelligibile* (i.e., the idea of the bridle) is contrasted with the *freno
fattibile* (the real bridle) and with the *freno imitabile* (the imitated
bridle). Cf. also p. 192:

Due parole ancora voglio soggiungere, o Guazzo, per sigillo
del mio discorso. Quante cose noi vediamo tutto di dentro quest'
ampio teatro del Mondo, tutte secondo la dottrina di Socrate nel
Fedone sono imagini e ombre. Il cielo è simolacro della sua
idea. Le cose suttolunari sono ombre, come non permanenti nell'
esser loro e come fugaci. Oltra che se noi andiamo considerando

214

l'huomo secondo le parti sue, che sono innumerabili, possiamo innumerabilmente dire, questa parte non è huomo, nè quella altresì: ma vna volta sola diciamo del tutto, questo è huomo. Così del cauallo, così de gli altri animali, e di tutti i composti auiene. Et de gli elementi dice il Timeo, che le loro parti son due, la materia e la forma, e che 'l fuoco non è detto fuoco, e l' acqua acqua, e i' aria aria, e la terra terra per la materia, ma per la forma: e che perciò questo è detto fuoco, e quello acqua, e quello aria, e quell' altro terra, non secondo il tutto, ma secondo vna sola parte: onde il tutto non è ueramente fuoco, ma igneo, nè acqua, ma acqueo, nè aria ma aereo, nè terra, ma terreo. Pero conclude il Timeo, che sopra queste imbrattate e mancanti forme della materia, altre ve n' hà pure, e separate, e intiere: che *sono l' idee;* e di queste dice Socrate nel Fedone, che le *naturali sono imagini e simolacri.*

Perhaps the most interesting thing is the discussion of the difference proposed in the *Sophist* between "eikastic" and "phantastic" imitation. This contrast was not understood by Comanini according to the proper Platonic interpretation (cf. pp. 5 f. above), viz., as the contrast between objectively correct and *trompe l'œil* imitation (as in the example of the statues placed high above eye level), but, corresponding to the more modern significance of φαντασία (already current in late antiquity; cf. the remark of Philostratus quoted on p. 185, n. 21), as the contrast between the representation of actually existing objects and the representation of actually nonexisting objects (i.e., those created by phantasy; pp. 25 ff.): *Una chiamata da lui nel Sofista rassomigliatrice overo icastica: e l'altra pur dal medesimo, e nel istesso Dialogo detta Fantastica. La prima è quella che imita le cose, le quali sono: la seconda è quella, che finge cose* non essistenti. The principal example of "eikastic" imitation, then, is portraiture: the principal example of "phantastic" imitation are the works of Arcimboldo (see p. 237, n. 69), who constructed human figures out of fruits, plants, and beasts. From this some difficult problems result (e.g., whether the representation of angels or God is "eikastic" or "phantastic," pp. 60 ff.); and with great perceptivity the principal difference between painter and poet is seen in the painter's greater success with "eikastic" representation: *più diletta l'imitatione fantastica del Poeta, che non fa l'icastica pur dell' istesso. Ma del Pittore accade tutto il contrario, perciò che più diletteuole è la sua imitatione icastica di quello, che la fantastica sia* (p. 81).

    52. *In ipsius mente* insidebat species (quoted p. 11 above).

53. *Sicut domus* praeexistit *in mente aedificatoris*, or *in quolibet artifice* praeexistit *ratio eorum, quae constituuntur per artem* (quoted on p. 40 and p. 196, n. 21). As far as the *praeconcipit* in the quotation from Thomas Aquinas's *Quodlibeta* (p. 196, n. 21) is concerned, the complete parallelism of that sentence to the others shows that the verb *praeconcipere* must be interpreted not in a psychological and functional but in a purely epistemological and theoretical sense: *praeconcipit aedificator* is completely synonymous with *praeexistit in mente aedificatoris*. To a mind trained in Aristotelianism this was obvious; for according to Aristotle the artist no more produces the form than he does the matter; but his achievement is limited to bringing the one into the other (cf. *Metaphysics*, VII.8).

54. Ficino (quoted pp. 210 f., n. 40): *innata, ingenita*.

55. Raphael (quoted p. 60 above): *mi viene nella mente*.

56. G. B. Armenini, *De' veri Precetti della Pittura* (Ravenna, 1587; quoted extensively on pp. 228 f., n. 31): *gli vien nascendo*.

57. Vasari (quoted p. 61 above): *si cava*.

58. Fil. Baldinucci, *Vocabolario Toscano dell arte del disegno* (1681), p. 72: Idea *f. Perfetta cognizione dell' obietto intelligibile, acquistata e confermata per dottrina e per uso. Usano questa parola i nostri Artefici, quando vogliono esprimere opera di bel capriccio e d'invenzione.* Cf. also Fr. Pacheco, *Arte de la pintura* (1648), p. 164: *Las hermosas ideas, que tiene acqueridas el valente artefice.*

59. Armenini (quoted on pp. 228 f., n. 31): *si forma e scolpisce.*

60. In Karel van Mander's didactic poem (ed. R. Hoecker [1915], pp. 252–53), the verse *Ons Ide' hier toonen most haer ghewelden* (X.30; by the way, the verse is not to be translated "Here Idea must show us its power" but "Our Idea must here show its power") defines Idea—in the margin—as follows: *imaginacy oft ghedact;* thus "Idea" equals "imagination or thought." Cf. also XII.4 (pp. 266–67): van Mander does not reprove good masters who without further preparation paint from their minds that which *in hun Ide' is gheschildert te vooren* (cf. the quotation from Vasari on p. 217, n. 64).

61. Vasari (quoted p. 61 above); in this place the meanings "imaginative content" and "imaginative ability" appear side by side in the same sentence. Closely related to Vasari's definition is that of Raff. Borghini, *Il Riposo* (Florence, 1594), pp. 136–37.

62. See for example G. P. Lomazzo, *Trattato dell' arte della pittura* (Milan, 1584), II.14, 158: . . . *le cose immaginate* . . . *nell' Idea.*

63. Guido Reni (quoted p. 160 above).

64. Vasari, I, 148: *La scoltura è un arte, che levando il super-fluo della materia suggetta la riduce a quella forma, che nell' idea dello artefice è disegnata.*

65. See pp. 107 ff.

66. Quoted p. 160 above.

67. Pacheco, pp. 164 f.: *Porque este exemplar no se à de perder de vista jamas. I este es el lugar donde prometimos hablar deste punto. I toda la fuerça de estudios no echa fuere este original* . . . *porque con los precetos i la buena i hermosa manera viene bien el juizio i elecion de las bellissimas obras de Dios i de la Naturaleza. I aqui se an de ajustar i corregir los buenos pensamientos del Pintor.* I cuando esto faltare, o no se hallare con la belleza que conviene, o por incomodad de lugar o de tiempo, bien admirablemente el valerse de las hermosas ideas, que tiene aquiridas el valiente artefice. *Como lo diò a entender Rafael de Urbino* . . . [here the letter to Castiglione follows]. *De manera que la perfecion consiste en* passar de las Ideas a lo natural, i de lo natural a las Ideas. *buscando siempre lo mejor i mas seguro i perfeto. Asi lo hazia tambien su maestro del mismo Rafael, Leonardo de Uinci, varon de sutilissimo ingenio atendiendo a seguir los antiguos, el cual primero que se pusiesse a inventar cualquier istoria, investigava todos los efetos proprios i naturales de cualquier figura, conforme a su Idea.* There follows the story of Zeuxis and the five maidens told in a beautiful poem.

68. In fact Pacheco (cf. preceding note) as well as Bellori (see p. 156) illustrates the theory of Ideas by the story of the Crotonian maidens. It is especially interesting that Franciscus Junius (*De pictura veterum*, s.v. "Zeuxis") translated τέλειον καλόν, the expression used by Dionysius of Halicarnassus in this context, directly with "idea": κἀκ πολλῶν μερῶν συλλογίσαντι συνέθηκεν ἡ τέχνη τέλειον καλόν is rendered as *ars construxit opus perfectae pulchritudinis ideam repraesentans.* Cf. also Fil. Baldinucci's Academy speech of 5 January 1691 (1692), repr. in the 1724 edition of his *Notizie de' professori del disegno*, XXI, 124 ff.: *io leggo . . . che Zeusi volendo dipignere per gli Crotoniati la figura d'Elena in modo, che rappresentar potesse la* più perfetta idea della beltà femminile . . . *scelse dai Corpi delle cinque Vergini quanto elle aveano di perfetto e di vago. . . . Ma queste* [scil. *parole*] *debbono intendersi non come sentesi talvolta dire anche in pubblico da qualche semplice . . . cioè che Zeusi vedendo una perfetta parte in alcuna delle fanciulle, quella copiasse nel suo Quadro, come vedevala nell' originale, ed appresso a*

questa un' altra di altre fanciulle, e vadasi così discorrendo; sapendosi molto bene, *che un bell' occhio intanto fa mostra di sua bellezza, in quanto egli è* adattato al proprio viso, *e che una bella bocca, accomodata sopra volto non suo, perde il pregio della sua bellezza, la quale in sustanza da null' altro ridonda, che da un complesso di parti proporzionati al loro tutto.* . . . *Onde convien dire, che Zeusi, dopo aver presa dai corpi* . . . *la più bella proporzione universale, scorgendo l'inclinazione, che avea alcuna parte a quel bello, che egli andava immaginando col pensiero, col caricarla e scaricarla riducessela con somma proporzione a quel* tutto di bellezza, *che gli andavasi col pensiero immaginando.* Here Baldinucci meets the objections of Bernini, who felt strongly that the natural unity of a living organism is indivisible and therefore had declared the whole Zeuxis anecdote to be a "fable" (thus, agreeing almost verbatim with the quotation just given, in Fil. Baldinucci, *Vita del Cav. Gio. Lor Bernini*, ed. Burda and Pollak [1912], p. 237). Baldinucci rescues the election theory by replacing the mechanical joining together with an intellectual thinking together; but just this makes the *idea della beltà femminile* obtained in this way an eclectic notion that is derived *a posteriori.* — In addition, for reasons similar to Bernini's, Baco of Verulam opposed the election theory (which was also extremely repugnant to Wilhelm Heinse's conception of genius): if an ancient artist had actually proceeded as Zeuxis is said to have done, the result would hardly have satisfied anyone except himself; cf. S. van Hoogstraaten's polemic against this interpretation, *Inleyding tot de Hooge Schoole der Schilderkonst* (1678), VIII.1, 279 f.

69. See pp. 107 ff.

70. Cf. Guido Reni's letter quoted on p. 160 above.

71. Cf. Petrarch, Sonnet LVIII:

> Quanto giunse a Simon l' alto Concetto,
> Ch' a mio nome gli pose in man lo stile. . . .

72. Thus, for instance, in an architectural project in Cesariano's edn. of Vitruvius (Como, 1520): idea *octogonae hecubae phalae et pyramidatae.* Cf. also the book titles favored in Romance countries since the middle of the sixteenth century, such as Giulio Camillo's *Idea del Teatro* (1550), G. P. Lomazzo's *Idea del Tempio della pittura* (1590), and Roger de Piles's *L'Idée du peintre parfait* (1699).

73. Cf. p. 186, n. 27 above. From this it is understandable that the Scholastically oriented Mannerist theory of art, which on the one

hand considered "subject" equivalent to "idea," on the other hand "idea" equivalent to "form" (or "species"), could in many cases come to use the expression *forma* precisely where today the expression "content" would be used. On this cf. also F. Saxl, *Antike Götter in der Spätrenaissance: Ein Freskenzyklus und ein Discorso des Jacopo Zucchi*, Studien der Bibliothek Warburg, Nr. 8 (Leipzig and Berlin, 1927).

74. Pacheco (quoted p. 217, n. 67). Pacheco shows the double meaning of the term "idea" most clearly: in the passage quoted in n. 67 it appears as a specific notion of beauty, and it is illustrated by the story of Zeuxis and the Crotonian maidens; in the discussion of *invención* quoted on pp. 225 f., n. 28, it appears as *conceto o imagen de lo, que se hà de obrar*. Following the new speculative direction of art theory, mainly as he found it in Zuccari, Pacheco here discusses "idea" according to the Scholastic-Peripatetic theory of knowledge and, as Zuccari himself did, treats it as a "theological" concept.

75. Baldinucci, *Vocabolario* (quoted p. 216, n. 58).

76. Giordano Bruno, *Eroici Furori*, I.1 (*Opere*, ed. A. Wagner [1830], II, 315; mentioned in Schlosser, *Materialien zur Quellenkunde*, VI, 110, and O. Walzel, *Vom Geistesleben alter und neuer Zeit* [1922], pp. 75 ff.): *Conchiudi bene, che la poesia non nasce da le regole se non per leggerissimo accidente; ma le regole derivano da le poesie: e però tanti son geni e specie di vere regole, quanti son geni e specie di veri poeti.*

CHAPTER 5

1. For this tripartite division we are indebted to Walter Friedlaender, *Mannerism and Anti-Mannerism in Italian Painting* (New York, 1957).

2. But purely inductive "naturalism" found at least one noteworthy champion: Bernard Palissy, the French artisan, natural scientist, and theoretician, who in many respects followed Leonardo, indeed occasionally plagiarized him; E. Kris is preparing a more detailed account of Palissy.

3. Cf. E. Panofsky, in *Zeitschrift für Aesthetik und allgemeine Kunstwissenschaft*, XIV (1920), 321 ff.

4. Lomazzo, *Trattato dell' arte della pittura*, VI.34, p. 363, in a representation of the Crucifixion one figure is supposed to be shown *in atto che ti guardi piangente, come che ti voglia dire la causa del*

suo dolore et moverti a participar della doglia sua. Alberti, *Della pittura*, p. 123: *Et piacemi sia nella storia, chie admonisca et insegni ad noi quello che ivi si facci; o chiami con la mano a vedere; o con viso cruccioso et con li occhi turbati minacci, che niuno verso loro vada . . . o te inviti ad piagnere con loro insieme o a ridere. . . .* Countless parallels of this kind—also in other art theorists from the sixteenth to the eighteenth centuries—show that art theory is and must be one of the most conservative disciplines in many respects.

5. Cf. Schlosser, *Materialien zur Quellenkunde der Kunstgeschichte*, IV, 17 ff.; VI, 45 ff.; VI, 57 ff.

6. It is significant that this epoch had such an enthusiasm for a *vollgepfropftes* (overcrowded) painting like Dürer's *Martyrdom of the Ten Thousand: con si bell' ordine, che lo sguardo nulla patisce della multitudine delle figure, ma gusta ogni cosa* (Comanini, *Il Figino*, p. 250).

7. Ascanio Condivi, *Vita di Michelangelo Buonarroti* (1553), ch. 52; new edn. in Karl Frey, *Sammlung ausgewählter Biographien Vasaris*, II (1887), 192.

8. Leonardo, *Trattato della pittura*, Nrs. 267 ff.

9. Lomazzo, I.1, p. 23; cf. also VI.4, p. 296.

10. Borghini, *Il Riposo* (1594), p. 150.

11. Zuccari, *Idea*, II.6, pp. 133 ff.; for the expression *Disegno interno e pratico artificiale* see below, pp. 226 ff. Zuccari's polemic is of course very unjust in so far as Dürer himself emphatically rejected any attempt to "dream up" (*erdichten*) a system of proportions (Lange-Fuhse, p. 351, Nrs. 4 ff.) and expressly stated that it is "not always necessary to measure every single thing in every way." Rather he wished exact measurement to be considered only a means toward achieving an "intuitive sense of proportion" (*Angenmass*; Lange-Fuhse, p. 230, Nrs. 16 ff.). But at any rate this vehement protest is a characteristic symptom of a specifically Mannerist attitude toward art; it also appears—even if usually in a more moderate form—in many other writers of the same period. For example, to the passage by Borghini quoted on p. 74 above and the passages by Vincenzo Danti quoted on p. 221, n. 13, may be added the remarks by Comanini, who appends to the discussion of Vitruvius's proportions the following restrictions: *Vero è, che bene spesso è necessario al Pittore operante, hauere (come diceua Michel Angelo) il compasso dentro gli occhi: non potendosi così di leggier osseruare la misura col compasso nel far gli scorti; quantunque Alberto Durero habbia insegnato la maniera di scortar con linee. Ma oltre, che questa sua regola è poco*

vsata, io stimo, che sia ancora di poco e forse di niun giouamento à chi opera (op. cit., p. 231). In Dutch art theory Willem Goeree, *Naturlijk en schilderkonstig ontwerp der Menschkunde* (1682), p. 45, may be mentioned as a critic of Dürer. It should be noted, however, that Zuccari was apparently the only author who tried to base this protest against the mathematical method not only on the "object" (namely, the mobility of the bodies to be represented) but also on the "subject" (namely, the need for freedom of the artistic spirit).

12. Cf. B. Schweitzer, in *Mitteilungen des deutschen archaeologischen Instituts, römische Abteilung*, XXXIII (1918), 45 ff.

13. Vincenzo Danti, *Il primo libro del Trattato delle perfette proporzioni* (1567; excerpt in Schlosser, *Jahrbuch der Kunstsammlungen des Allerhöchsten Kaiserhauses*, XXXI [1913], 14 ff., ch. XI; in the new printing [Florence, 1830] available to me, pp. 47 ff.): *Che il modo d'operare nell' arti del disegno non vale sotto alcuna misura di quantità perfettamente, come vogliono alcuni.* For architecture he admits the possibility of certain norms of measurement, but for painting and sculpture he does not consider them to be suitable: *È ben vero, che alcuni antichi et moderni hanno con molta diligenza scritto sopra il ritrarre il corpo humano; ma questo si è veduto manifestamente non poter servire; perchè hanno voluto con il mezzo della misura determinata circa la quantità comporre la sua regola, la qual misura nel corpo humano non ha luogo perfetto, per ciò che egli è dal suo principio al suo fine mobile.*

14. Danti, preface and ch. XVI (in new printing, pp. 12 ff. and 95).

15. Zuccari, *Idea*, II.2, p. 110, where an even more extensive discussion of the *regola e simmetria del corpo umano* is promised: *Onde vediamo, che i corpi umani sono vari di forme e di proporzioni; altri magni, altri grassi, altri asciutti, altri pastosi, e teneri, altri di proporzione di sette teste, altri di otto, altri di nove e mezza, altri di dieci, come è l'Apollo nel Belvedere di Roma: cosi le Ninfe, e le Vergini Vestali. D'otto e mezza, e nove teste dagli antichi furono figurati Giove, Giunone, Plutone, Nettuno, ed altri simili: di nove, e nove e mezza, come Marte, Ercole, Saturno e Mercurio. Di sette, e sette e mezza Bacco, Sileno, Pan, Fauni e Silvani. Ma la più commune e bella proporzione del corpo umano e di nove teste in dieci, come più a pieno di queste regole e simmetria del corpo umano ne tratteremo a parte nella scuola del Disegno, che appresso questo secondo libro disegniamo porre.*

16. Lomazzo, *Trattato*, I, ch. 5–8. Cf. also Panofsky, "Die

Entwicklung der Proportionslehre als Abbild der Stilentwicklung,"
Monatshefte für Kunstwissenschaft, XIV (1921), pp. 188–219. In
ch. 20 and 21 the proportions of a horse are given, in ch. 22 to 28
those of architecture. In II, 7 ff., the theory of expressive movements
is treated, and in ch. 22–23 even the possible movements of plants
and garments are described.

17. Danti, ch. XVI (in new printing, pp. 90 ff.), and more often,
e.g., p. 73: . . . *si harebbe à osservare in tutte le cose, che il disegno
mette in opera, cioè cercar sempre di fare le cose, come* dovrebbono
essere, e non in quello modo che sono.

18. Danti, ch. XVI (pp. 93 ff.): *E così quell' artefice, che col
mezzo di queste due strade* [scil. *ritrarre* and *imitare*] *camminerà
nell' arte nostra, cioè nelle cose, che hanno in se imperfezione e che
harebbono à essere perfette, col imitare, e nelle perfette col ritrarre,
sarà nella vera e buona via del disegno.* That, as Schlosser says, Danti
believes *ritrarre* to be sufficient for the representation of *corpi inani-
mati* (plants and dumb animals) is not quite correct. Actually Danti
admitted that representation is the easier the lower the object stands
in the hierarchy of things, and that therefore an artist who only
knows how to reproduce inanimate objects is not to be counted among
"true" artists (p. 92). He maintained, however—for plants, even
with special emphasis (ch. XIII, esp. pp. 72 f.)—that in case of
necessity (i.e., if the natural object to be represented is actually imperfect), the "imitating" (i.e., in his terminology: the idealizing)
procedure should be applied everywhere.

19. *De' veri Precetti della Pittura* (1587), II.3, p. 88; quoted in
K. Birch-Hirschfeld, *Die Lehre von der Malerei im Cinquecento*
(1912), p. 107. On this cf. the remark by Jul. Caes. Scaliger,
Esotericae Exercitationes . . . ad Cardanum, CCCVII.11 (p. 937
in the Frankfurt edn. of 1576), which was already used by Junius:
Mavultque [*sapiens*] *pulchram imaginem, quam naturali similem
designatam. Naturam enim in eo superat ars, quia multis eventis a
primo homine symmetria illa depravata fuit. At nihil impedit plasten,
quominus attollat, deprimat, addat, demat, torqueat, dirigat. Equi-
dem ita censeo: nullum umquam corpus tam affabre fuisse a Natura
factum (duo scilicet excipio: unum primi hominis, alterum veri hominis, veri Dei) quam perfecte finguntur hodie doctis artificum mani-
bus.*

20. *Trattato*, VI.50, p. 434 (quoted in Birch-Hirschfeld, p. 92),
on feminine portraits: *Nelle femine maggiormente và osseruato con
esquisita diligenza la bellezza, leuando quanto si può con l'arte gli*

errori della natura. In relation to masculine portraits it is also demanded that disproportion and discoloration be softened, but with the limitation *ma di tal modo e con tal temperamento, che'l ritratto non perda la similitudine* (I.2; Birch-Hirschfeld, p. 90). Vasari still vacillated between demanding absolute truth to nature (IV, 464 f.) and recognizing the principle of idealization (VIII, 24), but he ultimately considered the most worthwhile goal to be a reconciliation of these two (IV, 463). — It is interesting to compare such prescriptions with related remarks by Alberti (pp. 119 f.) which became standard in later writing (Lomazzo still refers to the same ancient examples, the pictures of Antigonus and Pericles, p. 434): *Le parti brutte a vedere del corpo et l'altre simili quali porgono poca gratia, si cuoprano col panno, con qualche fronde et con la mano. Dipignievano li antiqui l'immagine d'Antigono solo da quella parte del viso, ove non era manchamento dell' occhio; et dicono, che a Pericle era suo capo lungho et brutto, et per questo dai pictori et dalli sculptori non come li altri era col capo armato ritratto. Et dice Plutarco, li antiqui pictori dipigniendo i Rè, se in loro era qualche vitio non volerlo però essere notato, ma quanto potevano, servando la similitudine, emendavano. Cosi adunque desidero in ogni storia servarsi, quanto dissi, modestia et verecundia.* . . . Alberti places the emphasis not so much on *correcting* "mistakes" as on *concealing* them, which does not at all hurt truth to nature; and closely connected with this, he treats the whole matter not from the point of view of "beauty" but of "propriety" (which is also shown by the placement of the passage concerned in the second rather than in the third book of his treatise). The demand to remove bodily defects from view was as important for him as the demand to cover the "indecent" parts of the body and fell under the general categories of *decorum, modestia,* and *verecundia;* he understood by "defects" not so much "lack of beauty" as outright deficiency or deformity such as the lack of an eye.

21. L. Dolce, *L'Aretino: Dialogo della pittura* (1557), new edn. ed. Ciampoli (Lanciano, 1913), p. 43. There is a German translation by C. Cerri (Vienna, 1871), p. 51.

22. *Disegno* was defined by Borghini (II, 106) and also by Baldinucci (*Vocabolario,* p. 51) in almost literal agreement with Vasari (quoted p. 61 above). The conceptualistic interpretation of *disegno* was intensified (namely, by completely ignoring the impression from nature which Vasari always referred to) by Armenini (I.4, p. 37), who pretended to repeat the opinion of others when he designated *disegno* as *artificiosa industria dell' intelletto col mettere in*

223

atto le sue forze secondo la bella Idea. He summarized his view of it thus: *che il dissegno sia come vn viuo lume di bello ingegno, e che egli sia di tanta forza e cosi necessario all vniuersale, che colui, che n' è intieramente priuo, sia quasi che vn cieco, io dico, per quanto alla mente nostra ne apporta l'occhio visiuo al conoscere quello, ch' è di garbato nel mondo e di decente.* This view was shared, above all, by Zuccari (quoted pp. 226–229, nn. 30–31) and by Francesco Bisagno (*Trattato della pittura* [Venice, 1642], p. 14), who identifies himself with Zuccari after having quoted the opinions of others. — At the same time Mannerism knew yet another definition, which refers more to the visual than to the conceptual meaning of the act of "designing" but also stresses the spontaneity rather than the receptivity of the practitioner. It was quoted by both Armenini and Bisagno: *Altri poi dicono più tosto dover essere* [scil. *il Disegno*] *una scienza di bella e regolata proporzione di tutto quello che si vede, con ordinato componimento, del quale si discerne il garbo per le sue debite misure;* both of these authors quote it, however, only *referendo,* not *asserendo.* Lomazzo (*Trattato,* I.1, p. 24; presumably Armenini's source) however, advocated a similar view as his own, but found it necessary to support it by profound metaphysical and cosmological reasons: *il medesimo vuol dire quantità proportionata, quanto disegno.*

23. It is characteristic of this conceptualistic attitude to art, which became prevalent about the middle of the century, that A. Francesco Doni (*Il desegno* [1549], pp. 8 f.) described the personification of "sculpture" in the image of Dürer's *Melencolia* (cf. Schlosser, *Materialien zur Quellenkunde,* II, 26).

24. Armenini; quoted pp. 223 f., n. 22.

25. Cf. Schlosser, *Materialien zur Quellenkunde,* VI, 118. The relation between *disegno,* spontaneously arising in the mind, and *pittura,* which merely executes this *disegno,* found vivid expression in a painting by Guercino (Dresden Gallery, Nr. 369), already mentioned by Birch-Hirschfeld (p. 31): *Pittura* is a beautiful young woman who paints a Cupid according to a drawing held before her by *Disegno,* a wise old thinker. A relation analogous to that between *disegno* and *pittura* exists of course between *disegno* and the two other "arts of design," sculpture and architecture; Vasari had already designated *disegno* as the *padre delle tre arti nostri.* An aftereffect of this interpretation can be seen in the view that reaches into the most recent aesthetics, according to which "drawing" claims primacy over "coloring," in contrast to which it, as Lomazzo once expressed it

(*Trattato*, I.1, p. 24), must be considered the "substantive" part of painting.

26. Lomazzo, *Trattato*, Proemio, p. 8: *Perciochè poniąmo ch' un Rè commetta ad un pittore e ad un scultore, che tutti due facciano di lui un ritratto, non è dubbio che l'uno e l'altro hauerà nel suo intelletto la medesima idea e forma di quel Rè.* If here the "idea" of that which is to be portrayed is, according to the Scholastic theory of knowledge championed by Zuccari as well as by Lomazzo, not only a suprareal but also a suprasubjective notion (and therefore theoretically the same for all artists), it takes on a thoroughly personal character with Bernini: *Bernini a dit, que jusqu'ici il avait presque toujours travaillé d'imagination . . . qu'il ne regardait principalement que là-dedans, montrant son front, où il a dit qu'était* l'idée *de sa* Majesté [*scil.* Louis XIV]; *que autrement il n'aurait fait qu'une copie au lieu d'un original . . .* (Chantelou, "Journal du voyage du Cav. Bernin en France," *Gazette des Beaux-Arts* [1885], p. 73).

27. Cf. von Obernitz, *Vasaris allgemeine Kunstanschauung auf dem Gebiet der Malerei* (1897), p. 9.

28. In many respects related to Zuccari—without even considering Lomazzo's *Trattato!*—is the Spaniard Fr. Pacheco, who was mentioned in this connection on p. 219, n. 74. His thoroughly Scholastic theory of the idea set forth in his discussion of invention (pp. 170 ff.) follows: *Que no es la pintura cosa hecha a caso, sino por elecion i arte del Maestro. Que para mover la mano a la execucion, se necessita de exemplar o idea interior: la cual reside en su imaginacion i entendimiento del exemplar exterior i objetivo, que se ofrece a los ojos. . . . . I esplicando esto, mas por menor lo que los filosofos llaman exemplar, llaman los* Teologos *Idea.* (*Autor deste nombre fue Platon, si creemos a* Tulio *i a* Seneca.) *Este exemplar o Idea, o es exterior o interior, i—por otros nombres—objetivo o formal. El exterior es la imagen, señal o escrito, que se pone a la vista. Deste hablò Dios, cuando dixo a Moisen: mira: „obra segun el exemplar, que es visto en el monte."* El interior es la imagen que haze la imaginativa, i el conceto que forma el entendimiento. Ambas cosas incaminan al artifice, a que con el lapiz o pinzel imite lo, que està en la imaginacion, o la figura exterior. En este sentido dizen los Teologos, que es la Idea de Dios su entendimiento: viva representacion de las cosas posibles. Tel que, a nostro modo de entender, dirigiò la mano deste Señor, para que las sacasse a luz: pasandolas del ser possible al actual, labor maravillosa, que cantò Boecio (lib. de consol.):*

„*Tu cuncta superno* | *ducis ab exemplo pulchrum pulcherrimus ipse* | *mundum mente gerens*"

> *Tu, que al modelo de tu sacra Idea*
> *Sacas a luz cuanto los ojos miran,*
> *I al orbe bello en tu concepto vivo*
> *Tu mas hermoso retretado tienes.*

En consequencia desto difine la idea Santo Tomas, o [forma] interior o exemplar, diziendo: „*Idea es la forma interior, que forma el entendimiento. I a quien imitas el efecto por voluntad del artifice*" (*qu. 2 de veritate*). *De donde se infiere, que no tienen ideas sino los agentes intelectuales, Angeles i ombres; i estos no* [in the text: *ne*] *se approvechon dallas sino cuando libremente obran.*

Es pues, segun lo dicho, la idea un conceto o imagen de lo que se à de obrar, i a cuya imitacion el artifice haze otra cosa semejante, mirando como a dechado la imagen, que tiene en el entendimiento. De suerte que cuando el artifice mira un Templo segun su Arquitectura o materialidad, entiende el Templo, mas cuando entiende la imagen, que à formado su juizio del Templo, entonces entiende la idea de l'arte, sino del Soberano Artifice o de su sostituto.

Sacò Dios a luz, cuanto vemos, imitando su idea; en tanto pintor, en cuanto dirigido de su viva imagen dava ser a lo exterior a semejança de su interior modelo, favoreciendo tanto las imagines, objeto i fin de la Pintura. . . .

29. Cf. W. Fränger, *Die Bildanalysen des Roland Fréart de Chambray* (diss. Heidelberg, 1917), p. 23; Birch-Hirschfeld, pp. 19, 27; H. Voss, *Die Spätrenaissance in Florenz und Rom* (1920), pp. 464 f.

30. Zuccari, *Idea*, I.3, pp. 38 ff.: *Ma prima che si tratti di qualsivoglia cosa, è necessario dichiarare il nome suo, come insegna il principe de' filosofi Aristotele nella sua Logica, altrimenti sarebbe un camminare per una strada incognita senza guida, o entrare nel laberinto di Dedalo senza filo. Però cominciando da questo capo, dichiarerò, che cosa io intenda per questo nome* Disegno interno, *e seguendo la comune intelligenza così appresso de' dotti come del volgo, dirò, che per Disegno interno intendo il concetto formato nella mente nostra per poter conoscere qualsivoglia cosa, ed operar di fuori conforme alla cosa intesa; in quella maniera, che noi altri pittori volendo disegnare o dipingere qualche degna istoria, com per esempio quella della Salutazione Angelica fatta a Maria Vergine, quando il Messaggier celeste le annunziò, che sarebbe madre di Dio, formiamo*

prima nella mente nostra un concetto di quanto allora potiamo pensare, che occorresse così in Cielo, come in Terra, sì dal canto dell' Angelo Legato, come da quello di Maria Vergine, a cui si faceva la Legazione, e da quello di Dio, che fu il Legante. Poi conforme a questo concetto interno andiamo con lo stile formando e disegnando in carta, e poi co' pennelli, e colori in tela, o in muro colorando. Ben è vero, che per questo nome di Disegno interno *io non intendo solamente il concetto interno formato nella mente del pittore, ma anco quel concetto, che forma qualsivoglia intelletto; sebbene per maggior chiarezza, e capacità de' miei conprofessori ho così nel principio dichiarato questo nome del Disegno interno in noi soli; ma se vogliamo più compitamente e comunemente dichiarare il nome di questo Disegno interno, diremo, che è il concetto e l' idea, che per conoscere e operare forma chissisia. Ed io in questo Trattato ragiono di questo concetto interno formato da chissisia sotto nome particolare di Disegno, e non uso il nome d'*intenzione, *come adoprano i logici e filosofi, o di esemplare o* idea, *com' usano i teologi, questo è perchè io tratto di ciò come pittore e ragiono principalmente a' pittori, scultori ed architetti, a' quali è necessaria la cognizione e scorta di questo Disegno per potere bene operare. E sanno tutti gl' intendenti, che si devono usare i nomi conforme alle professioni, di cui si ragiona. Niuno dunque si maravigli, se lasciando gli altri nomi a logici, filosofi e teologi, adopro questo di* Disegno *ragionando con miei conprofessori.* Cf. also II.15, p. 192: *Dieci attribuzioni del Disegno interno ed esterno: 1. Oggetto commune interno di tutte le intelligenze umane. 2. Ultimo termine d'ogni compita cognizione umana. 3. Forma espressiva di tutte le forme intellettive e sensitive. 4. Esemplare interno di tutti i concetti artificiali prodottivi. 5. Quasi un altro Nume, un altra Natura produttiva, in cui vivono le cose artificiali. 6. Una scintilla ardente della divinità in noi. 7. Luce interna ed esterna dell' intelletto. 8. Primo motore interno e principio e fine delle nostre operazioni. 9. Alimento e vita d'ogni scienza e pratica. 10. Augumento d'ogni virtù e sprone di gloria, dal quale finalmente vengono apportati tutti gli comodi dell' uomo dal proprio artificio ed industria umana.* — On Zuccari's terminology it should be remarked that, although on p. 96 he heavily reproached Vasari for using the term "idea" in the sense of "imaginative ability" instead of in the sense of "imaginative content," he himself used the term *disegno* (= idea) in exactly the same double significance: he designated the process as well as the object of the act of "designing" as *disegno*. [In order to use a similarly equivocal expression *disegno* is translated in the orig. Ger. of this book mostly with *Vorstellung*. In the present Eng. tr. the Ital. *disegno* is rendered as "design" (both nominally and verbally), the Ger. *Vorstellung* almost always as "notion" throughout the book.—Tr.]

31. Zuccari, *Idea*, I.3, p. 40: *E principalmente dico, che Disegno non è materia, non è corpo, non è accidente di sostanza alcuna, ma è forma, idea, ordine, regola, o oggetto dell' intelletto, in cui sono espresse le cose intese; e questo si trova in tutte le cose esterne, tanto divine, quanto umane, come appresso dichiareremo. Ora seguendo la dottrina de' filosofi, dico, che il Disegno interno in generale è un' idea e forma nell' intelletto rappresentante espressamente e distintamente la cosa intesa da quello, che pure è termine ed oggetto di esso. E per meglio anco capire questa definizione si dee osservare, che essendovi due sorte d'operazioni, cioè altre esterne, come il disegnare, il lineare, il formare, il dipingere, lo scolpire, il fabbricare, ed altre interne, come l' intendere, e il volere, siccome e necessario, che tutte le operazioni esterne abbiano un termine . . . così anco è necessario, che l' operazioni interne abbiano un termine, acciocchè sieno anch' esse compite e perfete; il qual termine altro non è, che la cosa intesa; come per esempio, s' io voglio intendere, che cosa sia il leone, e necessario, che il leone da me conosciuto sia termine di questa mia intellezione; non dico il leone, che corre per la selva, e dà la caccia agli altri animali per sostentarsi, che questo è fuora di me; ma dico una forma spirituale formata nell' intelletto mio, che rappresenta la natura e forma del leone espressamente, e distintamente ad esso intelletto, nella qual forma o idolo della mente vede e conosce chiaramente l' intelletto non pure il leone semplice nella forma e natura sua, ma anco tutti i leoni. E di quì si vede non pur la convenienza fra le operazioni esterne ed interne, cioè che ambedue hanno un termine appartato, acciocchè sieno compite e perfette, ma anche in particolare (più a proposito nostro) la differenza loro; e ove il termine dell' operazione esterna è cosa materiale, come la figura disegnata o dipinta, la statua, il tempio o il teatro, il termine dell' operazione interna dell' intelletto è una forma spirituale rappresentante la cosa intesa.* Cf. Armenini, p. 137: *Deue prima il Pittore hauer nella mente vna bellissima Idea per le cose, ch' egli oprar vuole, accioch' egli non faccia cosa, che sia senza consideratione e pensamento; ma che cosa sia Idea, diremo breuemente, fra i Pittori non douer esser altro, che la* forma apparente delle cose create, concette nell' animo *del Pittore, onde l' idea dell' huomo è esso* huomo vniuersale, *al cui sembiante sono fatti poi gli huomini. Altri dissero poi l'Idee essere le similitudini delle cose fatte da Dio, percioche prima ch' egli creasse, scolpì nella mente le cose,*

ch' egli crear voleua, e le dipinse. Così l' Idea del Pittore si può dire essere quella imagine, *che prima egli si forma e scolpisce nella mente di quella cosa, che o dissegnare o dipingere voglia, la qual subito dato il soggetto gli vien nascendo.*

32. Zuccari, *Idea*, II.1, p. 101: *Dico dunque, che il Disegno esterno altro non è, che quello, che appare circonscritto di forma senza sostanza di corpo: semplice lineamento, circonscrizione, misurazione e figura di qualsivoglia cosa immaginata e reale; il qual Disegno così formato e circonscritto con linea è esempio e forma dell' immagine ideale. La linea dunque è proprio corpo e sostanza visiva del Disegno esterno, in qualsivoglia maniera formato; nè qui mi occorre a dichiarare, che cosa sia linea, e come nasca dal punto, retta o curva, come vogliono i mattematici. Ma dico bene, mentre essi vogliono sottoporre ad essa linea o lineamenti il Disegno o la pittura, fanno un grandissimo errore; essendochè la linea è semplice operazione a formare qualsivoglia cosa sottoposta al concetto e al Disegno universale, come appunto, diremo, i colori alla pittura, e la materia solida alla scultura, e simili. Però essa linea, come cosa morta, non è la scienza del Disegno, nè della pittura; ma operazione di esso. Ma tornando al nostro proposito, questa immagine ideale formata nella mente e poi espressa e dichiarata per linea, o in altra maniera visiva, è detta volgarmente Disegno, perchè segna e mostra al senso e all' intelletto la forma di quella cosa formata nella mente e impressa nell' idea.*

33. Zuccari, *Idea*, I.7, p. 51 (*Scintilla della Divinità*), or II.14, p. 183 (*Scintilla divina nell' anima nostra impressa*). Cf. also II.1, p. 102: *È l' anima e virtù interna e scintilla divina; e per maggior intelligenza diremo quello spiraculo di luce infuso nell' anima nostra, come immagine del Creatore, è quella virtù formativa, che noi chiamiamo anima del Disegno, concetto, idea. Questo concetto e quest' idea uniti all' anima, come specie ed immagine divina, immortale, che è quella, che avviva i sensi e tutti i concetti nell' intelligenza dell' intelletto.*

34. Zuccari, *Idea*, I.5, pp. 44 f.: *Platone dunque pose l'idee in Dio, nella mente e nell' intelletto suo divino* [Neoplatonic-Patristic reinterpretation of Plato!]; *onde egli solo intende tutte le forme rappresentanti qualsivoglia cosa del Mondo. Ma è da avvertirsi intorno a questo, acciocchè talora anco noi non cadessimo in errore, o peggior di quello; che Platone non pose l' idee, o forme rappresentanti tutte le cose di Dio, come in lui distinte a guisa di quelle, che sono nell' intelletto creato, angelico, o umano, ma per queste idee*

intese l' istessa natura divina, la quale a guisa di specchio da se stessa
come atto purissimo rappresenta tutte le cose più chiaramente e per-
fettamente che non sono rappresentate le nostre al senso; e questa
interpretazione è la più dotta e la più vera. Sicchè trovandosi in Dio
l' idee, anche in sua divina Maestà si trova il disegno interno. Ed
oltre le autorità filosofiche, addurrò quello che da' teologi mi fu
mostrato essere stato scritto dall' angelico Dottore s. Tommaso nella
prima parte, alla questione 15. all' articolo primo, cioè che è neces-
sario poner l' idee, che se queste non s' intendono, niuno può esser
sapiente; posciachè l' idea nella lingua Greca suona l' istesso che
forma nella Latina, onde per l'idee s' intendono le forme realmente
distinte da quelle cose, che sono esistenti in se stesse. E queste forme
sono necessarie, sendo che in tutte le cose, che non sono generate a
caso, è necessario la forma esser fine della generazione; perchè l'
agente non opera per la forma, se non in quanto la similitudine della
forma è in esso. Il che avviene in due modi. . . .

35. Zuccari, *Idea*, I.6, pp. 46 ff.

36. Ibid., I.7, p. 50.

37. Ibid., II.16, p. 196.

38. Ibid., II.15, p. 185.

39. On earlier attempts at the absurdly vast expansion of the term *disegno*, which became almost sacrosanct by joining it with the Idea concept, see pp. 223 f., n. 22.

40. Ibid., I.8–9, pp. 52 ff.

41. Ibid., I.10, pp. 59 ff. Cf. Thomas Aquinas, *Physica*, II.4 (Fretté-Maré, XXII, p. 348): *ars imitatur naturam. . . . Eius autem, quod ars imitatur naturam, ratio est, quia principium opera-tionis artificialis cognitio est. . . . Idea autem res naturales imita-biles sunt per artem, quia ab aliquo principio intellectivo tota natura ordinatur ad finem suum, ut sic opus naturae videatur esse opus in-telligentiae, dum per determinata media ad certos fines procedit: quod etiam in operando ars imitatur.* Understood in this sense, *imitazione* can naturally include the "idealizing" representation also, since the expression cannot be interpreted everywhere—least of all in Aristotle and Thomas Aquinas—in the sense of so-called "real-ism." Danti (cf. p. 81 and p. 222, n. 18) even used *imitare* (in contrast to mere *ritrarre*) to mean the "idealizing" way of reproduc-ing nature. To Zuccari's (Aristotelian-Scholastic) solution of the problem of imitation, cf. Lomazzo, *Trattato*, I.1, p. 22: *Oltre di ciò ha anco d'usar il pittore queste linee proportionate con certo modo e regola, la quale non è altro che quella, che vsa e con che procede*

l'istessa Natura in fare vn suo composito; doue prima presuppone la materia, *che è vna cosa senza forma, senza bellezza e senza termine, e poi nella materia introduce la* forma, *che è vna cosa bella e terminata.* The difference between Lomazzo and Zuccari consists, then, in this: Lomazzo, even though in contrast to the older authors his interests had become more speculative, nevertheless proceeded in the *Trattato* very much according to the older, practically directed theory of art; he wished to instruct the artist directly, and his speculation was no more than an introduction to and an embellishment of concrete prescriptions, which he took for the most part from older sources; Zuccari, however, was the first writer so fascinated by the purely speculative problem that he dedicated a whole tome to a systematic discussion of it and almost completely renounced the directly useful, the practically applicable.

42. Zuccari, *Idea*, I.11, pp. 63 ff.: *Ecco la necessità, che tiene l' anima nostra dei sensi per intendere e principalmente per formare il suo Disegno interno. E perchè gli esempi facilitano le cose, io apporterò un esempio in che modo nella mente nostra si formi il Disegno.*

Però dico, che siccome per formare il fuoco il fucile batte la pietra, dalla pietra n' escon faville, le faville accendon l' esca, poi appressandosi all' esca i solfanelli, s' accende la lucerna: così la virtù intellettiva batte la pietra dei concetti nella mente umana; e il primo concetto, che sfavilla, accende l' esca dell' immaginazione, e move i fantasmi e le immaginazioni ideali; il qual primo concetto è interminato e confuso, nè della facoltà dell' anima o intelletto agente e possibile è inteso. Ma questa favilla diviene a poco a poco forma, idea, e fantasma reale e spirito formato di quell' anima speculativa e formativa; poi s' accendono i sensi a guisa di solfanelli, e accendono la lucerna dell' intelletto agente e possibile, la quale accesa diffonde il suo lume in ispeculazione e divisione di tutte le cose; onde ne nascono poi idee più chiare e giudizî più certi, presso de' quali cresce l' intelligenza intellettiva nell' intelletto alla cognizione o formazione delle cose; e dalle forme nasce l' ordine e la regola, e dall' ordine e regola l' esperienza e la pratica: e così vien fatta luminosa e chiara questa lucerna. It is highly significant that Zuccari, in his excerpt from Thomas Aquinas quoted in n. 41 above, left out the sentence *Omnis autem nostra cognitio est per sensus a rebus sensilibus et naturalibus accepta. . . .* Moreover cf. p. 195, n. 14, and p. 210, n. 39.

43. Ibid., II.11, p. 164.

44. Cf. Schlosser, *Materialien zur Quellenkunde*, VI, 117.

45. Cf. the differentiation (already stressed by Schlosser, *Materialien*, VI, 118) between good and bad artists; the good ones need no model, the bad ones, however, do (lowest of all are those artists who use other artists' works as models). Zuccari, *Idea*, II.3, p. 115: *Questo sebbene è necessario assolutamente alle operazioni nostre di pittura, scultura ed architettura a perfezionarli: nientedimeno è necessario con esso Disegno esterno naturale principalmente l' interno intellettivo sensitivo; ma quello come meno esemplare proprio è perfetto. Nel che anco consiste la differenza fra i pittori eccellenti, scultori ed architetti ed altri di nostra professione di poca eccellenza, che dove questi non sanno disegnare, scolpire nè fabbricare senza la scorta del Disegno, esterno esemplare, quelli operano queste stesse cose senz' altra interna scorta di altra intelligenza, come vediamo per esperienza.*

46. Zuccari, *Idea*, II.4, pp. 118 ff. Even such *capricci* must have their rules and measurements (p. 121); cf. Pacheco's interesting discussions (pp. 225 f., n. 28), according to which creatures alien to nature, such as chimeras, etc., are in truth only new combinations of forms that in themselves are natural.

47. Ibid., II.1, pp. 101 ff.; II.3, p. 114. *Spirito*, according to the view common throughout the Renaissance, is a mediator between *corpo* and *anima*.

48. Ibid., II.6, p. 132.

49. Naturally this did not prevent Zuccari (ibid., II.2, pp. 109 f.) from telling the indispensable legend about the Crotonian maidens—but without systematically connecting the advice to "select," which is attached to this legend, with his whole point of view. He expressly cautioned that such a selection should not interfere with the "imitation of nature": *E perchè quasi tutti gli individui naturali patiscono qualche imperfezione, e rarissimi sono i perfetti, massime il corpo umano, che spesso è manchevole in proporzione e disposizione di qualche membro, è necessario al pittore e allo scultore acquistare la buona cognizione delle parti e simmetria del corpo umano, e d'esso corpo scegliere le parti più belle e le più graziose, per formarne una figura di tutta eccellenza, ad imitazione pure della Natura nelle sue più belle e perfette opere.*

50. There is not very much more Platonism or Neoplatonism in Zuccari's *Idea* than had been absorbed into Thomism: his basic attitude is thoroughly High Scholastic and Aristotelian.

51. Aristotelians—even Lomazzo in his *Trattato*—were ap-

parently satisfied now, as they had been earlier, with a purely phenomenal definition of beauty as συμμετρία and εὔχροια. Thus Julius Caesar Scaliger, for instance, determined even poetic *pulchritudo* as follows: *species excitata ex partium modo, figura, situ, numero, colore. Modum partium appello debitam quantitatem* (quoted by Brinckschulte, p. 46). Alongside "harmony" another criterion of beauty was often cited: "the mean" (*Mittelmass*); but in the last analysis both of these postulates amount to the same thing; cf. Panofsky, *Dürers Kunsttheorie*, pp. 140 ff.

52. Cf. Vincenzo Danti, ch. VII–VIII, pp. 37 ff. (also Schlosser, in *Jahrbuch der kunsthistorischen Sammlungen*, XXXI [1913], 14 ff.; and idem, *Materialien*, VI, 119 f.): besides the "external" beauty resulting from the perfect proportion of the visible, corporeal shape there is an "internal" beauty, designated as *grazia*, which consists in the *attezza . . . di poter ben discorrere e ben conoscere e giudicare le cose;* this *grazia* results from the perfect proportion of that which is corporeal but not visible, namely, the parts of the brain; both kinds of beauty, however, are alike in that they please only because they are an expression of the "good," which in turn *depende dal sommo buono.* With Danti, then, the spirit of Platonizing metaphysics—shown not only in the derivation of the beautiful from the good and in the explanation of ugliness by the resistance of matter, but also by the axiomatic recognition of the fact that "internal" beauty can be concealed beneath "external" ugliness (*essendo stata molte volte veduta in huomini brutti*), as is the case with Plato's Socrates—is obviously mixed with the spirit of Peripatetic natural philosophy and Socratic rationalism. "Internal" beauty is reduced to a good relationship of the parts of the brain and "perfect proportion" is equated with perfect appropriateness: *la proporzione non è altro, che la perfezione d'un composto di cose nell' attezza, che se le conviene, per conseguire il suo fine* (V, 31). With Danti, therefore, that is beautiful which most perfectly fulfills its natural purpose, its natural τέλος. For instance, that tree is most beautiful whose top best fulfills the duty of shielding the root from excessive sunlight and too much rain, thereby guaranteeing the greatest possible fruitfulness of the whole plant. This teleological theory of beauty may ultimately derive from the Socratic equation of καλόν with χρήσιμον and can also be documented in Scholasticism (Thomas Aquinas, *Summa Theol.*, I.2.54.1c) as well as in eleventh-century Arabic philosophy (Al-Ghazali, *Das Elixir der Glückseligkeit*, German translation by H. Ritter [1923], pp. 147 ff.). But the

thought that it is the function of art to realize the ἄνθρωπος τέλειος or the ἵππος τέλειος was foreign to both the Arabs and the Scholastics.

53. Thus R. Borghini, p. 122, where beauty is further connected with a good disposition of the four humors. That an author like Castiglione already considered physical beauty to be a radiation of divine grace and accordingly an expression of internal goodness was pointed out on pp. 211 f., n. 45; but significantly it was not until fifty years later that this conception invaded the theory of art.

54. Besides Lomazzo (quoted pp. 140 ff.) mention may be made of Cesare Ripa, *Iconologia* (Rome, 1603), s.v. *Bellezza: Si dipinge la Bellezza con la testa ascosa frà le nuuole, perchè non è cosa, della quale più difficilmente si possa parlare con mortal lingua e che meno si possa conoscere con l'intelletto humano, quanto la Bellezza, la quale nelle cose create non è altro (metaforicamente parlando) che* vn *splendore che deriua della luce della faccia di Dio, come diffiniscono i Platonici, essendo la prima Bellezza vna cosa con essa, la quale poi, communicandosi in qualche modo l'Idea per benignità di lui alle sue creature, è caggione, che esse intendano in qualche parte la Bellezza.* Francesco Scannelli refers to Ripa and Lomazzo for the following way of defining beauty in his *Il Microcosmo della Pittura* (Cesena, 1657), I.17, p. 107: . . . *non essere . . . la tanto desiderata bellezza, che riflesso di supremo lume, e come raggio della divinità, la quale m'appare composta con buona Simetria di parti e concordata con la soauità de' colori, lasciata in terra per reliquia e Caparra della vita Celeste ed immortale.* The relationship of the Neoplatonic-metaphysical definition of beauty to the classic-phenomenal is especially clear here.

55. Cf. Zuccari, quoted p. 232, n. 49; also Alberti, quoted pp. 57 f.; and Dolce, quoted pp. 81 f.

56. Zuccari, *Idea*, I.10, p. 59: *materia esterna, atta a produrre quegli effetti* and *materie soggetti e capaci della pittura*, etc. The reason for the defectiveness of certain natural and artistic objects is not the resistance of matter but the inadequacy of the *agens* (i.e., the forming and effecting power); e.g., I.10, p. 60, which explains how works of art fall short of natural objects: *Sebben pare, che l'imiti nel dipingere o scolpire un animale, che non è pero imitarlo propriamente, ma piuttosto ritrarlo o scolpirlo; e di questo n' è causa la differenza, che si trova tra l'arte Divina producente le cose naturali, e l'arte nostra producendo le cose artificiali, che quella è più perfetta, generale e di virtù infinita, condizioni, che mancano all' arte nostra; il che è anco cagionato dalla differenza del Disegno Divino ed umano,*

che quello è perfettissimo e di virtù infinita, e il nostro è imperfetto [cf. Leonardo da Vinci's remarks to the contrary, quoted p. 248, n. 37!]; *e però ove il nostro può esser causa di alquanti effetti minori e di poco momento, quello è causa di effetti grandissimi e importantissimi.* Further, II.6, pp. 132 ff., which, in order to prevent conclusions about art as such from single poor works of art, draws attention to the fact that nature herself sometimes creates deformities: *Deve dunque ciascheduno lodare e pregiare la pittura, nè deve avvilirla nè i suoi nobili professori da un fine particolare ed a essa ed a loro per accidente: oppure perchè talora si vedono delle pitture disgraziate, che fanno vergogna a sì nobil professione, posciachè a questo modo dovremmo ancora biasimare l'opere della Natura e la Natura istessa, poichè bene spesso vediamo della mostruosità nell' opere di essa; eppur sappiamo, che sebbene ella si trova in alcune cose manchevole per difetti di alcuni agenti, in se stessa è però perfetta, quando opera col mezzo d'agenti perfetti: e l'istesso potiamo dire dell' arte della pittura.* Cf. Aristotle, *Physics*, I.8.199, and Thomas Aquinas's commentary (Fretté-Maré, XXII, 375).

57. Cf. Carlo Ridolfi, *Le Maraviglie dell' Arte* (1648), I, 3 (quoted in Birch-Hirschfeld, p. 107): *E perchè avviene, che i naturali corpi nella loro produttione pèr la prava dispositione della materia rimanghino spesso di molti difetti impressi, questo solo offitio e dignità è conceduto alla Pittura, di ridurli a quello stato primiero, che furono dall' eterno Facitore prodotti, e come dispensiera della divina gratia recargli i gradi della perfettione e della bellezza.* Further Vinc. Danti (cf. Schlosser, *loc. cit.*), Bellori (quoted p. 154), and even Vasari (*Proemio delle Vite* = I, 216): *Perciochè il Divino architetto del tempo e della natura, come perfettissimo, volle mostrare nella imperfezione della materia la via del levare e del aggiungere nel medesimo modo, che sogliono fare i buoni scultori e pittori. . . .*

58. Ridolfi, quoted in the preceding note.

59. Vinc. Danti, XVI, 91.

60. It needs no special emphasis that neither in Lomazzo nor in other writers did the surrender to Neoplatonism exclude an Aristotelian influence, which was not only not avoided but assimilated by the very members of the Florentine *Academia Platonica*. It can be demonstrated, however, that the Aristotelian-Scholastic elements, predominating in Lomazzo's *Trattato*, tended to be superseded by Neoplatonic tendencies in his *Idea del Tempio della Pittura*.

61. Milan, 1590.

62. Cf. Lomazzo himself, *Trattato*, VI.9, pp. 310 f. (theory of the four humors or temperaments); II.7, pp. 110 ff. (planets). Further, Zuccari, *Idea*, II.15, pp. 187 ff.

63. Lomazzo, *Idea* . . . , ch. 26, pp. 72 ff.: *Dal modo di conoscere e constituire le proporzioni secondo la bellezza*.

64. On this view cf. that which was hinted at on pp. 199–201, n. 27. Its roots lie in late Hellenism; see H. Ritter, in *Vorträge der Bibliothek Warburg*, I (1922), 94 ff.

65. Thus the *formulae idearum* are, as it were, reproductions of the actual Ideas, which, understood according to the strict definition, can reside only in suprahuman Intelligences. The view that the cognition of the beautiful is made possible only by referring earthly appearances back to the Ideas is also suggested by Cesare Ripa's remark quoted on p. 234, n. 54.

66. Namely, the sentence *E prima abbiamo da sapere, che la bellezza non è altro che una certa grazia vivace e spiritale*. It has been said that in this sentence Lomazzo defined beauty as "grace in motion," and this has been associated with the Mannerist preference for strong, free movement. Recently Lomazzo's statement has even been contrasted with the "Florentine" interpretation of beauty as a *convenienza* based on proper proportion; cf. Birch-Hirschfeld, p. 40; W. Weisbach, in *Zeitschrift für bildende Kunst*, new ser., XXX (1919), 161 ff.; Giacomo Vesco, in *L'arte*, XXII (1919), 98. The very next clause, however (*la quale prima s'infonde negli Angeli* . . .), should have aroused skepticism about this interpretation. Actually Lomazzo's sentence is a verbatim quotation from Ficino's corresponding chapter; Lomazzo simply anticipated Ficino's final definition by placing it at the beginning of his own exposition. — Even Lionello Venturi, in his otherwise very instructive book *La critica e l'arte di Leonardo da Vinci* (1919), pp. 111 ff., goes astray in explaining Lomazzo's light metaphysics—taken from Ficino and ultimately rooted in Christian Neoplatonism—as an especially profound interpretation of the Leonardesque *chiaroscuro*.

67. In Appendix I, Lomazzo's ch. 26 is juxtaposed with the excerpts borrowed from Ficino's commentary on Plato's *Symposium*. Subsequently I have discovered that the relation between Lomazzo and Ficino has already been pointed out in a small, theosophically oriented tract by Paul Vulliard, *De la conception idéologique et esthétique des dieux à l'époque de la Renaissance* (Paris, 1907), p. 30.

68. Cesare Ripa's *Iconologia* (cf. p. 234, n. 54), perhaps not

unworthy of more thorough investigation, and illustrating with special clarity the inner relationship of Mannerism to the Middle Ages, suffices to characterize this tendency of the epoch. The illustration on p. 69 shows how even the Idea concept could be the object of allegorical-symbolical representation (Ripa, Venice edition of 1645, pp. 362 ff. [vacat in the Roman edition of 1603]): *Vna bellissima donna solleuata in aria, sarà nuda, ma ricoperta da vn candido e sottilissimo velo, che tenga in cima del capo vna fiamma viuace di fuoco, haurà cinta la fronte de vn cerchio d'oro contesto di gioie splendidissimo; terrà in braccio la figura della Natura, alla quale come fanciulla dia il latte, che con l'indice della destra mano accenni vn bellissimo paese, che vi stia sotto, doue siano dipinte Città, Monti, Piani, Acque, Piante, Albori, uccelli in aria e altre cose terrestri.* The continuation of the text—which again appeals primarily to Thomas Aquinas but also draws on countless other ancient and medieval philosophers—goes on to explain, as always in such books and according to good medieval custom, the single constituent parts of the pictorial representation: "Idea" must float in the air, because she is immaterial and unchangeable; she must be naked, because (according to Ficino!) she represents a *sostanza semplicissima;* the white veil indicates her purity and genuineness, the fire means the "good," the golden circlet "spiritual perfection"; she nourishes "Nature," in order to indicate the "world soul" that shines from the spirit of God as radiance from light; and she points to a landscape, because the entire terrestrial world depends on the world of Ideas.

69. Comanini's *Il Figino* provides curious examples of both. On the one hand (pp. 45 ff.) reference is made to Arcimboldo's *capricci*, already mentioned on p. 215 (in n. 51); these were invented strictly according to the principles of allegory ("Autumn," for example, might consist only of fruits, "Flora" of flowers; and if a human countenance were constructed out of beasts, then the elephant had to form the cheeks because these, on account of blushing, are the *locus* of the "modesty" which already characterizes the elephant in the *Physiologus*). On the other hand (pp. 252 ff.), we find the truly amusing interpretation, already rejected by Lor. Pignoria, of a Mithras-relief as an "Allegory of perfect husbandry": Mithras with his Phrygian cap is a *contadino giouane;* the butchered steer means the ploughed-up earth; the snake means the cleverness which the farmer must apply in order to accomplish his work well and at the right time; Cautes and Cautopates are day and night (one

sees how Comanini's interpretation—completely without basis—
sometimes accidentally agrees with that which today seems histori-
cally "correct"); and it is uncertain whether the scorpion by its hiber-
nation symbolizes the generative power of the earth or whether by
its living in nocturnal dampness it symbolizes the dew. — Arcimboldo's *capricci* were already mentioned by Lomazzo in *Idea del
Tempio*, ch. 37, pp. 137 ff.; and their predecessors seem to be carica-
tures such as those well-known phallic medals mocking Paolo Giovio.

70. Cf. M. Dvořák, in *Jahrbuch für Kunstgeschichte*, I [XV]
(1922), 22 ff.

CHAPTER 6

1. On the occasional opposition to the Raphael cult, that is indi-
visibly bound up with classicism, cf. Schlosser, *Materialien zur
Quellenkunde*, VIII, 6 ff.; and esp. the interesting essay by
O. Kutschera-Woborski, in *Mitteilungen der Gesellschaft für
vervielfält. Kunst* (1919), pp. 9 ff.

2. See pp. 47 ff. and pp. 202 ff., n. 2.

3. See p. 204, n. 3.

4. The art theory of the Renaissance, too, is essentially opposed to
a mere imitative "realism." Yet the postulate of beauty is, at the beginning, appended to the demand for correctness as a sort of amend-
ment or reservation. This is especially clear with Alberti (cf. pp.
204 f., nn. 8 and 9). The original intention was chiefly—as is only
natural—to oppose medieval alienation from nature. Alberti characteristically even adduced the perennial anecdote of the Crotonian
maidens not to refute the "realists" but those who "think they can
create something beautiful from their own free invention."

5. On the term *maniera*, in addition to Bellori's statements
quoted below in Appendix II, pp. 172 ff., cf. for instance Fil. Baldinucci, *Vocabolario Toscano dell' arte del disegno* (1681), XXI, 122:
ed in ogni altro [*scil.* except Michelangelo, Raphael, and Andrea del
Sarto] *scuopresi talora alquanto di quel difetto, che dicesi Maniera
o Ammanierato, che è quanto dire debolezza d'intelligenza e più
della mano nell' obbedire al vero;* also the letter of the Marchese
Giustiniani mentioned on p. 240, n. 6 (Bottari, *Raccolta*, VI, 250):
*Decimo è il modo di dipignere, come si dice, di maniera, cioè che il
pittore con lunga pratica del disegno e di colorire, di sua fantasia*

senza alcun esemplare forma in pittura quel che ha nella fantasia . . . nel qual modo ha dipinto a' tempi nostri il Barocci, il Romanelli, il Passignano e Giuseppe d'Arpino. . . . ed in questo modo molti altri hanno a olio fatto opere assai vaghe e degne di lode. This specific definition of *maniera* as an artistic practice alien or foreign to nature is, however, not the original one. At first *maniera (di fare)* meant nothing more than "manner of working," so that it was possible to speak of *maniera buona* as well as of *maniera cattiva* or *goffa,* and as a rule the expression was used to designate the special artistic character of a nation, an era, or a certain master: *maniera antica, maniera moderna, maniera greca, maniera tedesca, maniera di Donatello* (unfortunately John Grace Freeman's *The "maniera" of Vasari* [London, 1867] was not available to me). The statements by Bellori, Baldinucci, and Giustiniani thus show that in the seventeenth century the term *maniera,* until then a completely colorless expression that could only be used in connection with an adjective or a possessive, began to take on a unique and derogatory significance that enabled it to be used without specification. *Dipingnere di maniera* came to mean painting "by rote," or, to avoid a mixed metaphor, to paint "off-hand." And only this total emancipation from the natural model, not the emulation of other masters, is the mark of the "Mannerist," according to the original sense of the term. Thus Goethe: "He discovers for himself a certain mode, makes himself a language, in order to render in his own way that which he has apprehended with his soul, to give to an object that he has often repeated his own characteristic form, without having nature itself before him when he repeats it, and without even remembering nature quite clearly." — Now, classicistic theory condemned everything that was "subjective" and "phantastic," but despite all its admonitions to "idealism" it nevertheless demanded from art a thorough "naturalness" and "correctness" based on concrete observation. Within this art theory the term *maniera,* now burdened with the specific meaning of production foreign to nature, took on that pejorative quality that it has had until today. The negative revaluation of the concept *maniera* was apparently accomplished by the circle around Bellori; with Giustiniani the censorious aftertaste is completely lacking, while Bellori and Baldinucci already spoke of *vitio, difetto,* and *ammanierato* (= "mannered"). And perhaps it is precisely this negative revaluation that forced the theory of art to look for another expression, neutral as to value, which would indicate nothing more than the special artistic way of eras, peoples, and persons, as earlier the now derogative term *maniera* had done. Thus the same circle about Bellori that refashioned the term *maniera* into an invective, also took the step that seems so obvious to us but in truth was hardly taken before the middle of the seventeenth century: they borrowed the term "style" from poetics and rhetoric and claimed it for works of representational art; cf. Poussin's art-theoretical maxims given by Bellori, *Vite de' pittori, scultori et architetti moderni* (Rome, 1672), pp. 460 ff.: *Della Materia, del Concetto, della Struttura, e dello Stile. . . . Lo stile è vna maniera particolare e industria di dipingere e disegnare, nata dal particolare genio di ciascuno nell' applicatione e nell' vso dell' idee, il quale stile, maniera o gusto si tiene della parte della natura e dell' ingegno.* Here the expression "style" is used apparently for the first time to designate the individual ways of pictorial representation that so far had been designated by the term *maniera;* in fact, "style" at first could not be defined otherwise than as *maniera particolare*. General acceptance of this term, new to the theory of the representational arts, came slowly, and above all outside France. In Germany, for instance, Joh. Fr. Christ still used the term *goût* in place of it (cf. Poussin's *gusto*); but the final triumph of the term "style" was probably decided for the Germans by Winckelmann.

6. Interesting by contrast with this is the letter of the Marchese Vinc. Giustiniani (Bottari, *Raccolta*, VI, 247 ff.), who saw in the art of Caravaggio a union of *dipingere di maniera* with *dipingere con avere gli oggetti naturali d'avanti*, and thus the highest possible form of painting. His letter, very important for understanding artistic practice and art education at that time, differentiates twelve *gradi* or *modi* of painting: (1) mechanical copy *con spolveri*, (2) free copy on the basis of simple observation or with the help of optical apparatuses, such as the *graticola* (graticule) first mentioned by Alberti, (3) copying everything that presents itself to the eye, but especially antique or modern statues and good paintings, (4) single studies of heads, hands, etc., (5) painted representation of flowers or other small objects—*ed il Caravaggio disse, che tanta manifattura gli era a fare un quadro buono di fiori, come di figure*, (6) architectural renderings and *vedute*, (7) invention of grand subjects, including landscape painting, be it in the grandiose manner of Titian, Raphael, the Carracci, and Reni or in the minute manner of Civetta, Breughel, and Bril, (8) grotesques, (9) painting or etching *con furore di disegno e d'istoria data dalla Natura* (Polidoro da Caravaggio and Tempesta), (10) *dipingere di maniera* (see pp.

238 ff., n. 5), (11) painting from the model, (12) a combination of the tenth and eleventh steps, reached only by the foremost masters, among contemporaries by Caravaggio, the Carracci, Guido Reni, and others.

7. Bellori, p. 212.

8. Bertolotti, *Artisti Lombardi a Roma* (1881), II, 59.

9. Letter of Marchese Giustiniani quoted p. 240, n. 6.

10. Thus Bernini's verdict; Chantelou, "Journal du voyage du Cav. Bernin en France," *Gazette des Beaux-Arts* (1885), p. 190.

11. Bellori, quoted pp. 166, 168.

12. Luigi Scaramuccia, *Le finezze de' Pennelli Italiani* (1674), p. 76: *Per finirlo è stato quest' Huomo vn gran Soggetto, mà non Ideale, che vuol dire non saper far cosa alcuna senza il naturale auanti.* Cf. also Giov. Baglione, *Le Vite de Pittori, Scultori ed Architetti* (1642), p. 139. Caravaggio, he says, had a good *maniera, che presa havea nel colorire dal naturale, benchè egli nel rappresentar le cose non hauesse molto giudicio di scieglere il buono e lasciare il cattiuo;* cf. also Scannelli, *Il Microcosmo della Pittura* (1657), I.7, pp. 52 f.: *provisto di particolar genio, mediante il quale daua con l'opere a vedere vna straordinaria e veramente singolare immitatione del vero, e nel communicar forza e rileuo al dipinto non inferiore, e forsi ad ogni altro supremo, priuo però della necessaria base del buon disegno, si palesò poscia d'inuentione mancante, e come del tutto* ignudo di bella idea, *gratia, decoro, Architettura, Prospettiua ed altri simili conueneuoli fondamenti.*

13. Bellori actually spoke of the *corruzione di nostra età:* what the Renaissance believed it already possessed, he believed he had to fight for again.

14. Bellori, quoted p. 168.

15. Thus Bellori, quoted pp. 170, 172. Painters and sculptors were directed to antiquity as a guide to nature, architects as an antidote against the modern Baroque *à la* Boromini. On Goethe's statement *Die Antike gehört zur Natur, und, wenn sie anspricht, zur natürlichen Natur,* cf. Panofsky, "Dürers Stellung zur Antike," *Jahrbuch für Kunstgeschichte,* I [XV] (1922), 43 ff. (also separately publ.; Eng. tr. "Albrecht Dürer and Classical Antiquity," in *Meaning and the Visual Arts* [Garden City, N. Y., 1955], pp. 236–94).

16. On this cf. Schlosser, *Materialien zur Quellenkunde,* VII, 11 ff., and lately Kutschera-Woborsky (above, n. 1), pp. 22 ff.

17. O. Walzel's statement (*Vom Geistesleben alter und neuer*

Zeit [1922], p. 5) "Wherever Raphael's phrase [*scil.* the dictum about the *certa idea*] appears, it is used as a weapon against naturalistic art" needs a certain amplification, since Bellori, and with him the entire classicistic theory, used the phrase not only against "naturalism" but also against "mannerism."

18. Bellori's *L'Idea . . .* is given *in extenso* in Appendix II (pp. 154 ff.) as the basic document of the classicistic attitude to art.

19. Cf. p. 252, n. 35.

20. Evidence for this and for the following is found in Appendix II. On the pair of concepts *pittori icastici* and *pittori fantastici*, cf. pp. 212 ff., n. 51. Bellori (and also Junius) accepted Comanini's faulty interpretation (see ch. IV, n. 51), but differed from him quite deeply (which follows from his basic attitude) in disapproving of both the *pittori fantastici* and the *pittori icastici*—especially the *facitori di ritratti*, as he scornfully put it—whereas Comanini still gave his *placet* to the representatives of "eikastic" imitation.

21. It should be noted, however, that Bellori borrowed those citations, which had not as yet become the common property of art theorists, from the compilation by Franciscus Junius, *De pictura veterum* (above all I.3 and II.2), which first appeared in 1637; Hoogstraaten, *Inlevding tot de Hooge Schoole der Schilderkonst* (1678), VIII.3, pp. 286 ff., also made full use of Junius's book.

22. Bellori is the "predecessor of Winckelmann" not only as an antiquarian but also as an art theorist. Winckelmann's theory of the "ideally beautiful" as he expounds it in *Geschichte der Kunst des Altertums*, IV.2.33 ff., thoroughly agrees—except for the somewhat stronger Neoplatonic impact, which is to be explained perhaps more as an influence of Raphael Mengs than as an influence of Shaftesbury —with the content of Bellori's *Idea* (to which Winckelmann also owes his acquaintance with the letters of Raphael and Guido Reni); he frankly recognizes this indebtedness in *Anmerkungen zur Geschichte der Kunst des Altertums* (1767), p. 36. — By contrast to Winckelmann, it is even more remarkable that Poussin's theory of beauty is purely Neoplatonic, thus deviating greatly from that of Bellori. While the great German archaeologist took up the dead Bellori's thoughts and carried them further, the great French painter, who had close personal contacts with Bellori, borrowed his theory of the beautiful almost verbatim from either Ficino's commentary on the *Symposium* or Lomazzo's *Idea del Tempio della pittura* (to which his attention could have been directed by Hilaire Pader, translator of Lomazzo and well known to Poussin). So inescapable

was the charm of this Neoplatonic metaphysics that not even the clear mind of the great French classicist could tear itself away from it. Poussin's sentences (to which the passage by Ficino [or Lomazzo] repr. pp. 128 ff. should be compared) run as follows (Bellori, *Vite de' pittori . . .* , pp. 461 f.): *Della idea della bellezza. L'idea della Bellezza non discende nella materia, che non sia preparata il più che sia possibile; questa preparazione consiste in trè cose, nell' ordine, nel modo e nella specie overo forma. L'ordine significa l'interuallo delle parti, il modo hà rispetto alla quantità, la forma consiste nelle linee e ne' colori. Non basta l'ordine e l'interuallo delle parti, e che tutti li membri del corpo habbiano il loro sito naturale, se non si aggiunge il modo, che dia a ciascun membro la debita grandezza proportionata al corpo, e se non vi concorre la specie, accioche le linee sieno fatte con gratia e con soaue concordia di lumi vicino all' ombre. E da tutte queste cose si vede manifestamente, che la bellezza è in tutto lontana dalla materia del corpo, la quale ad esso mai s'auuicino, se non sarà disposta con queste preparationi incorporee.* The conclusion (*E qui si conclude, che la Pittura altro non è che vna idea delle cose incorporee, quantunque dimostri li corpi rappresentando solo l'ordine, e 'l modo delle specie delle cose, e la medesima è più intenta all' idea del bello che a tutte l'altre*) is evident as soon as art is credited with the ability to realize the *bellezza* defined in the preceding sentences; as we already know, such was not as yet the case with Ficino. Here is another instance to show that the utterances of theorizing artists must be used with the greatest caution. Certainly the very fact of such a borrowing is very important—even more, of course, the individual development of that which is borrowed—but it is always necessary to test carefully before declaring statements like Poussin's to be an artist's "independent epistemological insights" and accepting them as a direct manifestation of his artistic intentions (thus K. Gerstenberg, *Die ideale Landschaftsmalerei* [1923], p. 108. On the other hand, Fränger, *Die Bildanalysen des Roland Fréart de Chambray* [diss. Heidelberg, 1917], p. 33, goes too far when he—misunderstanding the special relationship of Poussin's theory with the metaphysics of Ficino [or Lomazzo]—sees in them only a deposit of the "generally circulated" Platonism and accordingly incorrectly interprets the concept *preparazione*, which can be understood only from the doctrine of the mystical influences connecting the sublunar with the translunar world.)

23. On the conception of the "Ideal," cf. Cassirer, "Eidos und Eidolon: Das Problem des Schönen und der Kunst in Platos Dialo-

gen," *Vorträge der Bibliothek Warburg*, II:1 (1922–23), 1–27; further, Schlosser, *Materialien zur Quellenkunde*, passim, and in *Jahrbuch der Kunstsammlungen des Allerhöchsten Kaiserhauses*, XXXIX (1910–11), p. 249. Bellori was not so shortsighted as to claim an absolutely universal (i.e., undifferentiatable) validity for the Ideal; rather it is individualized insofar as the "Idea" is a generic notion which—while having general validity within its class—lends truly "exemplary" expression to certain *types* of habitual appearance (such as strength, grace, fieriness) as well as to types of psychological states (such as anger, grief, or love).

24. Perhaps even stronger than in Bellori, this intolerant character of the classicistic position manifests itself in such French theorists as Félibien, Du Fresnoy, Fréart de Chambray; (cf. also, Fränger, *op. cit.*, and esp. A. Fontaine, *Les doctrines d'art en France de Poussin à Diderot* [1909]). Conversely, there rises here for the first time the opposition of the "modernists" like Charles Perrault, of the "painterly" artists like Philippe de Champaigne, and particularly of the "amateurs" like Roger de Piles; cf. Schlosser, *Materialien zur Quellenkunde*, IX, 28 ff.

25. Cf. also Bernini's great Academy speech on 5 Sept. 1665 (Chantelou, p. 134).

26. Lomazzo, *Trattato*, I.1, p. 19; quoted in Birch-Hirschfeld, *Die Lehre von der Malerei im Cinquecento* (1912), p. 22. In the same context he even uses the old phrase *simia della natura* (of course in a laudatory sense).

27. Dion Chrysostom, Ὑπὲρ τοῦ Ἴλιον μὴ ἁλῶναι, in v. Arnim's edn. (1893 ff.), I, 115 ff.

CHAPTER 7

1. *Michelangelo: eine Renaissancestudie* (1892).

2. *Die Rätsel Michelangelos* (1908).

3. *Michelangelo*, II (1903), esp. 191 ff.

4. *Vita di Michelangelo Buonarroti* (1553), ch. 56, p. 204.

5. Karl Frey, *Die Dichtungen des Michelagniolo Buonarroti* (1897), CLXXII (= Ces. Guasti, *Le Rime di Michelangelo Buonarroti* [1863], p. 291), and elsewhere.

6. Petrarch, I, Canzone IX:

> Gentil mia Donna, io veggio
> Nel mover de' vostr' occhi un dolce lume,
> Che mi mostra la via, ch' al Ciel conduce. . . .

Cf. Michelangelo (Frey, CIX, 19): *Veggio co' bei vostr' occhi un dolce lume.* . . .

7. Frey, LXIV.

8. Frey, CIX, 105; cf. inter alia also XXXIV, XCII, LXXV. On the "light metaphysics" expressed here again and again, cf. ch. III, nn. 2 and 27, ch. IV, n. 29, and pp. 93 ff.

9. Frey, CIX, 99.

10. Frey, XCIV. At times, however, the passion for the "empirically beautiful" breaks through and unhesitatingly tears down the barriers of Platonic training: Frey, CIX, 104.

11. Frey, LXXV.

12. Frey, XCI.

13. Frey, CIX, 24; cf. CXLVI.

14. Frey, XCI; cf. XLIII, LXIV, and Guasti, p. 27.

15. Cf. pp. 188 f., n. 43 above. To quote only the founder of modern art theory, Alberti had already said: *Alii solum detrahentes, veluti qui superflua discutiendo quaesitam hominis figuram intra marmoris glebam inditam atque absconditam producunt in lucem* (p. 171). The corresponding passage in Vasari was quoted, in another context, on p. 217, n. 64.

16. Cf. Borinski, *Die Antike in Poetik und Kunsttheorie*, pp. 169 f.

17. Frey, LXXXIV (cf. also CXXXIV and Guasti, p. 171):

> . . . Simil di me model di poca stima
> Mio parto fu, per cosa alta e perfetta
> Da voi rinascer po', Donna alta e degna,
> Se 'l poco accresce e mio soverchio lima
> Vostra mercè. . . .

Such a redefinition of the borrowed thought (cf. pp. 188 f., n. 43) can be compared to the equally subjective and erotic allegorisation of antique myths, characteristic of Michelangelo the artist and his circle; cf. Panofsky, in *Jahrbuch für Kunstgeschichte*, I [XV] (1922), Buchbesprechungen, col. i ff., particularly col. 49 ff. With Schiller, who also sometimes used the marble block simile, this subjective-erotic mood gives way to an objective-ethical one: *Ein Marmorblock, obgleich er leblos ist und bleibt, kann darum nichtsdestoweniger lebende Gestalt durch Architekt und Bildhauer werden; ein Mensch, wiewohl er lebt und Gestalt hat, ist darum noch lange keine lebende Gestalt (Über die ästhetische Erziehung des Menschen,* Letter 15). And with a theologian, Geiler von Kaisersberg, the ancient notion of ἀφαίρεσις is raised not to a simile for the perfection of man's own being, but to a simile for a purification of the *visio Dei:* *Ein bildhauwer wen er wil ein bild hauwen vnd machen, so nimpt er ein lindinbaum oder ein ander holtz, vnd thut nüt dann das er hinweg thut, stets hauwet er daruon . . . vnd würt von dem selben vonthun ein semlich hübsch kostlich wol geziert bild. Ein maler der musz zuthun, wil er ein bild malen. . . .* Thus the pious person, "as a sculptor," should divorce from his conception of God everything visible and concrete and therefore imperfect, be it angels, saints, heaven, or earth, in order to gain a pure and perfect idea of the Supreme Being (*Brosamlein* [Strassburg, 1517], fol. XLIIII^v).

18. Frey, LXXXIII.

19. Cf. Frey, LXV.

20. Another sonnet, which treats the same problem in the form of a dialogue between the poet and Eros (Frey, XXXII), shows a remarkable parallel with Giordano Bruno: *Intendo, che non è figura o la specie sensibilmente o intelligibilmente representata, la qual per sè muove; perche, mentre alcuno sta mirando la figura manifesta a gli occhi, non viene ancora ad amare; ma da quello instante, che l'animo concipe in se stesso quella figurata non più visibile, ma cogitabile, non più dividua, ma individua, non più sotto specie di cosa, ma sotto specie di buono bello, allora subito nasce l'amore* (*Eroici Furori,* I.4, in *Opere,* ed. A. Wagner [1830], II, 345 ff.).

21. See p. 212, n. 50.

22. *Forma,* a third expression often equated with "idea," does not concern us here. For Michelangelo it meant either simply "shape" (e.g., Frey, CIX, 61) or, as in Scholastic-Peripatetic usage (*anima est forma corporis*), soul; thus, e.g., in Frey, CIX, 105:

> Per ritornar la donde venne fora
> L'immortal forma al tuo carcer terreno. . . .

This explanation (cf. also Scheffler, p. 92 n. 2) is confirmed by the fact that in exactly the same context *immortal forma* can be replaced by *alma diva* (Frey, CXXIII; cf. also CIX, 103, lines 4–6).

23. See pp. 198 f., n. 26.

24. Thus Frey, XXXIV, line 3; XXXVI, st. 10, line 4; LXII, line 3; CIX, 1, line 12; CIX, 25, line 7; CIX, 103, line 2. In addition the word *imagine* or *imago* also occurs, of course, in the more concrete meaning of an actual, painted or sculpted image; e.g., Frey, LXV, line 3; CIX, 53, line 2; CIX, 92, line 3.

25. Thus Frey, CIX, 59, line 2; CXLIV, line 2.

26. Frey, CIX, 87, lines 1 ff.

27. Frey, CXLI, line 7. The expressions *imagine* and *concetto* are contrasted with each other very clearly in Frey, CIX, 50:

> Negli anni molti e nelle molte prove
> Cercando, il saggio al buon concetto arriva
> D'una imagine viva,
> Vicino a morte, in pietra alpestra e dura.

Concetto, therefore, is the Idea of the *imagine*, the latter being realized in stone according to the former. Cf. also Frey, CXLVI: *S'a tuo nome ho concetto alcuna imago.*

28. G. Milanesi, *Le lettere di Michelangelo Buonarroti* (1875), Nrs. 464 and 465.

29. *Due Lezioni di messer Benedetto Varchi* (1549). The first lecture commenting on the sonnet is reprinted in Guasti, pp. LXXXV ff., from which I quote.

30. Varchi, p. XCIV.

31. Ibid. Varchi, clearly hinting at Francesco Berni's verse quoted on p. 115 above, explicitly stresses the Aristotelian element in Michelangelo's thought—an element perhaps too little emphasized in recent literature: *che egli è nuovo Apollo e Apelle e non dice parole, ma cose, tratte non solo del mezzo di Platone, ma d'Aristotile* (Varchi, p. CXI).

32. In a youthful love poem (Frey, IV) Michelangelo reinterpreted the "election theory" in a metaphysical, even theological sense: the "selection of the best" is carried out not by man but (in order to create the beloved) by God, for Whom that which is already created and that which is to be created are not opposites:

> Colui, che 'l tutto fè, fece ogni parte,
> E poi di tutto la più bella scelse,
> Per mostrar quivi le sue cose excelse
> Com' ha fatt' or con la sua divin' arte.

33. Lange and Fuhse, *Dürers schriftlicher Nachlass* (1893), p. 227; Ficino, *Comm. in Sympos.* (*Opera*, II, 1336), can be compared to this figure of speech:

Dürer	Ficino
Daraus wirdet der versammlet heimlich Schatz des Herzen offenbar. . . .	*Qua inclinatione gravatus thesaurum penetralibus suis absconditum negligit.*

Dürer's train of thought is, however, so different that the existence of a relationship (in the sense of direct dependence) seems rather questionable.

34. Lange and Fuhse, p. 297, Nrs. 27 ff.; quite similar, p. 295, Nrs. 8 ff.

35. Ficino, *Libri de vita triplici*, I.6 (*Opera*, I, 498); Dürer's corresponding sentence, *dann es will kummen van den öberen Eingiessungen* (Lange and Fuhse, p. 297, Nr. 20), has already been compared with Ficino's statement by Karl Giehlow, in *Mitteilungen der Gesellschaft für vervielfält. Kunst* (1904), p. 68.

36. Dürer (Lange and Fuhse, p. 298, Nr. 1 = p. 295, Nr. 13): *Dann ein guter Maler ist inwendig voller Figur, und obs müglich wär, dass er ewiglich lebte, so hätt' er aus den inneren Ideen, dovan Plato schreibt, allweg etwas Neus durch die Werk auszugiessen.* Seneca (*Epist.* LXV.7; quoted complete, pp. 19 ff. above): *Haec exemplaria rerum omnium Deus intra se habet . . . plenus his figuris est, quas Plato ideas appellat. . . .*

37. Statements similar to those by Vasari, Zuccari, Pacheco, and Bellori are infinite in number (cf. e.g., Lomazzo, *Trattato*, II.14, p. 159: *Però questo solo essercitio stimo io al debbol mio giudicio essere il più eccellente e divino che sia al mondo, poi che l'artifice viene quasi à dimostrarsi quasi* vn' altro Dio). Two beautiful sentences by Leonardo (*Trattato*, Nrs. 13 and 68) may be added here: *Come il pittore è Signore d'ogni sorte di gente e di tutte le cose. Se 'l pittore vol vedere bellezze, che lo innamorino, egli n'è signore di generarle, et se vol vedere cose mostruose, che spaventino, o' che sieno buffonesche e risibili, o' veramente compassionevoli, ei n'è signore e Dio* [in a marginal note added about 1550: *creatore*]. . . . *e in effetto, ciò ch' è nell uniuerso per essentia, presentia o' immaginatione, esso lo ha primo nella mente e poi nelle mani; e quelle sono di tanta eccellentia, che in pari tempi generano una proportionata armonia in un' solo sguardo, qual' fanno le cose;* and, agreeing almost verbatim with Dürer's statement: *La deità che ha la scientia del pittore fa, che la mente del pittore si trasmuta in una similitudine di mente diuina, imperochè con libera potestà discorre alla generatione di diuerse essentie, di uarij animali, pianti, frutti, paesi, campagne,* etc. . . .

38. Just as the intellect "causes the perceptible world to be either not an object of experience at all or to be a nature" (Kant, *Prolegomena*, §38), so, we may say, the artistic consciousness

causes the sensory world to be either not an object of artistic representation at all or to be a "figuration." The following difference, however, must be remembered. The laws which the intellect "prescribes" to the perceptible world and by obeying which the perceptible world becomes "nature," are universal; the laws which the artistic consciousness "prescribes" to the perceptible world and by obeying which the perceptible world becomes "figuration" must be considered to be individual—or to use an expression recently suggested by H. Noack, *Die systematische und methodische Bedeutung des Stilbegriffs* (diss. Hamburg, 1923), "idiomatic."

APPENDIX I

1. Marsiglio Ficino, *Sopra lo amore o ver convito di Platone* (Florence, 1544), Or. V, ch. 3–6, pp. 94 ff. (cf. orig. Latin text in *Opera*, II, 1336 ff.). In his elaboration of this chapter Lomazzo left out much (particularly everything concerned with acoustic beauty), added much, and partly rearranged what he retained of the original. It was therefore not possible to print parallel passages facing each other, as is customary, but rather the following procedure had to be adopted: the passages by Ficino that were omitted by Lomazzo have been placed in brackets, as well as the passages in Lomazzo that do not occur in Ficino. The remaining passages, that is, those in which Lomazzo depends upon Ficino, are indicated by italics.

2. From Ficino, ch. 3 (op. cit., p. 94). It is evident that Ficino defines beauty in this passage as a proportion only in order to reduce (in the sense of Plotinus) the equation *bellezza = proporzione* to the absurd.

3. With this expression cf. pp. 39 ff. and p. 196, n. 21.

4. Compare with this discussion the almost word-for-word passage in Plotinus, *Ennead*, I.6.3, partially quoted on p. 187, n. 40.

5. The body measurements given by Ficino are derived partly from the well-known canon of Vitruvius (thus the determination of the length of the whole body as eight lengths of the head, the division of the face into three lengths of the nose, and the outspread arms equaling the length of the body) and partly, apparently, from a tradition that goes back to the Middle Ages as it can be found on the one hand in the writings of artists and on the other hand in cosmological literature. From the latter is derived particularly the tendency to equalize various single measurements that in themselves

are disparate, such as may be encountered with Pomponius Gauricus and (in an altered sense) with Leonardo. On this see Panofsky, *Monatshefte für Kunstwissenschaft*, XV (1921).

6. G. P. Lomazzo, *Idea del Tempio della Pittura* (1590), ch. 26; in the 2d edn. (Bologna), from which the quotation is taken, pp. 72 ff.

7. Instead of the *e* ("and") in the chapter title, there is merely a comma; the table of contents (p. xi), on the contrary, correctly has the *e*.

APPENDIX II

1. Gio. Pietro Bellori, *Le vite de' Pittori, Scultori et Architetti moderni* (Rome, 1672), I, 3–13. The introduction to the vita of Annibale Carracci (pp. 19–21), which in content is directly connected with the discourse on Idea, is included here. We believe we are rendering a service to the reader and partly preparing the way for a future new edition of Bellori by verifying insofar as possible the passages quoted.

2. The expression *emendare* (according to Schlosser, *Materialien zur Quellenkunde*, IX, 88, a "school expression with philological shading"), is used in the same way by L. B. Alberti, p. 119 (quoted pp. 222 f., n. 20).

3. Cicero, *Orator*, II.7 ff., quoted pp. 11 f.; compare above with pp. 13 ff. and pp. 105 ff.

4. Proclus, *Comm. in Tim.*, II.122B: οὐδὲ εἰ λάβοις τὸν ὑπὸ φύσεως δεδημιουργημένον ἄνθρωπον καὶ τὸν ὑπὸ τῆς ἀνδριαντοποιητικῆς κατεσκευασμένον, πάντως ὁ ἐκ τῆς φύσεως κατὰ τὸ σχῆμα σεμνότερος· πολλὰ γὰρ ἡ τέχνη μᾶλλον ἀκριβοῖ. Bellori, apparently led astray by Junius, interpreted this passage too broadly: Proclos says only that natural man is *not necessarily more beautiful* than the one artistically represented, for in many ways art is more exact.

5. Overbeck, *Schriftquellen*, 1667–69. During the Renaissance this passage was used as a reference in all writing dealing in any way with aesthetics.

6. Cicero, *De inventione*, II.1.1.

7. Maximus Tyrius, Φιλοσοφούμενα, XVII.3 (ed. Hobein, p. 211): ὅνπερ τρόπον καὶ τοῖς τὰ ἀγάλματα τούτοις διαπλάττουσιν, οἳ παντὸς παρ' ἑκάστου καλὸν συναγαγόντες, κατὰ τὴν τέχνην ἐκ διαφόρων σωμάτων ἀθροίσαντες εἰς μίμησιν μίαν, κάλλος ἓν ὑγιὲς

καὶ ἄρτιον καὶ ἡρμοσμένον αὐτὸ αὐτῷ ἐξειργάσαντο. καὶ οὐκ ἂν εὗρες σῶμα ἀκριβὲς κατὰ ἀλήθειαν ἀγάλματι ὅμοιον. ὀρέγονται μὲν γὰρ αἱ τέχναι τοῦ καλλίστου.

8. Xenophon, Ἀπομνημ III.10.1; cf. p. 184, n. 15.

9. Lucian, Φιλοψεύδ, 18 and 20 ("ἀνθρωποποιός"); Quintilian, *Inst. Or.*, XII.10.9 (here among other things the criticism is repeated by Alberti that he strove more for similarity than beauty); Pliny, *Epist.* III.6.

10. Aristotle, *Poetics*, 2: Πολύγνωτος μὲν γὰρ κρείττους, Παύσων δὲ χείρους, Διονύσιος δὲ ὁμοίους εἴκαζεν. Pliny, *Natural History*, XXXV.113, calls the artist ἀνθρωπογράφος, because he *nihil aliud quam homines pinxit*.

11. Aristotle, *Poetics*, 2, and *Politics*, VIII.5.7.

12. Pliny, *Natural History*, XXXV.112.

13. Pliny, *Natural History*, XXXIV.65. Characteristically Bellori understood this passage as precisely the reverse of what was intended: Lysippus, according to the correct meaning, claimed that he did not represent men as they are but as they seem to be (*quales viderentur esse*). He must therefore be rightly classified as an "illusionist."

14. Aristotle, *Poetics*, 2.

15. Cicero, *Orator*, II.9.

16. Seneca (the Elder!), *Rhet. Controv.* X.34.

17. Philostratus, *Apollonius of Tyana*, VI.19; in Kayser's edn., τὰ Σωζόμενα (2d edn., 1853), p. 118; cf. p. 185, n. 21.

18. Alberti, op. cit., pp. 151, 153 (cf. pp. 48 f).

19. Leonardo da Vinci, *Trattato della Pittura*, passages from 88 and 89, also 53 (the interior dialogues of the painter with himself).

20. Cf. pp. 59 f. The sentence *il gran maestro . . .* is a quote from Dante, as we know.

21. Ovid, *Metam.*, XII.397.

22. Ovid, *Ars amandi*, III.401.

23. Philostratus, Ἡρωικός, 725 (ed. Kayser, p. 317).

24. Philostratus, Ἡρωικός, 739 (ed. Kayser, p. 324).

25. Ariosto, *Orlando Furioso*, X.96 (cf. also VII.11 and XI.69 ff.).

26. Ovid, *Metam.*, IV.671.

27. Marino, *La galleria distinta* (Milan, 1620), p. 82 (according to information from Prof. Walter Friedlaender, of Freiburg).

28. Lodovico Castelvetro, *Poetica d'Aristotele vulgarizzata et*

sposta, II.1 (in the Basel edn. [1576], p. 72, accessible to us): "But since Aristotle uses the example of delight, that one takes from the imitation in painting, in order to make us understand the delight that one takes in the imitation in poetry, one must realize that this is not the best example in the world, inasmuch as painting delights less in ways that only poetry delights us highly, and painting delights more and completely in ways that poetry not only does not delight but even displeases. Therefore painting . . . must be divided into two parts: one, when it represents something certain and known, such as a certain and particular man, let us say, Philip of Austria, the King of Spain, and secondly when it imitates something uncertain and unknown, such as an unknown man and in general"; it is much more enjoyable—continuing this train of thought—to see represented in a painting a definite & recognized personality than an unknown "ordinary man" (for the former requires more effort & skill to paint, and the painter is seriously reproached for each tiny dissimilarity). In poetry it would be the other way around, so that the principles of pictorial and poetic "imitation" could be considered diametrically opposed: with the former there is "an outward resemblance, which is apparent to the eyes," and with the latter there is an "internal resemblance, which is manifest to the intellect."

29. With this Platonic expression, which for example, Junius also misinterpreted in the same way as Comanini and Bellori, cf. pp. 212 ff., n. 51, and p. 242, n. 20, as well as pp. 5 f.

30. Aristotle, *Poetics*, XV.11 (1454B).

31. Philo, *De opificio mundi*, ch. IV; cf. p. 193, n. 5.

32. Ovid, *Metam.*, III.158.

33. Tasso, *Gerusalemme liberata*, XVI.10.

34. Aristotle, *Physics*, I.8.199: Οἶον εἰ οἰκία τῶν φύσει γιγνομένων ἦν, οὕτως ἂν ἐγίγνετο ὡς νῦν ὑπὸ τέχνης . . . . It is of course far from Aristotle's intention to make a value judgment of architectural creation, in the sense of Bellori's *perfettione*. He intends by comparing natural creation with artistic creation merely to prove the teleological purposefulness of natural processes, the τινος ἕνεκα γίγνεσθαι (cf. also at this point the most instructive commentary of Thomas Aquinas, in Fretté-Maré, XXII, 373 ff.)

35. Compare for instance *Phaedon*, XIX (75A): Ἀλλὰ μὲν καὶ τόδε ὁμολογοῦμεν μὴ ἄλλοθεν αὐτὸ ἐννενοηκέναι μηδὲ δυνατὸν εἶναι ἐννοῆσαι, ἀλλ' ἐκ τοῦ ἰδεῖν ἢ ἅψασθαι ἢ ἔκ τινος ἄλλης τῶν αἰσθήσεων. . . . Of course sensual perception is for Plato only the occasion for, not the origin of, understanding, which can only be achieved when

the spirit goes beyond sensual perception to that which, if it is equal, cannot appear to be unequal, and vice versa; that is, to the Ideas.

36. Quintilian, *Inst. Or.*, II.17.9: *Illud admonere satis est omnia, quae ars consummaverit, a natura initia duxisse.*

37. Plato, *Sophists*, 236 ff. Also the concept μίμησις φανταστικὴ is found in Bellori in a redefined form, of course: φαντασία is for him (just as it is for Comanini) not the sensual appearance but the voluntary inner notion; hence he saw the Mannerists as "fantastic" artists—whom Plato, rather, would have identified as so-called "realists." But the only difference between his conception and that of Comanini, let it be emphasized again, is that he disapproves of the goal of the *pittori icastici* (in his sense, the "simple imitation of nature") no less than the goal of the *pittori fantastici*.

38. On Critolaos the Peripatetic and his abuses against rhetoric, cf. Quintilian, *Inst. Or.*, II.15.23 (τριβή) and II.18.2 (κακοτεχνία and ἀτεχνία); see also Sextus Empiricus, πρὸς Ῥήτορας, passim (summary in *Philodemi voll. Rhet.*, ed. Sudhaus [suppl., 1895], pp. ix ff.).

39. Vitruvius, *De architectura*, VII.5.3–8, a tirade, which however is directed only against painted architectural structures of the so-called "fourth style"; naturally Bellori inveighs here against the specific "baroque" tendency in architecture, mainly represented by Boromini.

40. Probably *honori* ("honors").

INDEX

Index

Index

Index

Index

Neo-Scholastic theory of art, 91
Night, Michelangelo's, 117
Night Watch, 184n
Noack, H., 249n
Notiones anticipatae, 17
Νοῦς, the, and art, 27, 37
Numerus (equals rhythm), Augustine's category of, 192n
Nyssa, gardens of, 165

Obernitz, W. von, 212n
Object-subject problem. *See* Subject-object problem
Odysseus and Circe, Plotinus's parable of, 191n
Orator, Cicero's concept of the perfect, 11–13
Orcus, 31
Origen, 191n
Originality, role of, in Middle Ages, 205n
Overbeck, J., 181n, 184nn, 185n, 209n, 250n
Ovid, 163, 209n, 251nn, 252n

Pacheco, Francisco, 216n, 232n, 248n; on Idea, 217nn, 219n, 225–29n
Pacioli, Luca, 55
Pader, Hilaire, 242n
Pahlmann, 201n
Paideia (Education) vs. Techne (Sculpture), 183n
Painting/*pittura*, 13, 14–15, 183nn, 184n, 209n
  Zuccari's anti-mathematical theory of, 75ff, 220–21n; Bellori on, 154ff, 161ff, 175–77, 242n, 250n ff; and *disegno*, 82, 224–25n; Dürer's concept of, 123–25, 248nn; eicastic/icastic, 165; —— vs. phantastic (*pittori icastici* vs. *pittori fantastici*), 212–15n, 242n, 252–53n; Giustiniani's classifications of, 238–41; Greek, 175; and Idea, 154ff, 250n ff; Italian, decline of, 175–77; Leonardo da Vinci's concept of, 47–48, 248n; Lomazzo's idea of, 248n; Philostratus's theory of, 14; vs. poetry, 161ff, 251–52n; poietic vs. heuretic, Plato on,

Painting/*pittura* (*Continued*)
  3–4, Roman, 175; vs. sculpture, 183n, 188–89n, 212n; Seneca's concept of, 25, 47ff, 201n; Zuccari's theory of, 74–79, 92–93, 220–21n. *See also* Art; Art theory; portraiture
Palissy, Bernard, 219n
Pallas Athena, 173, 193n; Phidias's statue of, 5, 12
Panofsky, E., vii, 204nn, 206n, 207n, 210n, 219n, 221n, 233n, 241n, 245n, 250n
Paris (Trojan prince), 165
Parmigianino, 73
Parrhasius, 159, 189n
Passavant, Johann David, 212n
Patristic aesthetics, 191n ff
Patrizzi, 94
Pausanias, 159
Paulinus of Nola, 191n
Peiraeikos, 159
Pericles, picture of, 223n
Peripatetic philosophy, 37, 95, 233n; theory of Idea, 92, 98
Peruzzi, Baldassare, 73
Petrarch, 59, 115, 211n, 218n, 244n
Phantasy, 48, 59, 103, 239n; vs. imitation, 159–61. *See also* Eicastic vs. phantastic painting; *Pittori icastici* vs. *pittori fantastici*
Phidias, 5, 12, 16, 18, 26, 27, 159, 163, 165, 173, 182n, 185n, 190n
Philip of Austria, 252n
Philo, 37, 40, 167, 187n, 194n, 200n, 252n; concept of Idea, 37, 193n
Philosophy: Arabic, 233n; Greek, 16; Peripatetic, 37, 95, 233n; Stoic, 37
Philostratus, 163, 184nn, 185n, 215n, 251n; on painting, 14; on Phidias's sculpture of the gods, 16
Piero della Francesca, 74
Pignoria, L., 237n
Piles, Roger de, 218n, 244n
Pino, Paolo, 73
Pittori icastici vs. *pittori fantastici*, 212–15n, 242n, 252–53n

2 6 5

Index